RALPH WALDO EMERSON

RALPH WALDO EMERSON

HIS

LIFE, GENIUS, AND WRITINGS

A BIOGRAPHICAL SKETCH

TO WHICH ARE ADDED

PERSONAL RECOLLECTIONS OF HIS VISITS TO ENGLAND
EXTRACTS FROM UNPUBLISHED LETTERS
AND MISCELLANEOUS CHARACTERISTIC RECORDS

BY

ALEXANDER IRELAND

Second Edition, Largely Augmented

KENNIKAT PRESS
Port Washington, N. Y./London

RALPH WALDO EMERSON

First published in 1882
Reissued in 1972 by Kennikat Press
Library of Congress Catalog Card No: 72-160762
ISBN 0-8046-1581-0

Manufactured by Taylor Publishing Company   Dallas, Texas

Plutarch says that when Cicero, as a young man, visited the oracle at Delphi, the advice given him was to make his own genius, not the opinions of others, the guide of his life.

————

One who of such a height hath built his mind,
And reared the dwelling of his thoughts so strong,
As neither fear nor hope can shake the frame
Of his resolvèd powers,   .   .   .
    .   .   .   .   .   nor pierce to wrong
His settled peace, nor to disturb the same ;
    .   .   .   .
Which makes, that whatsoever here befalls,
He in the region of himself remains.

SAMUEL DANIEL (1562-1619).

PREFACE.

———

THE rapid sale (within twelve weeks) of the first edition
of this work has encouraged its author to prepare a
second, augmented to considerably more than double
its former size by the addition of matter which cannot
fail to be interesting to admirers of Emerson. The
"Biographical Sketch" has been increased from forty-
seven to one hundred and twenty-nine pages,—the
"Recollections of his three Visits to England," from
twenty-five to forty-one pages,—and the "Miscellaneous
Characteristic Records," from thirty-four to ninety-two
pages. An important addition has been made in the
shape of twenty-eight pages of Tributes to Emerson's life
and genius, delivered at a special meeting of the Massachusetts Historical Society, in Boston, in May last, by Dr. Ellis,
Judge Hoar, and Dr. Oliver Wendell Holmes, the well-
known author of "The Autocrat of the Breakfast Table,"
"Elsie Venner," "The Guardian Angel," and other works.
For the beautiful memorial volume containing these
addresses the author is indebted to the kindness of Dr.
Holmes. The volume is unknown in England, no notice
of it even having appeared on this side of the Atlantic.
Dr. Holmes's *éloge*, coming as it does from the heart of
one of Emerson's most intimate and cherished friends—

himself a man of rare genius—possesses a deep interest
not only on account of the spirit which pervades it, but
also for its consummate literary expression.

The reader of the following pages will find in them
many illustrative passages in connection with Emerson,
without which any account of his life and work, however
brief, would be inadequate. Among them may be
named—his friendly relations with Margaret Fuller, perhaps the most remarkable woman of culture of her time ;
exercising, during her unfortunately brief life, an acknowledged influence on the best thought of New England,—
his connection with "The Dial," the most remarkable
organ of high thought published in our time,—an account
of that singular social experiment, "The Brook Farm
Community," idealized by the weird genius of Hawthorne
in that saddest of fictions, "The Blithedale Romance,"—
the resignation of his pastoral charge in 1832, and his
sermon and farewell letter in connection therewith,—his
addresses on Robert Burns and Walter Scott,—and his
notable speech in Manchester in 1847, in which he gave
utterance to his confidence in, and admiration of, England.
Among the "Miscellaneous Characteristic Records" and
"Anecdotes" will be found some impressions and glimpses
that enable us, by a side-light, as it were, to see Emerson
almost face to face.

In the "Biographical Sketch," the author has
endeavoured to bring out in fuller detail some of
Emerson's characteristics as a thinker, writer, and public
lecturer, as well as his personal bearing in the family and
social circle. This has been done by freely using what

has been written about him by others—chiefly those who knew him well, and enjoyed his intimate friendship. Wherever he has found a vivid presentment of Emerson, the author has not hesitated to make use of it, and to incorporate it in his sketch, in order to add to the completeness of the picture. In this respect he has been but "a gatherer and disposer of other men's stuff." His object throughout has been to present a likeness of Emerson as true as he can make it—to the fidelity of which not merely his own opportunities of observation, but also the faithful reports of friends and life-long associates have contributed. In the pages which follow, the reader may see, through many different eyes, something of the personality and surroundings of the most original thinker and highest-reaching ethical teacher his country has produced—who, during a long, serene, and beautiful life—a life, the end and aim of which was "to make truth lovely, and manhood valorous"—has exercised on some of the most thoughtful minds of his age an influence probably not exceeded by that of any other writer of the century.

INGLEWOOD,
    BOWDON, CHESHIRE,
       October 21, 1882.

CONTENTS.

PAGE

RALPH WALDO EMERSON.

THE grave has scarcely closed over the remains of the great man whose renown all over the world is more firmly established than that of any Englishman of his time,* when the news comes to us that the foremost thinker and philosopher of America has joined the ranks of the majority. America has produced great soldiers, distinguished men of science, and poets of world-wide fame, but it is not too much to say that since the Declaration of Independence no man has so powerfully influenced the intellect of the nation as Ralph Waldo Emerson. On Thursday night, April 27th, at nine o'clock, at his house in Concord, Mass., surrounded by those dearest to him, this great man

---

* Charles Darwin died April 19th, 1882.

peaceably departed. He leaves a widow, a son—
Dr. Edward Emerson, of Concord,—and two
daughters. The eldest, Ellen—his devoted and
helpful companion whenever he left home, his
amanuensis in later years, and, as he sometimes
lovingly called her, his " memory "—is unmarried.
The youngest, Edith, is married to Colonel W. H.
Forbes, of Milton Hill, Mass., and has several
children. When they visited England in 1872,
bringing their children with them, Mr. Carlyle sat
for a likeness, with Emerson's grandson, Ralph,
then a fine boy of twelve or thirteen, standing by
his knee.

Ralph Waldo Emerson, the most original and
independent thinker and greatest moral teacher
that America has produced, was born at Boston
on May 25th, 1803. He was a legitimate product
of Puritanism. As far back as his family is traced
it has been represented by ministers of the old
faith of New England, the founder of it having
voyaged thither with his congregation from Glou-
cestershire, in England, in 1635, and each of these
ministers was associated with some phase of that
faith, whether Calvinism, Universalism, or Unitarianism. He sprang on both sides from clerical
stock, and his ancestry forms an indispensable
explanation and background of every page of his

writings. The Emerson family were intellectual, eloquent, with a strong individuality of character, robust and vigorous in their thinking—practical and philanthropic. His father was the Rev. William Emerson, pastor of the First (Unitarian) Church of Boston, and was noted for his vigorous mind, earnestness of purpose, and gentleness of manner. The boy lost his father when he was but eight years old. His mother was described as "a woman of great sensibility, modest, serene, and very devout. She was possessed of a thoroughly sincere nature, devoid of all sentimentalism, and of a temper the most even and placid—(one of her sons said that in his boyhood, when she came from her room in the morning, it seemed to him as if she always came from communion with God)—possessed great patience and fortitude, had the serenest trust in God, was of a discerning spirit, and a most courteous bearing, one who knew how to guide the affairs of her house, and to exercise the sweetest authority. Both her mind and her character were of a superior order, and they set their stamp upon manners of peculiar softness and natural grace and quiet dignity. Her sensible and kindly speech was always as good as the best instruction ; her smile, though it was ever ready, was a reward. Her dark, liquid eyes, from which old age did not take away the expression, were among the remembrances of all on whom they ever rested."

The subject of this memoir was the second of five brothers. William, the eldest, graduated at Harvard in 1820. Although wanting the genius of the others, he was said to have been "a man whom it was a privilege to know." Edward, the third brother, who gave early promise of the rarest and most brilliant qualities, was of a robust moral nature, and high-toned in his ideas of duty, and "incapable," as his brother Waldo said, "of self-indulgence." He died in 1834. Peter Bulkeley, the fourth brother, died in early life. Charles Chauncy, the youngest of the family, graduated at Harvard in 1828. He died of consumption in 1836. Both these young men possessed unusual gifts of intellect, and the little they did of literary work was of the very best. That exquisite poem, "The Dirge," by Ralph Waldo, expresses, with unsurpassed tenderness, his sense of their loss. Dr. Oliver Wendell Holmes speaks of Edward and Charles as young men of "exceptional and superior natural endowments. Edward was of the highest promise. Of Charles I knew something in my college days. A beautiful, high-souled, pure, exquisitely delicate nature in a slight but finely-wrought mortal frame, he was for me the very ideal of an embodied celestial intelligence.

. . . I felt as many have felt after being with his brother, Ralph Waldo, that I had entertained an angel visitant. The Fawn of Marvell's imagination survives in my memory as the fitting image to recall this beautiful youth, a soul glowing like the rose of morning with enthusiasm, a character white as the lilies in its purity."

Mary Emerson, Waldo's aunt, assisted his mother in bringing up the boys. She was "a woman of many remarkable qualities, high-toned in motive and conduct to the greatest degree, very conscientious, and with an unconventional regard of social forms." Waldo was greatly indebted to her. He once said that her influence upon his education had been as great as that of Greece or Rome. She was well read in theology, and a scholar of no mean abilities. In her old age she was described as "still retaining all the oddities and enthusiasms of her youth—a person at war with society as to all its decorums, who enters into conversation with everybody, and talks on every subject ; is sharp as a razor in her satire, and sees you through and through in a moment. She has read all her life in the most miscellaneous way ; and her appetite for metaphysics is insatiable. Her power over her young friends was almost despotic." There was another remarkable woman who exercised much influence on his early life—Sarah Bradford, afterwards the wife of Samuel Ripley. She, like his aunt, was a great lover of books, and "both of them were unusually well-informed for the time; under their lead he early came to love Plato." One of the earliest of the serious books he read was a translation of the "Pensées" of Pascal, which he used to carry to church with him, and to peruse diligently.

"In this pious and conscientious household," says Mr. Cooke,* "the mother and aunt exercised a rare influence over him and his brothers. The most careful economy had to be practised, and they grew up with the strictest regard for all that is good and true. They were carefully and conscientiously trained at home, especially in regard to every moral virtue. Honesty, probity, unselfishness—these virtues they had deeply instilled into them." At eight years of age he entered the public grammar-school, and soon after, the Latin School, in which he made good progress. This is apparent from a letter written to him, when he was eleven, by Miss Bradford, urging him to send her a translation from Virgil, and to

---

* "Ralph Waldo Emerson; his Life, Writings, and Philosophy," by George Willis Cooke. To this volume, which contains the fullest and most accurate record of Emerson's Life and Works yet published, the author of this Memoir has been much indebted during its compilation.

write her a letter in Latin or in Greek, or tell her
what most interests him in Rollin. In response, he
returned her a poetic version of part of the fifth
bucolic. He was fond of writing verses as school
exercises, and was an eager reader of books of
history. In one of his essays he takes us into his
confidence with regard to his habits of reading in
those early days, where he says, "The regular
course of studies, the years of academical and professional education, have not yielded me better
facts than some idle books under the bench at the
Latin School. What we do not call education is
more precious than that which we do call so."

Rufus Dawes, who knew Emerson as a boy,
gives us in his "Boyhood Memoirs" (1843) a
sight of the boy when he was about ten years
old :—" It is eight o'clock a.m. ; and the thin
gentleman in black, with a small jointed cane
under his arm, his eyes deeply sunken in his
head, has asked that spiritual-looking boy in blue
nankeen, who seems to be about ten years old,
to 'touch the bell ; '—it was a privilege to do
this;—and there he stands, that boy, whose image,
more than any others, is still deeply stamped upon
my mind, as I then saw him and loved him, I
knew not why, and thought him so angelic and
remarkable—feeling towards him more than a

boy's emotion—as if a new spring of brotherly affection had suddenly broken loose in my heart. There is no indication of turbulence and disquiet about him ; but with a happy combination of energy and gentleness, how truly is he the father of the man! He has touched the bell, and while he takes his seat among his fellows, he little dreams that in after times he will strike a different note."*

Young Emerson entered Harvard University in his fourteenth year, viz., in 1817. Edward Everett was then Professor of Greek Literature. His lecturing and Sunday preaching had a powerful influence upon the boy student. Ticknor was also a professor at

* Since the First Edition of this Memoir was published, the author of it has received from the venerable Dr. Furness, of Philadelphia— Emerson's schoolfellow and senior by about a year—a letter, from which he ventures to give the following extract, partly relating to the school-day period of their lives:—"The language of eulogy is apt to run wild, but I have no words to tell my sense of the greatness and worth of R. W. E. I cannot remember when I did not know and admire him. We learned our A B C together. We sate together at our writing school when he, ten years of age, and I eleven, wrote verses on our naval battles in the war of 1812. The only time I can remember when he played was (when we were some six or seven years old) on the floor of my mother's chamber. He lived always from the earliest in a serene world of letters. Never since Shakespeare has our English tongue been used with such beauty as by our great friend. . . . I have never presumed to analyse him. I have not needed to do so. 'The affections are their own justification.' The reverence, the love he inspired, bear witness to his rare worth.—Yours faithfully, W. H. FURNESS."

that time, and was an inspiring influence to the students. In the class before his (E.'s) were Furness and Gannett, (afterwards Dr. Channing's co-pastor). Every graduating class in the university elects a poet and an orator for its celebration, which is called "class-day," and Emerson was chosen as the poet of his class. In his junior year he received a Bowdoin prize for an essay on "The Character of Socrates," and in his senior year he again gained a prize, his subject being "The Present State of Ethical Philosophy." Among his companions he was already distinguished for literary attainments, and more especially for a certain charm in the delivery of his addresses. He was then described as "a slender, delicate youth, younger than most of his classmates, and of a sensitive, retiring nature." According to his own account he received but little instruction from his professors that was of value to him. His favourite study was Greek, and his translations of the classical authors were neat and happy. In mathematics he could make no headway, and in philosophy he did not get on very well. He was a great reader, and studied much outside of the prescribed course. Even before entering college he was well read. His favourite books were the old English poets and dramatists— Shakespeare and his contemporaries. Shakespeare

he knew almost by heart. Montaigne had special
attraction for him. When a boy, he found a
volume of his Essays among his father's books;
after leaving college it again came to his notice,
and he procured the remaining volumes. " I
remember the delight and wonder in which I
lived with him. It seemed to me as if I had myself
written the book in some former life, so sincerely
did he speak to my thought and experience."
Tillotson, St. Augustine, and Jeremy Taylor were
also among his favourite authors. In 1823 he began
the study of theology. At this time Dr. Channing's
conversation and preaching were an important influence. " The outcome of this eminent preacher's
most cherished ideas being a practical reliance on
the soul of man as a medium of truth and goodness,
Emerson eagerly embraced the essential spirit of
his teaching. To the young student the contact
with such a man was worth more than any formal
instruction." After graduation he entered upon
his studies in the Unitarian Divinity College
connected with the University. After he had
graduated from the Divinity College and been
"approbated" for the ministry, he was led to visit
the far South—South Carolina and Florida—on
account of impaired health. On his return he was
settled in 1829 as colleague to Henry Ware in the

pastorate of the Second Church (Unitarian) of Boston. A year afterwards Mr. Ware's health broke down, and he was compelled to go to Europe, whence he returned only to resign his charge, and Emerson then became sole minister of the church. He was afterwards appointed chaplain to the State Legislature. His preaching attracted considerable attention, though it brought no crowd. Many an old hearer afterwards remembered these discourses in reading his essays. A venerable lady of those days, a member of his congregation, when asked what was his chief characteristic as a minister, said : " On God's law doth he meditate day and night." In September, 1829, he married Helen Louisa Tucker, to whom he addressed a beautiful poem, " To Ellen at the South." She died of consumption in February, 1832.

Emerson's earliest appearance in print, we believe, was in an address, delivered in 1830, at the ordination of the Rev. H. B. Goodwin, as colleague of Dr. Ripley, in the Concord Church. " On this occasion," says Mr. Cooke, " Emerson took part, and gave 'the right hand of fellowship;' and it is the only discourse or address of his printed during his ministry. It indicates a general acceptance of the customs of the church, and a general reception of its most cherished ideas. In personally addressing his friend, he said,—'It is with sincere pleasure that I speak for the church on this occasion, and on the spot hallowed to all by so many patriotic, and, to me, by so many affectionate, recollections. I feel a peculiar, a personal right to welcome you hither to the home and the temple of my fathers. I believe the church whose pastor you are will forgive me the allusion, if I express the extreme interest which every man feels in the scene of the trials and labours of his ancestors. Five out of seven of your pre-decessors are my kindred. They are in the dust who bind my attachment to this place; but not all. I cannot help congratulating you that one survives, to be to you the true friend and venerable counsellor he has ever been to me.'"

Owing to a conscientious disinclination to con-duct the communion service, he decided to resign his pastorate. On September 9th, 1832, he preached a remarkable sermon on the subject, giving a history of the rite of the "Communion Supper," and setting forth his reasons for rejecting the commemoration of it in the sense generally entertained. This sermon has been described as "justifying all the praise accorded to his pulpit abilities — being dispassionate, truly religious, and very charming in its quiet and yet earnest style. The rite seemed to him a repudiation of that spiritual worship which Jesus taught, and a return to the forms from which he sought to liberate men." Mr. Frothingham, in his "Transcendentalism in New England," thus characterises the discourse: "It was a model of lucid, orderly, and simple statement; so plain that the young men and women of the congregation could understand it; so deep and elevated that experienced believers were fed; learned enough, without a taint of pedantry; bold, without a suggestion of audacity; reasonable, without critical sharpness or affectation of mental superiority; rising into natural eloquence in passages that contained pure thought, but for the most part flowing in unartificial sentences that exactly expressed the speaker's meaning and no more."

Many of Emerson's poems were written during these early years—a well-known one among the number beginning

Good-bye, proud world! I'm going home.

Mr. Cooke says it has been referred to the period after his leaving the pulpit, but he adds that this is incorrect. "It simply indicates the spirit and purpose of the young man, his genius, his high ideals, his love of a life of meditation, and his scorn for the shams and shows and low motives of the world. It was written before he left the ministry, and shows his intense love of nature, and the devoutness of his mind." Here are the concluding lines :—

> I am going to my own hearth-stone,
> Bosomed in yon green hills alone,—
> A secret nook in a pleasant land,
> Whose groves the frolic fairies planned ;
> Where arches green, the live-long day,
> Echo the blackbird's roundelay,
> And vulgar feet have never trod
> A spot that is sacred to Thought and God.
>
> O, when I am safe in my sylvan home,
> I tread on the pride of Greece and Rome ;
> And when I am stretched beneath the pines,
> Where the evening star so holy shines,
> I laugh at the lore and the pride of man,
> At the sophist schools, and the learnèd clan ;
> For what are they all, in their high conceit,
> When man in the bush with God may meet ?

After his resignation his health broke down, and he was advised to take a sea voyage. Unable to appear in the pulpit again, he addressed an affectionate letter of farewell to his congregation, dated 22nd December, 1832.* His health did not improve during the winter, and he embarked early in the spring of 1833 for Europe. He sailed up the

---

* The Sermon and Letter here alluded to contain so much that is characteristic of Emerson, even at this early period of his life, that extracts from both are given at the end of the volume. They will be read with interest by students of his mind and character.

Mediterranean in a vessel bound for Sicily, and went as far eastward as Malta. Returning through Italy, where he dined with Walter Savage Landor in Florence—finding him "noble and courteous, living in a cloud of pictures at his villa Gherardesca"— "If Goethe had been still living, I might have wandered into Germany also. Besides those I have named,—Coleridge, Wordsworth, De Quincey, and Carlyle—(for Scott was dead), there was not the man living whom I cared to behold, unless it were the Duke of Wellington, whom I saw in Westminster Abbey at the funeral of Wilberforce." He visited France, and in July reached London. He called on Coleridge, whom he describes in his "English Traits." In August of the same year (1833) he made a pilgrimage to Scotland. He remained some days in Edinburgh, and delivered a discourse in the Unitarian Chapel there, recollections of which happily still survive. Desirous of personally acknowledging to Carlyle his indebtedness for the spiritual benefit he had derived from certain of his writings—notably the concluding passage in the article on German Literature, and the paper entitled " Characteristics "—he found his way, after many hindrances, to Craigenputtock, among the desolate hills of the parish of Dunscore, in Dumfriesshire, where Carlyle was then living with his bright and

accomplished wife in perfect solitude, without a
person to speak to, or a post office within seven
miles. There he spent twenty-four hours, and
became acquainted with him at once. They
walked over miles of barren hills, and talked
upon all the great questions which interested
them most. The meeting is described in his
" English Traits," published twenty-three years
afterwards, and the account of it there given is
reprinted by Mr. Froude in his "Life of Carlyle,"
&c., lately issued. Carlyle and his wife often afterwards spoke of that visit, "when that supernal vision,
Waldo Emerson, dawned upon us," as if it had been
the coming of an angel. They regarded Emerson
as a "beautiful apparition" in their solitude. A
letter exists (reprinted in this volume), addressed to
the present writer, a few days after the visit, giving
an account of it, as well as of one to Wordsworth. This letter, written on the spur of the
moment, and not intended for publication, contains
some details not to be found in the more elaborate
and carefully-prepared account of these two
visits which he gave to the public so many
years later. Mr. Froude says of this visit : " The
fact itself of a young American having been so
affected by his writings as to have sought him
out on the Dunscore moors, was a homage of the

kind which he (Carlyle) could especially value and appreciate. The acquaintance then begun to their mutual pleasure ripened into a deep friendship, which has remained unclouded in spite of wide divergencies of opinion throughout their working lives, and continues warm as ever at the moment when I am writing these words (June 27, 1880), when the labours of both of them are over, and they wait in age and infirmity to be called away from a world to which they have given freely all that they had to give."

Emerson has the distinction of having been the first eminent literary man of either continent to appreciate and welcome "Sartor Resartus." The book was written in 1831 at Craigenputtock, but could find no publisher for two years. At last it appeared in "Fraser's Magazine" in successive chapters, in 1833-4 (Carlyle having to accept reduced remuneration); and it was not till 1838 that it appeared as a volume in England. While subscribers were complaining of the "intolerable balderdash" appearing from month to month in the magazine, under the title of "Sartor Resartus,"— "sentences which might be read backward or forward, for they are equally intelligible either way"— and threatening to withdraw their subscriptions if "that clotted nonsense" did not speedily cease,

Emerson was quietly collecting the successive
numbers with a view to its publication on completion. In 1836 the American edition of the work
appeared in Boston, and was sufficiently successful
to yield a profit of £150, which Emerson sent to
Carlyle—the most important sum which he had, up
to that time, received for any of his works. In
Emerson's modest preface to the book (on its first
appearance in the shape of a volume), occur these
memorable words—the earliest cordial recognition
of the originality and power of this now famous
work :—

> We believe, no book has been published for many years, written
> in a more sincere style of idiomatic English, or which discovers an
> equal mastery over all the riches of the language. The author
> makes ample amends for the occasional eccentricity of his genius,
> not only by frequent bursts of pure splendour, but by the wit and
> sense which never fail him. But what will chiefly commend the book
> to the discerning reader is the manifest design of the work, which
> is a Criticism upon the Spirit of the Age,—we had almost said, of
> the hour, in which we live ; exhibiting, in the most just and novel
> light, the present aspects of Religion, Politics, Literature, Arts,
> and Social Life. Under all his gaiety, the writer has an earnest
> meaning, and discovers an insight into the manifold wants and
> tendencies of human nature, which is very rare among our popular
> authors. The philanthropy and the purity of moral sentiment,
> which inspire the work, will find their way to the heart of every
> lover of virtue.

A similar service was done by Emerson some
years later in a few prefatory remarks to the

first American reprint of Carlyle's "Critical and Miscellaneous Essays." In this case also, the American collected reprint preceded the one in England. Emerson, in his preface, refers to the influence these Essays had exerted in New England, especially on inquiring youthful minds; how they spoke "with an emphasis that hindered them from sleep."

His health, which had always been delicate, and which in 1832 had been greatly affected by domestic bereavement (the death of his first wife) and the worry of controversy, was quite restored by the voyage and his subsequent travels. After his return to America he gave lectures before the Boston Lyceum,—his subjects being : " Water ;" "Michael Angelo ;" "Milton ;" "Luther ;" "George Fox ;" " Edmund Burke ;" also two lectures on " Italy," and three on " The Relation of Man to the Globe." In August, 1835, in a lecture before the American Institute of Instruction, his subject was the " Means of Inspiring a Taste for English Literature." In September of the same year he gave a historical address in Concord, it being the second centennial anniversary of the incorporation of that town. In September, 1835, he married Miss Lydia Jackson, of Plymouth. Her family was descended from one of the earliest Plymouth

settlers. In December, 1835, he gave a course of
ten lectures in Boston on " English Literature."
The first two were on the earlier authors, and
there were others on Chaucer, Bacon, Shakespeare,
and the subsequent great writers. In the last
lecture, he touched upon Byron, Scott, Dugald
Stewart, Mackintosh, and Coleridge. He placed
Coleridge among the sages of the world. In
succeeding seasons he gave courses on " The
Philosophy of History ; " " Human Culture ; "
" Human Life ; " " The Present Age ; " " The
Times ; " and other subjects. It is to be hoped
that many of these lectures, hitherto unprinted, will
be given to the world. At a meeting held in Concord in 1836, on the completion of a monument
to commemorate the Concord fight, a hymn
was written for the occasion by Emerson, and
read by Dr. Ripley, and sung to the tune of
the "Old Hundred." It contained the immortal
lines :—

> Here once the embattled farmers stood,
> And fired the shot heard round the world.

In 1835 he was reading Plato and Plutarch
more diligently than ever, and began to study
Plotinus and other writers of the same class. He
also read the writings of the German mystics,

including Jacob Bœhmen,* as well as of the English idealists, the poems of George Herbert (which he keenly relished), and the prose works of Ralph Cudworth, Henry More, Milton, Jeremy Taylor, and Coleridge.

In 1836 appeared "Nature," a little volume of only ninety-five pages, the contents consisting of an Introduction, and eight chapters, entitled, Nature, Commodity, Beauty, Language, Discipline, Idealism, Spirit, and Prospects. The spirit of its teachings is that nature exists only for the unfolding of a spiritual being. His ideas are in this little volume more systematically developed than elsewhere. They have been thus summarised :—" Every natural fact is a symbol of some spiritual fact. Nature becomes a means of expression for these spiritual truths and experiences, which could not otherwise be interpreted. Its laws, also, are moral laws when applicable to man ; and so they become to man the language of the Divine Will. Because the

* In a letter from Miss Elizabeth Peabody, of Boston, U.S., editor of "Æsthetic Papers," 1849, to the writer of this memoir (July 2, 1882), she says :—" His favourite book was Bœhmen's 'Way to Christ,' which I borrowed from him as late as 1860, and when he lent it to me he remarked, 'This is my *vade mecum*.' I have ever felt that Emerson was 'deeper in Christ' than any one I knew, more entirely 'one with him' in spirit than perhaps even Dr. Channing. They were the two souls from whom I have received most."

physical laws become moral laws the moment they are related to human conduct, Nature has a much higher purpose than that of beauty or language— in that it is a Discipline. It is in these views that Emerson's resemblance to Swedenborg is apparent, in his caring for Nature only as a symbol and revelation of spiritual realities." The volume attracted the attention and warmest enthusiasm of a few thinkers, but it met with but a small sale,—only 500 copies being disposed of in twelve years! The first edition of it is now one of the rarest books in America. A writer in " The Democratic Review " thus spoke of it:—" The highest intellectual culture and the simplest instinctive innocence have received it, and felt it to be a divine thought, borne on a stream of English undefiled, such as we had almost despaired could flow in this our world of grist and saw-mills." He finds evidence of "the highest imaginative power" in it, while "it proves to us that the only true and perfect mind is the poetic." Another writer says of it :—" It is replete with the deepest sentiment and the liveliest emotion. In it the heart predominates over the brain. The style is glowing rather than austere, rising not unfrequently to a lofty pitch of eloquence. It is inspired throughout by a glad spirit born of recovered health, a happy, new-found home, and pleasant domestic and social surroundings. It was the first great fruit of his genius, the ' first crushings ' of the grapes of his intellectual vineyard—for the reason that in it he more or less developed the germs of his speculations and theories." In England it met with even a heartier reception than in America. A remarkable lecture in Boston, on " War," in March, 1838, was afterwards printed in Miss Peabody's " Æsthetic Papers " in 1849.

An oration, entitled " The American Scholar," delivered before the Phi-Beta-Kappa Society, at Harvard, August 31, 1837; an address before the literary societies of Dartmouth, on " Literary Ethics ;" and a discourse before the senior class in Divinity College, Cambridge, on Sunday, July 15, 1838—won him wide notice for their originality, boldness, and power. They exercised an immense influence on the youthful mind of New England. A. B. Alcott, who was present at the first of these addresses, said of it :—" I believe that was the first adequate statement of the new views that really attracted general attention. I had the good fortune to hear that address ; and I shall not forget the delight with which I heard it, nor the mixed confusion, consternation, surprise, and wonder with which the audience listened to it." Lowell, who also heard it, says the delivery of this

lecture "was an event without any former parallel
in our literary annals, a scene to be always treasured
in the memory for its picturesqueness and its inspiration. What crowded and breathless aisles,
what windows clustering with eager heads, what
enthusiasm of approval, what silence of foregone
dissent!"

It was the last of the above addresses, however, which, like a trumpet-blast, most startled and
took by surprise the thoughtful minds of the country.
"It was Emerson's first, full, and direct expression
of his faith in moral power and self-trust, and his
repudiation of all commands laid on us from the
teachings of other men, unless their thought is
verified in our own nature." He said that the
office of the preacher was dying, and the church
tottering to its fall! "The real work of the pulpit
is not discharged. Preaching is the expression of
moral sentiment in application to the duties of life.
In how many churches, by how many prophets, tell
me, is man made sensible that he is a living soul.
. . . The true preacher can be known by this,
that he deals out to his people his life—life passed
through the fire of thought. Man is not made to
feel that he is an infinite soul; the life of to-day is
not touched; actual experience brings no lessons.
The redemption is to be sought in the Soul.

The present evils of the church are many, and need much to be put away. We need more faith. The old forms are good enough if new life be breathed into them. The remedy for these evils is—first, soul ; and second, soul ; and evermore soul."

This renowned address was warmly criticised, and as warmly defended, and Mr. Cooke tells us that the agitation caused by it reached such a height that the " Christian Examiner " thought it necessary in behalf of the Unitarians of the Divinity School to make a formal renunciation of the views given forth in it.*

The Rev. Henry Ware, then the most prominent professor in the School, addressed to Emerson a friendly expostulation against the doctrines of this discourse. In reply Emerson said : "What you say about the discourse at Divinity College is just what I might expect from your truth and charity, combined with your known opinions. I am not a stick or a stone, as one said in the old time, and could not feel but pain in saying some things in

* In the letter from Miss Elizabeth Peabody, quoted at p. 21, she says :—" Dr. Channing regarded the address at Divinity Hall as an entirely justifiable and needed criticism on the perfunctory character of service creeping over the Unitarian Churches at the time. He hailed the commotion of thought it stirred up as a sign that 'something did live in the embers' of that spirit which had developed Unitarianism out of the decaying Puritan Churches."

that place and presence which I supposed would meet with dissent, I may say, of dear friends and benefactors of mine. Yet, as my conviction is perfect in the substantial truth of the doctrines of this discourse, and is not very new, you will see at once that it must appear very important that it be spoken; and I thought I could not pay the nobleness of my friends so mean a compliment as to suppress my opposition to their supposed views, out of fear of offence. I would rather say to them—these things look thus to me, to you otherwise. Let us say our uttermost word, and let the all-pervading truth, as it surely will, judge between us. Either of us would, I doubt not, be willingly apprised of his error. Meantime, I shall be admonished, by this expression of your thought, to revise with greater care the 'address' before it is printed (for the use of the class); and I heartily thank you for this expression of your tried toleration and love." This was followed by a sermon against Emerson's views, delivered by Mr. Ware in the Divinity School, a copy of which was sent to the former, with a letter, the concluding sentences being these:—" I confess that I esteem it particularly unhappy to be thus brought into a sort of public opposition to you, for I have a thousand feelings which draw me toward you; but my situation, and the circumstances of the times, render it unavoidable ; and both you and I understand that we are to act on the maxim, 'Amicus Plato, amicus Socrates, sed magis amica Veritas.' (I believe I quote right.) We would gladly agree with all our friends ; but that being impossible, and it being also impossible to *choose* which of them we will differ from, we must submit to the common lot of thinkers, and make up in love of heart what we want in unity of judgment. But I am growing prosy, so I break off.—Yours very truly."

To this letter Emerson returned the following characteristic reply :—

" Concord, Oct. 8, 1838.

"My dear Sir,—I ought sooner to have acknowledged your kind letter of last week, and the sermon it accompanied. The letter was right manly and noble. The sermon, too, I have read with attention. If it assails any doctrine of mine,—perhaps I am not so quick to see it as writers generally,—certainly I did not feel any disposition to depart from my habitual contentment, that you should say your thought, whilst I say mine. I believe I must tell you what I think of my new position. It strikes me very oddly that good and wise men at Cambridge and Boston should think of raising me into an object of criticism. I have always been—from my very incapacity of methodical writing—a 'chartered libertine,' free to worship and free to rail,—lucky when I could make myself understood, but never esteemed near enough to the institutions and mind of society to deserve the notice of the masters of literature and religion.   I have appreciated fully the advantages of my position, for I well know there is no scholar less willing or less able than myself to be a polemic.   I could not give an account of myself, if challenged.   I could not possibly give you one of the 'arguments' you cruelly hint at, on which any doctrine of mine stands ; for I do not know what arguments are in reference to any expression of a thought.   I delight in telling what I think ; but if you ask me how I dare say so, or why it is so, I am the most helpless of mortal men. I do not even see that either of these questions admits of an answer.   So that in the present droll posture of my affairs, when I see myself suddenly raised to the importance of a heretic, I am very uneasy when I advert to the supposed duties of such a personage, who is to make good his thesis against all comers.   I certainly shall do no such thing.   I shall read what you and other good men write, as I have always done, glad when you speak my thoughts, and skipping the page that has nothing for me.   I shall go on just as before, seeing whatever I can, and telling what I see ; and, I suppose, with the same fortune that has hitherto attended me,—the joy of finding that my abler and better brothers, who work with the sympathy of society, loving and beloved, do now and then unexpectedly confirm my perceptions, and find my nonsense is only their own thought in motley,—and so I am your affectionate servant," &c.

Mr. M. D. Conway, writing about the address in question, which Theodore Parker pronounced to be " the noblest, the most inspiring strain I ever listened to," says,—" Little wonder that the New England shepherds, watching their flocks by night, should have been sore afraid when this light shone round about them. But their terror could not quench the star that had risen. ' It is no use,' said an eminent divine, when he had heard that the Faculty had passed a censure on the discourse, ' henceforth the young men will have a fifth gospel in their Testaments.' Among the young men who listened was one who went back to his little suburban parsonage, and entered that night in his private journal these words :—' In this Emerson surpassed himself as much as he surpasses others in a general way. I shall give no abstract,—so beautiful, so just, and terribly sublime was his picture of the Church in its present condition. My soul is roused, and this week I shall write the long-meditated sermons on the state of the Church and the duties of these times.' So under the electric touch of Emerson, rose the American John Knox—Theodore Parker."

The "address" became the subject of many sermons, pamphlets, and newspaper articles, while controversies and debates about it rose to a great height. The effect of all this was, in the words of Mr. Cooke, "to finally separate Emerson from the Unitarians, and to cause him to abandon the pulpit. He saw how strongly the Unitarians were wedded to the old forms, and he found himself more and more alienated from them. He could not continue to preach amidst controversy and objection, so he quietly withdrew to his work in a manner of his own." Henceforth he may be considered as having emancipated himself finally and for ever from the trammels of creed. Shaking off all traditions of creed and authority, "I stepped," to use his own words, "into the free and open world to utter my private thought to all who were willing to hear it." Thenceforth he became "the chartered libertine" of thought, as he sometimes humorously called himself. From this time the lecture platform was his pulpit. How admirably he filled it during a period of more than forty years;—how ennobling were his teachings, and how beneficent and far-reaching was their influence—the record of his life and work amply testifies.

About the end of 1836 there originated at Boston, in the house of the Rev. George Ripley, one of the most prominent of the Unitarian ministers in that town, a gathering of thoughtful persons for discussion and mutual inquiry. In this way gradually came together a number of friends "who entertained the same ideas, and had common hopes of a new era of truth and religion"—A. B. Alcott, Margaret Fuller, R. W. Emerson, George Ripley, F. H. Hedge, Dr. Channing, Convers Francis, James Freeman Clarke, J. S. Dwight, Elizabeth Peabody, W. H. Channing, Dr. C. Follen, C. A. Bartol, N. L. Frothingham, O. A. Brownson, Theodore Parker, Jones Very, Caleb Stetson, Charles S. Wheeler, R. Bartlett, S. J. May, George Bancroft, and others. Meetings were held four or five times a year, with very little form, from house to house, every one contributing something to the conversation. These meetings took place at various places—Boston, Chelsea, Concord, Milton, Newton, Watertown. Emerson was almost always present during the three or four years that the club met. The idea of publishing a quarterly journal was first discussed at one of the meetings in 1839. The

title, " The Dial," was suggested by Alcott.   No
one was willing to assume the editorship of the
projected periodical.   After much solicitation, Margaret Fuller consented to undertake what Emerson
called this "private and friendly service."   " Perhaps
no enterprise was undertaken more diffidently by
those interested in it.   When it began it concentrated a good deal of hope and affection."   She
was assisted in the editorship by Mr. George Ripley.

The first number of " The Dial " had a very characteristic address to its readers from Emerson's pen.
The purpose of the magazine was—the most various
expression of the best, the most cultivated, and the
freest thought of the time,—and was addressed to
those only who were able to find " entertainment "
in such literature.   " There were no facts for
popularity.   Each number was a symposium of
the most accomplished minds in the country ; it
originated in the hopes of the young."   Alcott
was only 40, Ripley 38, Emerson 37, Margaret
Fuller, Theodore Parker, W. H. Channing, and J.
Freeman Clarke 30, Bartol, Cranch, and Dwight 27,
Thoreau 23, and W. E. Channing 22.   Through
this organ Emerson, Ripley, Theodore Parker,
Henry D. Thoreau (unique among American literary
personalities), J. S. Dwight, W. H. Channing,
Margaret Fuller, C. P. Cranch, J. F. Clarke, F.

H. Hedge, J. R. Lowell, Elizabeth Peabody, A. B. Alcott, W. Ellery Channing, Thomas T. Stone, C. Lane, C. A. Dana, J. C. Cabot, and others,—all of them persons of high and varied culture,—gave utterance to their thoughts. Owing to the state of her health, Miss Fuller withdrew from the editorship, at the end of the second year, and Emerson became sole editor. Under his superintendence, "The Dial" became less literary and more reformatory.

In "The Dial" Emerson published "Man the Reformer," "English Reformers," "The Young American," "Lectures on the Times" (including "The Conservative," and "The Transcendentalist"), "The Senses and The Soul," "Thoughts on Modern Literature," "Prayers," "Tantalus," "Carlyle's 'Past and Present,'" "Thoughts on Art," "Walter Savage Landor," "Europe and European Books" (including remarks on Wordsworth and Tennyson, Novels by Bulwer, &c.), "The Tragic," "The Comic," "Letter to the Readers of 'The Dial'" (on Railroads and Air-Roads, Communities, Culture, The Position of Young Men, Bettina von Arnim, and Theodore Mandt's Account of Holderlin's "Hyperion"). Some of these articles have not been reproduced in any of his collected essays. Many of his finest poems made their first appearance

in this periodical, sometimes anonymously, and
sometimes with his own signature.

In "The Dial," Thoreau was first introduced to
the public. Almost every number contained some
contribution from his pen. To Emerson he owed his
introduction to literature. He wrote The Natural
History of Massachusetts, A Winter Walk, translated
Pindar, and the "Prometheus Bound" of Æschylus,
besides contributing many poems. Elizabeth Peabody furnished papers on Christ's Idea of Society,
and The West Roxbury Community, and Mrs.
George Ripley, one on Woman ; H. Tuckerman, a
paper on Music, Mr. J. R. Lowell, three Sonnets, and
Hedge, papers on The Art of Life—The Scholar's
Calling. Ripley criticised Brownson's Writings,
wrote a "Letter to a Theological Student," and
contributed Records of the Month. Parker wrote
on German Literature, the Pharisees, Primitive
Christianity, The Divine Presence in Nature and in
the Soul, Truth against the World, Thoughts on
Theology, A Lesson for the Day, and Thoughts
on Labour. Dwight, the foremost musical critic
of New England, gave accounts of concerts, and
wrote on the Religion of Beauty and Ideals of
Everyday Life. Alcott furnished some Orphic
Sayings and Days from a Diary. C. Lane contributed papers on James Pierrepont Greaves,

A. B. Alcott's Works, Social Tendencies, A Day with the Shakers, Brook Farm, Life in the Woods, and Millennial Church. W. H. Channing wrote Ernest the Seeker and other papers, and W. E. Channing contributed many poetical pieces. Margaret Fuller contributed much from the stores of her immense reading, and the rich treasures of her noble thought. Besides numerous pieces of miscellaneous criticism, she wrote a Short Essay on Critics, Goethe, the Great Composers, Menzel's View of Goethe, Canova, Romaic and Rhine Ballads, The Modern Drama (including a long criticism of John Sterling's tragedy, "Strafford"), Bettine Brentano, Dialogue, Allston's Pictures, Klopstock and Meta, Festus, and other subjects. The article on Goethe was alone "enough to establish her fame as a discerner of spirits." In the last volume appeared a remarkable article by her, entitled "The Great Lawsuit; Man *versus* Men—Woman *versus* Women." It was afterwards enlarged and published as a volume, "Woman in the Nineteenth Century," one of the most admirable works ever written on the opportunities and duties of women.

The paper called "Notes from the Journal of a Scholar" was from the pen of Charles Chauncy Emerson, Ralph Waldo's youngest brother, who

died in 1836, and is full of subtle power. Edward
B. Emerson's beautiful poem, "The Last Farewell," written while sailing out of Boston Harbour,
for the West Indies—a voyage from which he
never returned,—appeared in "The Dial," many
years after his death. In his latest volume of
poems, Ralph Waldo gives "The Last Farewell"
a place, adding some memorial verses to this
"brother of the brief but blazing star, born for the
noblest life." This memorial poem is one of the
best of its kind in the language. Under the head-
ing "Ethnical Scriptures" were given from time to
time selections from the oldest ethical and religious
writings of men, exclusive of the Hebrew and Greek
Scriptures,—the object being "to bring together
the grand expressions of the moral sentiment in
different ages and races, the rules for the guidance
of life, and the bursts of piety and of abandonment
to the Invisible and Eternal." Seven of this series
of selections appeared ; from Veeshnoo Sarma,
The Laws of Menu, Sayings of Confucius, The
Desatir (from the Persian Prophets), The Chinese
Four Books, Hermes Trismegistus, and The Chal-
dæan Oracles. The magazine existed for four
years—1841-4. A complete set of the four volumes
is now an almost unattainable rarity. Even odd
numbers of it fetch a high price. In a recent

American literary periodical, it has been suggested that there should be a reprint of these volumes. An originally subscribed-for copy is in the possession of the writer of this memoir, which is rendered unique and very precious by having the authorship of each article indicated in Emerson's own handwriting.

"The Dial," says Mr. Cooke, "was a most notable effort toward a truer life, and a fresher expression of thought, and its influence has doubtless been very great. It is the memorial of an intellectual impulse which the national life of America has never lost. Emerson has written of it with sound sense, giving interesting hints of its purpose. He has always spoken of it in a modest manner, giving to others whatever honour and fame the quarterly has produced. In fact, he was its chief contributor, its trusted adviser, from the first ; and he did far more than any other to give it whatever of value and influence it had. . . . It was the first American periodical to assume a character and aim of its own. . . . Its influence was wholesome and vigorous. It quickened thought, gave its writers freedom of expression, and greatly stimulated originality. The school of writers which it formed and brought before the public has been the most productive and helpful we have yet seen in this country. Such has been the value of this short-lived quarterly, it already has a fame and honour quite its own, which are likely to increase in the future. Emerson thus wrote about it :—

It had its origin in a club of speculative students, who found the air in America getting a little too close and stagnant; and the agitation had, perhaps, the fault of being too secondary and bookish in its origin, or caught, not from primary instincts, but from English, and still more from German, books. The journal was commenced with much hope, and liberal promises of many co-operators. But the workmen of sufficient culture for a poetical and philosophical magazine were too few; and as the pages were filled by unpaid contributors, each of whom had, according to the usage and necessity of this country, some paying employment, the journal did not get his best work, but his second best. Its scattered writers had not digested their theories into a distinct dogma, still less into a practical measure which the public could grasp; and the magazine was so eclectic and miscellaneous that each of its readers and writers valued only a small portion of it. For these reasons it never had a large circulation, and it was discontinued after four years. But "The Dial" betrayed, through all its juvenility, timidity, and conventional rubbish, some sparks of the true love and hope, and of the piety to spiritual law, which had moved its friends and founders; and it was received by its early subscribers with almost a religious welcome. Many years after it was brought to a close, Margaret was surprised in England by very warm testimony to its merits ; and in 1848 the writer of these pages found it holding the same affectionate place in many a private book-shelf in England and Scotland which it had secured at home. Good or bad, it cost a good deal of precious labour from those who served it, and from Margaret most of all. As editor, she received a compensation for the first years, which was intended to be two hundred dollars per annum, but which, I fear, never reached that amount.

But it made no difference to her exertion. She put so much

heart into it that she bravely undertook to open, in "The Dial," the subjects which most attracted her ; and she treated, in turn, Goethe and Beethoven, the Rhine and the Romaic Ballads, the Poems of John Sterling, and several pieces of sentiment, with a spirit which spared no labour; and when the hard conditions of journalism held her to an inevitable day, she submitted to jeopardizing a long-cherished subject by treating it in the crude and forced article for the month. I remember, after she had been compelled by ill-health to relinquish the journal into my hands, my grateful wonder at the facility with which she assumed the preparation of laborious articles that might have daunted the most practiced scribe.

The first series of Emerson's "Essays," to which Mr. Carlyle contributed a preface, was published in 1841. It contained "Self-Reliance," "Compensation," "Spiritual Laws," "Love," "Friendship," "The Over-Soul," and "Intellect." Some of his very best essays are in this volume, nearly every one of them rising to the highest level of his ability as a thinker and worker. He was here more truly himself than in any other book he has published, though single essays in the succeeding volumes reach the height almost constantly maintained in this. Here are a few characteristic sentences from Carlyle's Preface, which was the first signal recognition of Emerson's genius and powers by an English writer of high authority.

At the present time it can be predicted, what some years ago it could not be, that a certain number of human creatures will be found extant in England to whom the words of a man speaking from the heart of him, in what fashion soever, under what obstructions soever, will be welcome ;—welcome, perhaps, as a brother's voice, to "wanderers in the labyrinthic Night ! " For these, and not for any other class of persons, is this little book reprinted and recommended.

The name of Ralph Waldo Emerson is not entirely new in England : distinguished Travellers bring us tidings of such a man ; fractions of his writings have found their way into the hands of the curious here; fitful hints that there is, in New England, some spiritual Notability called Emerson, glide through Reviews and Magazines. Whether these hints were true or not true, readers are now to judge for themselves a little better.

Emerson's writings and speakings amount to something :—and yet hitherto, as seems to me, this Emerson is perhaps far less notable for what he has spoken or done, than for the many things he has not spoken and has forborne to do. With uncommon interest I have learned that this, and in such a never-resting locomotive country too, is one of those rare men who have withal the invaluable talent of sitting still ! That an educated man of good gifts and opportunities, after looking at the public arena, and even trying, not with ill success, what its tasks and its prizes might amount to, should retire for long years into rustic obscurity ; and, amid the all-pervading jingle of dollars and loud chaffering of ambitions and promotions, should quietly, with cheerful deliberateness, sit down to spend *his* life not in Mammon-worship, or the hunt for reputation, influence, place or any outward advantage whatsoever : this, when we get notice of it, is a thing really worth noting.

For myself I have looked over with no common feeling to this brave Emerson, seated by his rustic hearth, on the other side of the Ocean (yet not altogether parted from me either), silently communing with his own soul, and with the God's World it finds itself alive in yonder. . . . The words of such a man, what words he finds good to speak, are worth attending to. By degrees a small circle of living souls eager to hear is gathered. The silence of this man has to become speech : may this too, in its due season, prosper for him !— Emerson has gone to lecture, various times, to special audiences, in Boston, and occasionally elsewhere. Three of those Lectures, already printed, are known to some here ; as is the little Pamphlet, called "Nature," of somewhat earlier date. It may be said, a great meaning lies in these pieces, which as yet finds no adequate expression for itself.

That this little Book has no "system," and points or stretches far beyond all systems, is one of its merits. We will call it the soliloquy of a true soul, alone under the stars, in this day. In England as elsewhere the voice of a true soul, *any* voice of such, may be welcome to some. . . . That one man more, in the most modern dialect of this year 1841, recognises the oldest everlasting truths : here is a thing worth seeing, among the others. One man more who knows, and believes of very certainty, that Man's Soul is still alive, that God's Universe is still godlike, that of all Ages of Miracles ever seen, or dreamt of, by far the most miraculous is this age in this hour ; and who with all these devout beliefs has dared, like a valiant man, to bid chimeras, " *Be* chimerical ; disappear, and let us have an end of you ! "—is not this worth something ?

What Emerson's talent is, we will not altogether estimate by this Book. The utterance is abrupt, fitful ; the great idea not yet embodied struggles towards an embodiment. Yet everywhere there is the true heart of a man ; which is the parent of all talent ; which without much talent cannot exist. A breath as of the green country,—all the welcomer that it is *New*-England country, not second-hand but first-hand country,—meets us wholesomely everywhere in these *Essays :* the authentic green Earth is there, with her mountains, rivers, with her mills and farms. Sharp gleams of insight arrest us by their pure intellectuality ; here and there, in heroic rusticism, a tone of modest manfulness, of mild invincibility, low-voiced but lion-strong, makes us too thrill with a noble pride. Talent ? Such ideas as dwell in this man, how can they ever speak themselves with *enough* of talent ? The talent is not the chief question here. The idea, that is the chief question. Of the living acorn you do not ask first, How *large* an acorn art thou ? The smallest living acorn is fit to be the parent of oaktrees without end,—could clothe all New England with oaktrees by and by. You ask it, first of all : Art thou a living acorn ? Certain, now, that thou art not a dead mushroom, as the most are ?—But, on the whole, our Book is short; the Preface should not grow too long. Closing these questionable parables and intimations, let me in plain English recommend this little Book as the Book of an original veridical man, worthy the acquaintance of those who delight in such; and so: Welcome to it whom it may concern!

In 1841 he delivered an address at Concord, on the anniversary of the emancipation of the negroes in the West Indies. "Man the Reformer," a lecture, was read before the Mechanics' Apprentices' Library Association, at the Masonic Temple, Boston, 25th January, 1841; and "The Method of Nature," an address to the Society of the Adelphi, in Waterville College, Maine, on August 11th, 1841. Three addresses, viz., "Lecture on the Times," "The Conservative," "The Transcendentalist," were read at the Masonic Temple, Boston, in December, 1841. "Man the Reformer," and the last three addresses on "The Times," were afterwards printed in "The Dial."

About this time (1841) originated the notable experiment of the Brook Farm Community, with which Emerson sympathised, but which he never joined, although he frequently visited the farm. It was one of the many movements of the day, pointing to a new order of things. To all these movements he gave his sympathy, "in so far as they expressed a genuine purpose, and showed a candid desire to make life richer with truth." The social and educational reformation of mankind by means of temperance, the common and normal school, associated living, and other agencies, was advocated at conventions of all kinds, and in the press. A society called "The Friends of Universal Progress" held conventions in Boston to revitalize the old church forms and doctrines, and to discuss the institutions of the Sabbath, the church, and the ministry. Almost all of Emerson's friends were connected with these various movements. The Brook Farm men and women he loved, " and thoroughly sympathised with their anxious desire to make life better; but he saw the folly of their experiment, and its weaknesses, and he quickly discovered the evils which it fostered in place of those it attempted to escape. His sense of humour was always a restraining and sanitary influence in his character. He saw the ridiculous, the incongruous side of Brook Farm ; and his humour, his rare perception of the fitness of things, led him to see that finely-conceived reform in its real light." Among those who took a leading part in the experiment was the Rev. George Ripley. Nathaniel Hawthorne was one of the first to take up the scheme, and his published note-books contain passages of deep interest in connection with it. In the "Blithedale Romance" his weird pen has thrown a halo of imagination, romance, and sentiment about Brook Farm ; although he disclaims any purpose to describe persons or events connected with it, and expressed a hope that someone might yet do justice to a movement so full of earnest aspiration, whose aim was " to simplify economics, combine leisure for study with healthful and honest toil, avert unjust collisions of caste, equalise refinements, awaken generous affections, diffuse courtesy, and sweeten and sanctify life as a whole." Margaret Fuller, "sympathising with the heroism that prompted the scheme, considered it as premature, but she gave her friends connected with it the cheer of her encouragement and the light of her counsel. She visited them often ; entering genially into their trials and pleasures, and missing no chance to drop good seed in every furrow upturned by the ploughshare or softened by the rain." Her intimate friend, W. H. Channing, said of her in relation to this movement :—" In the secluded yet intensely animated circle of those co-workers, I frequently met her during several succeeding years, and rejoice to bear witness to the justice, magnanimity, wisdom, patience, and many-sided good will that governed her every thought and deed." An account of the Brook Farm experiment is given by Mr. O. B. Frothingham in his " Transcendentalism in New

England," from which some extracts are given towards the end of this volume. To these the attention of the reader is specially called, as they afford a vivid picture of the aims and aspirations of a circle which included many of Emerson's most valued friends.

In 1842 he lost a most promising child, called Waldo. This domestic loss he has bewailed in his "Threnody," a poem of unequalled tenderness and beauty, some passages of which vividly express feelings known only to those who have lost a bright and precocious child. Margaret Fuller knew this child, and said of him, "I hoped more from him than from any living being. I cannot yet reconcile myself to the thought that the sun shines upon the grave of the beautiful blue-eyed boy, and that I shall see him no more. Five years he was an angel to us, and I know not that any person was ever more the theme of thought to us. . . . I loved him more than any child I ever knew, as he was of nature more fair and noble. You would be surprised to know how dear he was to my imagination." A few of the opening lines will perhaps induce readers to become acquainted with the whole poem, which occupies fourteen pages. In order fully to appreciate this poem, the reader should know that the second part, beginning " The deep Heart answered, ' Weepest thou ? ' " was written three years after the first.

The South-wind brings
Life, sunshine, and desire,
And on every mount and meadow
Breathes aromatic fire ;
But over the dead he has no power,
The lost, the lost, he cannot restore ;
And, looking over the hills, I mourn
The darling who shall not return.

I see my empty house,
I see my trees repair their boughs ;
And he, the wondrous child,
Whose silver warble wild
Outvalued every pulsing sound
Within the air's cerulean round,—
The hyacinthine boy, for whom
Morn well might break and April bloom,—
The gracious boy, who did adorn
The world whereinto he was born,
And by his countenance repay
The favour of the loving Day,—
Has disappeared from the Day's eye ;
Far and wide she cannot find him ;
My hopes pursue, they cannot bind him.
Returned this day, the south wind searches,
And finds young pines and budding birches ;
But finds not the budding man ;
Nature, who lost, cannot remake him ;
Fate let him fall, Fate can't retake him ;
Nature, Fate, men, him seek in vain.

A second series of " Essays " appeared in 1844, the English edition having a few prefatory words

by Carlyle. " I will wish the brave Emerson a fair
welcome among us again ; and leave him to speak
with his old friends and to make new." This series
contained nine papers—"The Poet," "Experience,"
"Character," "Manners," "Gifts," "Nature," "Politics," "Nominalist and Realist," and "New England
Reformers." In the essay " Nature " is incorpo-
rated a piece entitled " Tantalus," which originally
appeared in " The Dial." The last of these papers
was a lecture, read before the Society in Amory
Hall on March 3rd, 1844. " The Young American,"
a lecture read before the Mercantile Library Association, Boston, was delivered February 7th, 1844,
and printed in " The Dial," April, 1844. In 1846,
he published his first volume of Poems. The
London reprint of it in 1847 is disfigured by many
glaring typographical errors. In 1847, he wrote
the " Editor's Address " in the first number of the
" Massachusetts Quarterly Review ;" but did not
contribute any paper to it. He was announced
as one of its editors ; but the originator and real
editor was Theodore Parker. It existed for three
years. The address showed his interest in socialism,
in Swedenborg, and the future of America, and his
general attitude towards the reforms of the time.
In a closing paragraph he says the Review is to
be open especially to those " inspired pages" which

come of "inevitable utterances." "We entreat the aid of every lover of truth and right, and let principles entreat for us. We rely on the talents and industry of good men known to us, but much more on the magnetism of truth, which is multiplying and educating advocates for itself and friends for us. We rely on the truth for and against ourselves."

The publication of his two volumes of Essays, having stamped Emerson as a thinker of indisputable originality and power, his fame rapidly increased in this country, and many of his admirers became desirous that he should visit England, and deliver courses of lectures, as he had done in the great towns of his own land. He had now gained the ear of England, and many of the most thoughtful minds of both hemispheres had acknowledged his genius and power. For some time he hesitated, doubting whether his name would bring together any numerous company of hearers. Several letters passed on the subject. At length his hesitancy was overcome, and permission granted by him to the writer of this memoir to announce his visit, and his intention to read lectures to institutions, or to any gathering of friendly individuals who sympathised with his studies. Applications immediately flowed in from every part of the kingdom, and in many cases it was found impossible to comply with the wishes of the requisitionists, from a fear of enforcing too much labour on the lecturer. Had every offer that was made been accepted, his engagements would have extended over a much longer period than he was prepared to remain in England. At last he arrived at Liverpool on 22nd October, 1847. Carlyle was greatly delighted with the prospect of again seeing his friendly visitor— "the lonely, wayfaring man," as he described him— of 1833. A letter from Emerson, announcing the probable time of his sailing, had, by negligence at a country post-office, failed to be delivered to Carlyle in due course, and was not received until near the time of Emerson's expected arrival, thus depriving the former of the opportunity of responding with hospitable messages and invitations. This led to great trouble of mind in Carlyle, fearing, as he did, that it might subject him to the appearance of a want of hospitality—a possibility abhorrent to his feelings. His trouble was ended, however, by an arrangement being made to have his reply delivered to Emerson the instant he landed in England, which, it is needless to say, was faithfully carried out. His minute instructions and almost solemn injunctions in regard to this matter were delightfully characteristic of his high regard for Emerson. The reader will find them in a later page.

For some months he took up his residence in Manchester, from which, as a centre, he went forth to lecture in various towns in the midland and northern counties of England. His first course was delivered to the members of the Manchester Athenæum, the subject being "Representative Men, including Plato, Swedenborg, Montaigne, Shakespeare, and Napoleon." His next course was given in the Manchester Mechanics' Institution, the subjects being " Eloquence," " Domestic Life," " Reading," and "The Superlative in Manners and Literature." They excited great interest, and attracted crowded audiences. While in Manchester he delivered a remarkable speech at a soirée, held under the auspices of the Manchester Athenæum, Sir A. Alison being in the chair. Richard Cobden and other notabilities were present. His text was the indomitable " pluck" and steadfastness and grandeur of England, amid all her difficulties and trials. At that time English commerce and industry were in a very depressed condition. This speech, although comparatively brief, was carefully prepared for the occasion, and the importance he attached to it may be gathered from the fact that he printed it, *in extenso*, in his " English Traits," published nine years after. The speech is given at the end of this volume. He also visited

Edinburgh in February, 1848, where he lectured, and met many of its celebrities, including Robert Chambers, with whose geniality and kindly humour, and charming family environment, he was delighted. While in Edinburgh he was the guest of Dr. Samuel Brown. He spent two days at Ambleside with Miss Martineau and again visited Wordsworth— his first visit having been paid fifteen years before. A few records of his stay in London, and remarks on some of the people he met there, will be found in his " English Traits," one of the most brilliant and striking books ever written about England and its characteristics. In perusing this volume the reader will be charmed by its vigour, vivacity, and acuteness. There is nowhere in it any didactic dulness, or commonplace descriptions, as in many books of this class. In hanging over its pages, one experiences much the same feelings as if one were transplanted from a dead-level country to hilly pastures and wooded ridges, where the turf is elastic, and the air sharp, keen, and bracing.

His lectures in London were attended by the *élite* of the social and literary world of the metropolis. Mr. and Mrs. Carlyle, the Duchess of Sutherland, Lady Byron and her daughter Ada (Lady Lovelace), the Duke of Argyll, Dr. John Carlyle, William and

Mary Howitt, Douglas Jerrold, Mr. John Forster,
Thackeray, and many other distinguished persons
were among his hearers. The writer of this notice
can speak for the breathless attention of his audience,
and the evident all-absorbing interest with which
his discourses were listened to. The course consisted
of six lectures, on " The Minds and Manners of
the Nineteenth Century," " Power and Laws of
Thought," " Relation of Intellect to Natural Science,"
" Tendencies and Duties of Men of Thought,"
" Politics and Socialism," " Poetry and Eloquence,"
and " Natural Aristocracy." It was a remarkable
course. Only one or two of these lectures have
been printed. Not a few of his aristocratic audience must have winced under some of his keen
and searching reminders of duty. He uttered his
convictions with a daring independence, and gave
his judgments with a decisiveness of tone and
earnest solemnity of manner which might have
put kings in fear. He made his audience feel as if
he had got them well in hand, and did not mean
to let them go without giving them his "mind."
It was as if he had said (to use his own words, on
another occasion) :—" This you must accept as
fated, and final for your salvation. It is mankind's
Bill of Rights, the royal proclamation of Intellect,
descending the throne, and announcing its good

pleasure, that, hereafter, as *heretofore*, and now once for all, this world shall be governed by common sense and law of morals, or shall go to ruin." During the delivery of this course a letter appeared in the *London Examiner*, urging a repetition of it at a price sufficiently low to admit of poor literary men hearing Emerson. "This might be done by fixing some small admission charge, commensurate with the means of poets, critics, philosophers, historians, scholars, and the other divine paupers of that class. I feel that it ought to be done, because Emerson is a phenomenon whose like is not in the world, and to miss him is to lose an important, informing fact, out of the nineteenth century. If, therefore, you will insert this, the favour will at all events have been asked, and one conscience satisfied. It seems also probable that a very large attendance of thoughtful men would be secured, and that Emerson's stirrup-cup would be a cheering and full one, sweet and ruddy with international charity."

Three lectures were also given at Exeter Hall: "Napoleon," "Shakespeare," and "Domestic Life." At their conclusion Mr. Monckton Milnes (now Lord Houghton) made a speech complimentary to the lecturer, and to which the latter replied.

The first impression one had in listening to

him in public was that his manner was so singularly quiet and unimpassioned that you began to fear the beauty and force of his thoughts were about to be marred by what might almost be described as monotony of expression. But very soon was this apprehension dispelled. The mingled dignity, sweetness, and strength of his features, the earnestness of his manner and voice, and the evident depth and sincerity of his convictions gradually extorted your deepest attention, and made you feel that you were within the grip of no ordinary man, but of one "sprung of earth's first blood," with "titles manifold ;" and as he went on with serene self-possession and an air of conscious power, reading sentence after sentence, charged with well-weighed meaning, and set in words of faultless aptitude, you could no longer withstand his "so potent spell," but were forthwith compelled to surrender yourself to the fascination of his eloquence. He used little or no action, save occasionally a slight vibration of the body, as though rocking beneath the hand of some unseen power. The precious words dropped from his mouth in quick succession, and noiselessly sank into the hearts of his hearers, there to abide for ever, and, like the famed carbuncle in Eastern cave, shed a mild radiance on all things therein. Perhaps no orator ever succeeded with so little

exertion in éntrancing his audience, stealing away
each faculty, and leading the listeners captive at
his will. He abjured all force and excitement—
dispensing his regal sentences in all mildness, goodness, and truth ; but stealthily and surely he grew
upon you, from the smallest proportions, as it were;
steadily increasing, until he became a Titan, a
commanding power—

> To whom, as to the mountains and the stars,
> .The soul seems passive and submiss.

The moment he finished, he took up his MS. and
quietly glided away,—disappearing before his audience could give vent to their applause.

The French Revolution of 1848 happening while
he was in this country, he went over to Paris in
the spring of that year, and was present at several
meetings of the political clubs, which were then in
a state of fullest activity. He was accompanied by
Mr. W. E. Forster (the late Chief Secretary for
Ireland). In Paris he made the acquaintance of
the late Mr. James Oswald Murray, then resident
in that city. Mr. Murray, who was an artist, made
a crayon sketch of Emerson, which is in the possession of the present writer. It brings him, as he
then was, very vividly before the mind's eye. This
likeness has not been reproduced. His observations made during that visit were embodied in a

brilliant lecture on the French, which he delivered after his return to America, but which has never been published. Before sailing for America, in the summer of 1848, he spent a night in Manchester with the present writer, and had much to say of all he had seen and met. He overflowed with pleasant recollections of his visit, and spoke in the warmest terms of the kindness and consideration which he had everywhere experienced. He said he had not been aware there was so much kindness in the world. Would that some unseen but swift pen could have recorded all he said in these last rapidly-flying hours! Speaking of Carlyle, he repeated the words used in a letter written some months before: "The guiding genius of the man, and what constitutes his superiority over almost every other man of letters, is his commanding sense of justice, and incessant demand for sincerity." He spoke of De Quincey and Leigh Hunt as having the finest manners of any literary men he had ever met. His visit to Leigh Hunt is described in the "Recollections" which follow this memoir.

On the Sunday before he sailed for America, a large number of his friends and admirers from all parts of the country were invited to meet him at the hospitable mansion of Mr. and Mrs. Paulet (both since dead), near Liverpool whose guest he was. Among other notable persons gathered together on that occasion to spend a few hours in his company, and to listen to his rich experiences and recollections, was Arthur Hugh Clough, for whom Emerson had a most tender regard. In the following year the former met Margaret Fuller in Rome. He had become known to a select circle of scholars by his poem, "The Bothie of Tober-Na-Vuolich," which Kingsley eulogised, and Oxford pronounced "indecent, immoral, profane, and communistic." Mr. Emerson esteemed the poem highly, and was the means of procuring its re-publication in America. In a private letter, dated December 8th, 1862, he says: "I grieve that the good Clough, the generous and susceptible scholar, should die. I have read over his 'Bothie' again, so full of the wine of youth." In the autumn of 1852 Clough went to America, by Emerson's invitation, voyaging thither in company with Thackeray and Lowell. He settled at Cambridge, Massachusetts, where he was welcomed with remarkable cordiality, and formed many friendships which lasted to the end of his life. While in America he contributed several articles to the reviews and magazines, and undertook a revision of the translation, known as Dryden's, of Plutarch's "Lives" for an American publisher, which appeared in five volumes. In the following year he returned to England. He died at Florence in 1861, in his 43rd year.

"Representative Men," seven lectures, was published in 1850, the subjects being Uses of Great Men; Plato, or, The Philosopher; Plato, New Readings; Swedenborg, or, The Mystic; Montaigne, or, The Sceptic; Shakespeare, or, The Poet; Napoleon, or, The Man of the World; Goethe, or, The Writer. The "Essay on War," a lecture delivered in Boston, in March, 1838, was published in 1850, in Miss Elizabeth Peabody's "Æsthetic Papers." In 1852, in conjunction with W. H. Channing and J. Freeman Clarke, he wrote "Memoirs of Margaret Fuller," his contribution to the work being the chapters on her life while resident in Concord and Boston, and her wonderful powers of conversation. When Kossuth visited the United States in 1852 he went to Concord, where Emerson welcomed him. There was a procession, a review, and speeches in the town hall, the address of the occasion being made by Emerson. A lecture on The Anglo-American Race was given by him in New York in 1855. In 1856 he lectured in Boston on English Civilisation, France, Signs of the Times, Beauty, The Poets, The Scholar. In the same year he delivered an address before the Woman's Rights

Convention. "The aspiration of this century will be the code of the next," was one of his utterances on this subject. In 1863, when a Woman's Journal was proposed to be published in Boston, he wrote for it a short essay defining his position on this subject. The journal was not started, and the essay remained unprinted until it appeared in "The Woman's Journal" of March 26th, 1881. In 1856 he published " English Traits," a record of his impressions of England, already referred to, p. 16.

In January, 1855, he gave one of a course of anti-slavery lectures at Tremont Temple, Boston. "It was a strong and forcible address, full of fire, alive with magnetic power, plain and simple in style, and was listened to throughout with breathless interest. He charged the prevalent indifference to the wrongs of the slave to scepticism concerning great human duties and concerns." In the same year he delivered an address before the Anti-Slavery Society of New York, in which he declared that "an immoral law is void." Under the title of " Echoes of Harper's Ferry," he published in 1860 three speeches concerning John Brown, which he had delivered at Boston in 1859, at Concord later in the same year, and at Salem in 1860. In 1856, when Charles Sumner was assaulted by Brooks, a meeting of sympathy was held in Concord, and Emerson spoke with warm appreciation of the services of that senator.

At no time was he a leader in the actual battle against slavery, but as time went on and the struggle increased in intensity, his spoken word and pen became more and more conspicuous and powerful. In January, 1861, he made a speech at the annual meeting of the Massachusetts Anti-Slavery Society in Boston. The speakers were often disturbed by a mob, and it was with great difficulty they could be heard. Emerson was frequently interrupted by hisses and other demonstrations of disapproval. He said that "slavery is based on a crime of that fatal character that it decomposes men. The barbarism which has lately appeared wherever that question has been touched, and in the action of the States where it prevails, seems to stupefy the moral sense. The moral injury of slavery is infinitely greater than its pecuniary and political injury. I really do not think the pecuniary mischief of slavery, which is always shown by statistics, worthy to be named in comparison with this power to subvert the reason of men ; so that those who speak of it, who defend it, who act in its behalf, seem to have lost the moral sense." In speaking of the threatened seces-

sion, he used these emphatic words, appropriate for
the hour and occasion :—

In the great action now pending, all the forbearance, all the dis-
cretion possible, and yet all the firmness will be used by the representatives of the North, and by the people at home. No man of
patriotism, no man of natural sentiment, can undervalue the sacred
Union which we possess ; but if it is sundered, it will be because it
had already ceased to have a vital tension. The action of to-day
is only the ultimatum of what had already occurred. The bonds
had ceased to exist, because of this vital defect of slavery at the
South, actually separating them in sympathy, in thought, in character, from the people of the North ; and then, if the separation
had gone thus far, what is the use of a pretended tie ? As to con-
cessions, we have none to make. The monstrous concession made
at the formation of the Constitution is all that ever can be asked ;
it has blocked the civilisation and humanity of the times to this day.

He received an invitation to give an anti-slavery
lecture at Washington. This he delivered in February, 1862, to a very large audience. President
Lincoln, his cabinet, and the leading officials in the
capital were present. Next day Seward introduced
Lincoln to Emerson, and they had a long con-
ference on slavery. The lecture had deeply impressed the President. The effect produced by the
lecturer on his audience was described as most
powerful, and it was listened to with unbounded
enthusiasm. Those who had often heard Emerson
considered it as one of his greatest and best efforts,
and that he seemed inspired throughout its
delivery. The lecture was printed in the "Atlantic

Monthly," April, 1862. A meeting was held in Boston immediately after the President's proclamation came out, on September 22nd, 1862, at which Emerson spoke of Lincoln's difficulties, and the wisdom which characterised his action. The speech was given in the "Atlantic Monthly," November, 1862. Mr. Cooke thus speaks of it :— "It was a clear, strong, earnest address, full of sympathy for the blacks, and grandly true to the highest moral convictions. There were no conceits of language in it, but a plain directness and a simple power that were full of charm. It is well to recall these addresses, that we may so much the more clearly understand how practical and human is Emerson's genius. On these occasions he came directly to the subject in hand, uttered not a word but of the highest wisdom, and proclaimed in majestic words that moral law which is written in the nature of things." After the proclamation had been carried into effect, and emancipation became a fact, a great meeting of rejoicing was held in Boston. At this meeting Emerson read his "Boston Hymn." Not long after he published his "Voluntaries," celebrating the victories of Liberty. In April, 1865, a meeting took place at Concord, to express the universal grief felt on account of Lincoln's death. On this occasion he delivered an address, giving full expression to his thoughts about the war, the victory of the North, and his love of Lincoln. This fine oration is given *in extenso* at p. 152 of Mr. Cooke's book.

In 1859 he lectured on Morals, Conversation, Culture, Domestic Life, Natural Religion, The Law of Success, Originality, Criticism, Clubs, and Manners. In a publication called "The Dial, a Monthly Magazine for Literature, Philosophy, and Religion," started in 1860 by his young friend, M. D. Conway, in Cincinnati, Ohio, were first printed The Sacred Dance from the Persian, Twelve Quatrains, and the Essay on Domestic Life, previously delivered as a lecture, and which subsequently took its place as one of the essays in the volume entitled "Society and Solitude;" and by his permission was printed in the same periodical the Address on West Indian Emancipation, delivered in Concord in 1844.

In 1860, he lost his friend Theodore Parker, and in 1862, H. D. Thoreau. To the former he paid a noble tribute at a public meeting, closing with these words :—"His sudden and singular eminence, the importance of his name and influence, are the verdict of his country to his virtues. We have few such men to lose ; amiable and blameless at home ; feared abroad as the standard-bearer of liberty ; taking all the duties he could grasp ; and, more, refusing to spare himself. He has gone down in early glory to his grave, to be a living and enlarging power, wherever learning, wit, honest valour, and independence are honoured." At Thoreau's funeral he spoke about his rare genius—"a man made for the noblest society : he had in a short life exhausted the capabilities of this world : wherever there is knowledge, wherever there is virtue, wherever there is beauty, he will find a home." This address appeared in the "Atlantic Monthly," August, 1862. He assisted in editing Thoreau's Letters in 1865, and in preparing several other volumes from his manuscripts. Parker's congregation, after his death, asked Emerson to give them a sermon in Music Hall, which he was reluctant to do, "as he could no longer preach in the ordinary sense, and as he had long before abandoned all thought of ever preaching again. He was urged so strongly, however, that at last he consented. He said he was glad that Parker had made the place one of freedom ; that he had valued religion more than its forms. During several years he frequently appeared before the society—often on Sundays—giving lectures for the Parker fraternity." One of his sermons in Music Hall has been reported by Mr. M. D. Conway in " Fraser's Magazine," May,

1867, who says it was "the most impressive utterance he ever heard from Emerson. It produced an effect on those who heard it beyond anything that I ever witnessed, many being moved at times to tears. I went with pencil and paper, intending to take down as much as I could, but at the end of the hour occupied by it, the paper remained blank, and the pencil had been forgotten. I can, therefore, only produce the record of my impressions of it, as they were written down the same day."

" The Conduct of Life" was published in 1860. The nine Essays of which it consists had mostly been delivered as lectures during the previous half-dozen years. Their titles are—Fate, Power, Wealth, Culture, Behaviour, Worship, Considerations by the Way, Beauty, and Illusions. The first, sixth, seventh, and last of these were considered to be among his best efforts. While his previous books had sold slowly, this one went off rapidly—2,500 copies of it being disposed of within two days after its publication. In July, 1861, he gave an address before one of the societies of Tuft's College, the subject being the duties and attitude of students. In 1863 he wrote the "Biographical Sketch" preceding H. D. Thoreau's "Excursions," extending to thirty-three pages, and in 1864, an "Introductory Essay on Persian Poetry," prefixed to the "Gulistan" of Saadi, and afterwards printed in the "Atlantic Monthly," July, 1864. In November, 1864, he gave a course of Sunday Lectures before the Parker fraternity on " American Life "—the subjects being Public and Private Education, Social Aims, Resources, Table-Talk, Books, Character. Three of these lectures were reprinted—Books, in the volume entitled " Society and Solitude," and Social Aims and Resources, in a later volume called " Letters and Social Aims." The essay on Character was printed in the " North American Review" for 1866. In 1865, he spoke at "Commencement" Festival at Harvard, and lectured on Literature before one of the Amherst societies. In 1866, he gave a course of lectures at Boston on " Philosophy for the People ;" the subjects being Intellect, Instinct, Perception, Talent, Genius, Imagination, Taste, Laws of the Mind, Conduct of the Intellect, and Relation of Intellect to Morals. During the winter of the same year, he gave lectures on The Man of the World, Eloquence, Immortality, and an address on the reception of the Chinese Embassy. He said in the course of one of these lectures that John Brown gave at Charlestown the best speech made in the nineteenth century, and that Daniel Webster and Father Taylor were the only two men who had reached his ideal of oratory.

" May-day and other Poems " made its appearance in 1867. Many of the smaller pieces had appeared before in the "Atlantic Monthly." " The Rule of Life" was the subject of a lecture delivered to the Parker Fraternity in 1867. In the same year he attended the meeting for the organisation of the " Free Religious Association." The persons taking a lead in this movement had been largely influenced by his writings and lectures. " To study religion as a universal sentiment, to find the sources of its world-wide manifestation in man, to regard all its forms as expressions of the same fundamental principles—these objects of the new association had been for many years among his most cherished ideas." He delivered an address on the occasion, in which he said, " We are all very sensible—it is forced on us every day—of the feeling that the churches are outgrown, that the creeds are outgrown, that a technical theology no longer suits us. . . . The church is not large enough for the man. . . . The child, the young student, finds scope in his mathematics and chemistry, or natural history, because he finds a truth larger than he is—finds himself continually instructed. But in the churches every healthy and thoughtful mind finds itself in something less ; it is checked, cribbed, confined ; and the statistics of the American, the

English, and the German cities, showing that the mass of the population is leaving off going to church, indicate the necessity which should have been foreseen, that the church should always be new and extemporized, because it is eternal, and springs from the sentiment of men, or it does not exist."

In July, 1867, he was made an Overseer of Harvard University, and received the honorary degree of LL.D. At this time he gave his Phi-Beta-Kappa address on "The Progress of Culture," afterwards published in "Letters and Social Aims." Public opinion had at last come round to him, and his startling and — to the conservative element at Harvard—obnoxious and heretical Divinity-School address of 1838 was at length condoned, and the University "did herself the honour to forget his heresies, and accord to the great thinker a just recognition. It was a triumph on his part, nobly won and richly deserved. His critics had become his admirers, his heresies were forgotten ; his genius, his rare merits, his pure and noble life only were remembered." His address was full of hope and courage, and richly suggestive with those great ideas he had preached for so many years. It was a strong plea for the truest culture, as the great promise of the American people. His concluding sentences were : "When I look around me, and consider the sound material of which the cultivated class here is made up—what high personal worth, what love of men, what hope, is joined with rich information and practical power, and that the most distinguished by genius and culture are in this class of benefactors— I can not distrust this great knighthood of virtue, or doubt that the interests of science, of letters, of politics and humanity, are safe. I think these bands are strong enough to hold up the Republic. I read the promise of better times and of greater use."

"Society and Solitude," a volume containing twelve essays, was given to the public in 1870. The essays are—Society and Solitude, Civilization, Art, Eloquence, Domestic Life, Farming, Work and Days, Books, Clubs, Courage, Success, Old Age. Many of these papers had been long before given as lectures. The one on Art was printed in "The Dial," and that on Farming had been delivered in Concord in 1858. The papers on Books and Domestic Life had been delivered as lectures in England in 1847-8, and those on Society and Solitude and Old Age had appeared in early volumes of the "Atlantic Monthly," while the one on Civilization was a portion of the Washington Address of 1862. Colonel Higginson, an accomplished American author, said of these essays that there was in them " a greater variety and a more distinct organic life than in the earlier ones, while they are no less finished and scarcely less concentrated. It is not enough to say that such papers as these constitute the high-water mark of American literature ; it is not too much to say that they are unequalled in the literature of the age. Name, if one can, the Englishman or the Frenchman who, on themes like these, must not own himself second to Emerson."

In the spring of 1871 he visited California with a party of friends, and delivered some lectures while there. In the autumn of the same year he gave an address before the Massachusetts Historical Society on the hundredth anniversary of the birth of Walter Scott. The address will be found at the end of this volume. In the same year he gave six lectures and readings in Mechanics' Hall. "The first was on literature. In the last he spoke of the effects of culture on the soul, and its influence on the formation of ideas about life and destiny." The "Boston Journal" thus spoke of these lectures :—

The same consummate magnetism lingers around and upon every phrase ; there is the same thrilling earnestness of antithesis, the same delight and brooding over poetry and excellence of expression, as of old. There is no other man in America who can, by the mere force of what he says, enthrall and dominate an audience. Breathless attention is given, although now and then his voice falls away so that those seated farthest off have to strain every nerve to catch the words. The grand condensation, the unfaltering and almost cynical brevity of expression, are at first startling and vexatious ; but presently one yields to the charm, and finds his mind in the proper assenting mood. The loving tenderness with which Emerson lingers over a fine and thoroughly expressive phrase is beyond description. It thrills the whole audience ; arrests universal attention. The sacredness of the printed page is interpreted in a new and universal light. There is the same passionate adoration displayed over a fine line from a sonnet, or lavished upon one of Thoreau's quaint conceits, which Ingres bestowed upon a specimen of pure drawing. The innate and inexhaustible love of beauty, softening and permeating every utterance, infusing its delicate glow and its delicious harmony into each idea, and investing abstractions with the charms of real and vivid beings, triumphs over age and diffidence, gives to the austere and unworldly philosopher the bloom and enthusiasm of the lover and the poet.

In 1871 he wrote an introduction to Goodwin's translation of Plutarch's "Morals," in which he gave an account of the works of that author. In January, 1872, while in Washington, he visited Howard University, and spoke extemporaneously to the coloured students on books as a means of education, on the choice of a profession, and other kindred topics.

In 1872 he again visited Europe, accompanied by his daughter, arriving in November. After a short stay in London, they proceeded to Egypt, spending some time there, returning in the spring of 1873 to England, *via* Italy and France. During this visit he did not deliver any lectures. He resided for some weeks in London, and visited Professor Max Müller at Oxford. He spent a single day (8th May) in Edinburgh, his main object being to see Dr. J. Hutchison Stirling, author of " The Secret of Hegel." His two last days were spent under the roof of the writer of this memoir, and many of his old acquaintances and hearers of 1847-8 had thus an opportunity of meeting him. Mr. George W. Smalley, the able London correspondent of " The New York Tribune," writing about Emerson's last visit to England, said :—" I know no American,—indeed, there can be no other, who has in England a company of such friends and disciples as those who gather about Mr. Emerson ; no one for whom so many rare men and women have a reverence so affectionate ; no one who holds to the best section of English students, and of her most religious and cultivated minds, a relation so delightful to both. The incomparable charm of his manner and of his conversation remains what it always was, and marked always by the same sweetness, the same delicacy, mingled with the same penetration and force."

Previously to this, his last visit to Europe, his house at Concord was accidentally destroyed by fire. Fortunately, none of his books or manuscripts were injured. During his absence in Europe it was rebuilt. When he returned home in May, 1873, he was received with the greatest enthusiasm by his fellow-townsmen—the crowd accompanying him from the railway station to the newly-built house, which was an exact counterpart of the old home. A letter from one of his own family, written at the time, records that the citizens gathered at the railway terminus in crowds, and the school children were drawn up in two smiling rows, through which he passed, greeted by enthusiastic cheers and songs of welcome. All followed his carriage to the house, and sang " Home, sweet Home " to the music of the band. A few days afterwards, he invited all his townsmen and townswomen to call and see him in his restored home, and a large number of them availed themselves of the opportunity.

In October, 1873, he gave the " Dedication Address " in connection with a new Free Library in Concord, the gift of an enlightened citizen of the town. His subject was the uses and value of books and libraries, and in the course of his address he spoke of Thoreau and Hawthorne. At Faneuil Hall, December 16th, 1873, he read a poem on the centennial anniversary of the destruction of tea in Boston harbour. He read the poem a second time on the last day of the year before the Radical Club. At this meeting a reception was given him, at which many of his friends were present. His manner was described as " so gentle, that he seemed only reading to one person, and yet his voice was so distinct that it filled the room in its lowest tones."

In 1874 he was put in nomination for the Lord Rectorship of Glasgow University. Emerson received 500 votes, against 700 for Disraeli, who was elected. In a letter addressed to Dr. J. Hutchison Stirling, the honorary president in connection with the movement, he said :—" I count that vote as quite the fairest laurel that has ever fallen on me. Probably I have never seen one of these 500 young men ; and thus they show us that our recorded thoughts give the means of reaching those who think with us in other countries, and make closer alliances, sometimes, than life-long neighbourhood."

In 1875 appeared " Parnassus, a Selection of British and American Poetry, with prefatory remarks," of which it may be truly said that it is the best collection of English Poetry ever published. The only defect in the volume is the much-to-be-regretted absence of a few specimens of his own poems—attributable to Emerson's characteristic modesty. Any other selector—had he been a poet—would, in all probability, have given some specimens of his own verses ; *e.g.*, in a recent volume of " Selections of English Poetry," published in London, the editor obligingly presents the reader with eleven passages from Shakespeare, seven from Milton, and *thirteen* from his own works! Some of the selections in " Parnassus " have been inserted for their historical importance ; some for their weight of sense ; some for single couplets or lines, perhaps even for a word ; some for magic of style ; and others which—although in their structure betraying a defect of poetic ear—have nevertheless a wealth of truth which ought to have created melody. The arrangement is not chronological, but based upon the character of the subject, under the following heads :—Nature ; Human Life ; Intellectual ; Contemplative, Moral and Religious ; Heroic ; Portraits ; Narrative Poems and Ballads ; Songs ; Dirges and Pathetic Poems ; Comic and Humorous ; Poetry of Terror, and Oracles and Counsels. An index of authors, prefixed, with dates of birth and death, is a useful guide in many instances, especially as regards the period of the writings. It does not appear that the merits of an author's acknowledged—or perhaps we should say recognised—position had had much to do

with the copiousness of the extracts.   In his preface
he erroneously attributes to Landor a remark on
Wordsworth's beautiful poem, " Laodamia," which
was really made by another critic :—" It is a poem
that might be read aloud in Elysium, and the spirits
of departed heroes and sages would gather round
to listen to it."   The sentence occurs in " The
Spirit of the Age ; or Contemporary Portraits," by
William Hazlitt.

On 19th April, 1875, Emerson delivered a brief
address on the occasion of the hundredth anniversary
of the Concord fight.   " May-day and other Poems,"
being a second volume of Poems, was published in
1874 ; "Letters and Social Aims," containing
eleven essays — Poetry and Imagination, Social
Aims, Eloquence, Resources, The Comic, Quotation and Originality, Progress of Culture, Persian
Poetry, Inspiration, Greatness, and Immortality—
appeared in 1876.   Some of these essays are
equal to any that he has written—notably " The
Progress of Culture," and "Immortality."   Most of
the others had been given as lectures between 1860
and 1870.   " Fortune of the Republic " was the title
of a lecture delivered at the Old South Church, Boston, March 30, 1878, afterwards published in à thin
volume.   In the same year and in the same place
he gave a lecture on " The Superlative;" in 1879

one on " Memory," before the Concord School of
Philosophy ; another in Cambridge, on " Eloquence;" and one before the Harvard Divinity
School on " The Preacher." This was printed in
the " Unitarian Review " (1880). In 1880 he gave
his hundredth lecture before the Concord Lyceum,
on " New England Life and Letters;" and before
the School of Philosophy, " Natural Aristocracy."
In the autumn he read an essay before the members
of the Divinity School, and early in 1881 he read
a paper on " Carlyle " (written in 1848) before the
Massachusetts Historical Society.

In the " North American Review " will be found
the following prose essays and articles :—Michael
Angelo, Milton, Character, Demonology, Perpetual
Forces, The Sovereignty of Ethics. In the "Atlantic
Monthly" appeared, between 1858 and 1876, the
following articles and poems:—The Rommany Girl,
The Chartist's Complaint, Days, Brahma, *Illusions*,
Solitude and Society, Two Rivers, *Books*, *Persian
Poetry*, *Eloquence*, Waldeinsamkeit, Song of
Nature, *Culture*, The Test, *Old Age*, The Titmouse,
American Civilization, Compensation, *Thoreau*,
The President's Proclamation, Boston Hymn,
Voluntaries, *Saadi*, My Garden, Boston, Terminus,
Progress of Culture (Phi-Beta-Kappa Address,
Harv. Univ., 1867). The prose articles are indicated

by being printed in italics. It has been already mentioned that several of the above pieces have been included in successive volumes of his collected essays.

At the end of this volume the reader will find a list of the articles on Emerson and his writings which have appeared in the magazines and reviews of Great Britain and the United States, as well as indications of what has been written about him in France, Germany, and Holland.

Any sketch of the life and environment of Emerson, however brief, would be incomplete if it did not include some reference to that remarkable woman, Margaret Fuller, and to the influence which she exercised on the best men and women with whom she came in contact. The friendship which subsisted between her and Emerson was only terminated by her untimely death. Returning from Europe with her husband (Count D'Ossoli) and child, the vessel in which they sailed was wrecked on 16th June, 1850, within sight of her own New England shores—indeed, quite close to the beach. For twelve agonising hours they were face to face with death. She refused an attempt made by four of the crew to save her, lest she might have been parted from those dearest to her. She bravely preferred certain death to the chances of a life-long separation. To perish with them were better than to live without them. The terrible story has been told with intense power and sympathy by her friend, Mr. W. H. Channing, in that portion of her "Memoirs" written by him. A more thrilling narrative has never been written.

Of this woman of true genius and extraordinary acquirements, and whose conversation was of unrivalled fluency, power, and brilliancy, ample records remain. As a biography, giving the inward and outward life of a woman of the highest culture, and endowed with rare gifts of soul, her "Memoirs" written by Mr. Emerson, Mr. J. Freeman Clarke, and Mr. W. H. Channing, are of the deepest interest. They knew her intimately, and have performed their task with loving admiration and sympathy, and "with extraordinary frankness, courage, and delicacy." She was a good Greek, Latin, and Hebrew scholar, was well read in French, Italian, and German literature, and had studied ancient and modern Art carefully and diligently. She had a singular power of communicating her literary enthusiasm to her companions. She has left behind her several volumes containing the best of her literary work. It has been said of her that "she was plain in appearance, and that she had a faculty of unsheathing herself at the touch of a thought; and those who

came into right relations with her remember her as
almost beautiful. Her natural place was at the
centre of a circle where thoughts and truths were
being discovered, and which had not yet found
their channels in literature. With the finest
womanly sympathies she combined the strong
masculine intellect, and an individuality which
stimulated every other individuality. Her influence
was great in the intellectual activities of her day."

At first, Emerson reluctantly made her acquaintance, and for a time they were not much drawn to
each other. She said he was not fully responsive
to her 'outbursts of sentiment, and was cold and
unapproachable ; while he found in her too much
of the sybil. Afterwards, however, " she became,"
to use his own words, " an established friend and
frequent inmate of our house, and continued thenceforward for years to come once in three or four
months to spend a week or a fortnight with us.
She adopted all the people and all the interests she
found here. 'Your people shall be my people, and
yonder darling boy I shall cherish as my own.'
Her ready sympathies endeared her to my wife
and my mother, each of whom highly esteemed
her good sense and sincerity. She was an active,
inspiring companion and correspondent ; and all
the art, the thought, and the nobleness in New

England seemed at that moment related to her, and she to it. She was everywhere a welcome guest. The houses of her friends in town and country were open to her, and every hospitable attention eagerly offered. Her arrival was a holiday, and so was her abode. She stayed a few days, often a week, more seldom a month ; and all tasks that could be suspended were put aside to catch the favourable hour, in walking, riding, or boating, to talk with this joyful guest, who brought wit, anecdotes, love-stories, tragedies, oracles with her, and, with her broad web of relations to so many friends, seemed like the queen of some parliament of love, who carried the key to all confidences, and to whom every question had been finally referred. . . . The day was never long enough to exhaust her opulent memory ; and I, who knew her intimately for ten years, never saw her without surprise at her new powers. . . . Her talents were so various, and her conversation so rich and entertaining, that one might talk with her many times, by the parlour fire, before he discovered the strength which served as foundation to so much accomplishment and eloquence. . . . In the evening she would come to the library, and many and many a conversation was there held, whose details, if they could be preserved, would justify all encomiums. They interested me in every manner;—talent, memory, wit, stern introspection, poetic play, religion, the finest personal feeling, the aspects of the future,—each followed each in full activity, and left me, I remember, enriched and sometimes astonished by the gifts of my guest. Her topics were numerous, but the cardinal points of poetry, love, and religion were never far off. . . . It remains to say that all these powers and accomplishments found their best and only adequate channel in her conversation; a conversation which those who have heard it, unanimously, as far as I know, pronounced to be, in elegance, in range, in flexibility, and adroit transition, in depth, and cordiality, and in moral aim, altogether admirable; surprising and cheerful as a poem, and communicating its own civility and elevation like a charm to all hearers. . . . Whilst she embellished the moment, her conversation had the merit of being solid and true. She put her whole character into it, and had the power to inspire. The companion was made a thinker, and went away quite other than he came."

Miss Peabody tells a very characteristic anecdote relating to Emerson's first acquaintance with Margaret Fuller:—" Emerson had returned from Europe, had recovered his health, had married a second time, had settled at Concord, and he and I had gotten over being shy with each other ; but he had not gotten on as well with Margaret Fuller. Margaret wrote poetry, and people laughed about it, and said she wrote it in fits of exaltation, which she called 'intense times.' This gave Mr. Emerson, who was very simple and natural, a prejudice against her. One day, when visiting at his house, I expressed the wish that he could know Margaret better. Mrs. Emerson, who is the soul of disinterested kindness, proposed at once that Margaret be invited to come to their house. 'Oh, no,' cried Mr. Emerson, 'I don't want to know a lady who has "intense times," and writes poetry in them.' Then I went on and told how I had had the same prejudice ; how it all melted away when I conversed with her, and how, in talking with me, she had made the whole universe look larger. At this assurance Mr. Emerson's face suddenly lighted, and, turning to his wife, he exclaimed : 'Yes, Queenie, you are right. Invite her, by all means. Let us welcome any young woman whose converse can make the whole universe look larger to us.'"

With regard to the influence which Emerson had on her mind and character, we have her own estimate:—"His influence has been more beneficial to me than that of any American, and from him I first learned what is meant by an inward life.

Many other springs have since fed the stream of living waters, but he first opened the fountain. That the 'mind is its own place' was a dead phrase to me till he cast light upon my mind. Several of his sermons stand apart in memory, like land-marks of my spiritual history. It would take a volume to tell what this one influence did for me." And again :—" My inmost heart blesses the fate that gave me birth in the same clime and time, and that has drawn me into such a close bond with him as, it is my hopeful faith, will never be broken, but from sphere to sphere ever be hallowed. When I look forward to eternal growth, I am always aware that I am far larger and deeper for him."

Margaret Fuller has left a record of her impressions of Emerson's Lectures, too long for quotation in full, but from which it is worth while giving a few sentences : " Among his audience some there were—simple souls—whose life had been, perhaps, without clear light, yet still a search after truth for its own sake, who were able to recognise beneath his veil of words the still small voice of conscience, the vestal fires of lone religious hours, and the mild teachings of the summer woods. The charm of his elocution was great. His general manner was that of the reader, occasionally rising into direct address or invocation in passages where tenderness or majesty demanded more energy. At such times both eye and voice called on a remote future to give a worthy reply—a future which shall manifest more largely the universal soul as it was then manifest to his soul. The tone of the voice was a grave body tone, full and sweet rather than sonorous, yet flexible, and haunted by many modulations, as even instruments of wood and brass seem to become after they have been long played on with skill and taste; how much more so the human voice! In the most expressive passages it uttered notes of silvery clearness, winning, yet still more commanding. The words uttered in those tones floated awhile above us, then took root in the memory like winged seed. In the union of an even rustic plainness with lyric inspiration, religious dignity with philosophic calmness, keen sagacity in details with boldness of view, we saw what brought to mind the early poets and legislators of Greece— men who taught their fellows to plough and avoid moral evil, sing hymns to the gods, and watch the metamorphosis of nature. Here in civic Boston was such a man—one who could see man in his original grandeur and his original childishness, rooted in simple nature, raising to the heavens the brow and eye of a poet."

Something has been said in the preceding para-

graph with regard to Emerson's voice. Another
friend, Mr. E. Whipple, the well-known American
critic, alluding to this characteristic, says :—" Emerson's voice had a strange power, which affected me
more than any other voice I ever heard on the stage
or on the platform. It was pure thought translated
into purely intellectual tone,—the perfect music of
spiritual utterance. It is impossible to read his
verses adequately without bearing in mind his peculiar accent and emphasis; and some of the grandest
and most uplifting passages in his prose lose much
of their effect unless the reader can recall the tones
of his voice ;—a voice now, alas ! silent on earth for
ever, but worthy of being heard in that celestial
company which he, 'a spirit of the largest size and
divinest mettle,' has now exchanged for his earthly
companions. . . . His voice had the stern,
keen, penetrating sweetness which made it a fit
organ for his self-centred, commanding mind. Yet
though peculiar to himself, it had at the same time
an impersonal character, as though a spirit was
speaking through him." When strongly moved,
his voice would assume the deepest intensity, and
his whole frame tremble with emotion,—kindling,
as if by magnetic sympathy, the feelings of his
audience. Such was the case on a memorable
occasion. An eminent lawyer of Boston, Rufus

Choate, in defending slavery, spoke of the Declaration of Independence, popularly held to be inconsistent with slavery, as a series of "glittering generalities." In a lecture given afterwards, Emerson quoted some of Choate's phrases—as those declaring "all men are born equal," and are endowed with "inalienable rights,"—and then said with ineffable scorn—"These have been called glittering generalities; they are BLAZING UBIQUITIES." The impression produced by this indignant sentence was tremendous.

The writer of this memoir had the good fortune to spend an evening in Miss Fuller's company in the autumn of 1846. She had just arrived in England, with the intention of making a long-delayed tour in Europe, with some American friends by whom she was accompanied. She spent a few days in Liverpool, and it was in the house of Mrs. Ames, a lady well known in Liverpool and Manchester circles in those days, that the conversazione took place. Her conversation—or rather monologue—was so memorable as to warrant all that has been said of it by her friends. On this occasion she ranged over a great variety of topics, social, literary, artistic, and religious, with an ease and assured grasp which made the listener feel that he was under the spell of a mind of undoubted originality, of singular magnetic force, and of the widest culture and accomplishments. Among other subjects she spoke in the warmest manner of a book that had recently appeared, called " Margaret; a Tale of the Real and the Ideal," written by the Rev. Sylvester Judd, of Augusta, Maine, containing the material for half-a-dozen ordinary novels— " full of imagination, aromatic, poetical, pictur-esque, tender, and in the dress of fiction—setting forth the whole gospel of Transcendentalism in religion, political reform, social ethics, personal character, professional and private life." The subject of the story, which belongs to the years following the Revolutionary War, is the development of a beauti-ful female nature,—the embodiment of an inbred natural refinement and purity,—amidst the rudest and most boorish surroundings, with vivid pictures of the religious life and homely customs of a rough frontier country; a tale full of moral earnestness, and fidelity to local traits, with wonderfully real descrip-tions of the varying appearances of nature and the changes of human occupation. This strange story, which some critics consider one of the best of American romances, was the theme of much bril-liant and far-reaching comment, which she poured forth with a fluency and commanding eloquence that almost took the breath from some among her audience. She kindly lent the book to the present writer, and invited a correspondence regarding it. While in Liverpool she heard a discourse by the Rev. James Martineau, which called forth her warm admiration.

Every reader of Mr. Lowell knows his intensely humorous description of the characteristics of Emerson and Carlyle, in "A Fable for Critics." That keen and vigorous critic has said many admirable things in prose about Emerson, and any memoir of him would be incomplete and inadequate which did not include the following exquisitely expressed tribute to his genius and influence. "A lecturer now for something like a third of a century, one of the pioneers of the lecturing system, the charm of his voice, his manner, and his matter has never lost its power over his earlier hearers, and continually winds new ones in its enchanting meshes. . . . I have heard some great speakers and some accomplished orators, but never any that so moved and persuaded men as he. There is a kind of undertone in that rich baritone of his that sweeps our minds from their foothold into deep waters with a drift we can not and would not resist. And how artfully (for Emerson is a long-studied artist in these things) does the deliberate utterance, that seems waiting for the first word, seem to admit us partners in the labour of thought, and make us feel as if the glance of humour were a sudden suggestion; as if the perfect phrase lying written there on the desk were as unexpected to him as to us. . . . There is no man living to whom, as a writer, so many of us feel and thankfully acknowledge so great an indebtedness for ennobling impulses. We look upon him as one of the few men of genius whom our age has produced. Search for his eloquence in his books, and you will perchance miss it, but meanwhile you will find that it has kindled all your thoughts. For choice and pith of language he belongs to a better age than ours, and might rub shoulders with Fuller and Sir Thomas Browne—a diction at once so rich and so homely as his I know not where to match. It is like homespun cloth-of-gold. I know no one that can hold a promiscuous crowd in pleased attention so long as he. . . . 'Plain living and high thinking' speak to us in this altogether unique lay-preacher. We have shared in the beneficence of this varied culture, this fearless impartiality in criticism and speculation, this masculine sincerity, this sweetness of nature which rather stimulates than cloys, for a generation long. If ever there was a standing testimonial to the cumulative power and value of Character—we have it in this gracious and dig-

nified presence. What an antiseptic is a pure life!
At sixty-five he has that privilege of soul which
abolishes the calendar, and presents him to us
always the unwasted contemporary of his own
prime. . . . Who that saw the audience will
ever forget it, where every one still capable of fire,
or longing to renew in them the half-forgotten
sense of it, was gathered? Those faces, young and
old, agleam with pale intellectual light, eager with
pleased attention, flash upon me once more from
the deep recesses of the years with an exquisite
pathos. Ah, beautiful young eyes, brimming with
love and hope, wholly vanished now in that other
world we call the Past, or peering doubtfully
through the pensive gloaming of memory, your
light impoverishes these cheaper days! I hear
again that rustle of sensation, as they turned to
exchange glances over some pithier thought, some
keener flash of that humour which always played
about the horizon of his mind like heat-lightning,
and it seems now like the sad whisper of the
autumn leaves that are whirling around me. . . .
His younger hearers could not know how much they
owed to the benign impersonality, that quiet scorn
of everything ignoble, the never-sated hunger of
self-culture, that were personified in the man before
them. But the older knew how much the country's

intellectual emancipation was due to the stimulus
of his teaching and example, how constantly he had
kept burning the beacon of an ideal life above our
lower region of turmoil.   To him more than to all
other causes did the young martyrs of our Civil
War owe the sustaining strength of thoughtful
heroism that is so touching in every record of their
lives.   Those who are grateful to Mr. Emerson, as
many of us are, for what they feel to be most
valuable in their culture, or perhaps I should say
their impulse, are grateful not so much for any
direct teachings of his as for that inspiring *lift*
which only genius can give, and without which all
doctrine is chaff."   " I can never help applying to
him what Ben Jonson said of Bacon—'There happened in my time one noble speaker, who was full
of gravity in his speaking.   His language was nobly
censorious.   No man ever spoke more neatly, more
pressly, more weightily, or suffered less emptiness,
less idleness, in what he uttered.   No member of
his speech but consisted of his own graces.   His
hearers could not cough, or look aside from him,
without loss.   He commanded where he spoke.'"

Mr. Lowell gives a vivid description of the effect
produced by Emerson's speech at the Burns Cen-
tenary dinner at Boston in 1859.   "In that closely-
filed speech of his every word seemed to have just

dropped from the clouds. He looked far away over the heads of his hearers with a vague kind of expectation, as into some private heaven of invention, and the winged period came at last obedient to his spell. . . . Every sentence brought down the house, as I never saw one brought down before,—and it is not so easy to heat Scotsmen with a sentiment that has no hint of native brogue in it. I watched, for it was an interesting study, how the quick sympathy ran flashing from face to face down the long tables, like an electric spark thrilling as it went, and then exploded in a thunder of plaudits. I watched till tables and faces vanished, for I, too, found myself caught up in the common enthusiasm." This celebrated speech is reprinted in the latter portion of this volume.

From an Essay on Emerson by John Burroughs, the author of several volumes of rare merit, published in New York, and which it is surprising no London publisher has yet introduced to British readers, a few sentences are here given,—full of pith and just appreciation. Mr. Burroughs wields a racy pen, and there is the ring of the true metal in his delightful sketches of outdoor nature, mingled with chapters of a more purely literary character.

I know of no other writing that yields the reader so many strongly stamped medallion-like sayings and distinctions. There is a perpetual refining and recoining of the current wisdom of life and conversation. It is the old gold or silver or copper ; but how bright and new it looks in his pages ! Emerson loves facts, things, objects, as the workman his tools. He makes everything serve. The stress of expression is so great that he bends the most obdurate element to his purpose; as the bird, under her keen necessity, weaves the most contrary and diverse materials into her nest. He seems to like best material that is a little refractory ; it makes his page more piquant and stimulating. Within certain limits he loves roughness, but not to the expense of harmony. He has a wonderful hardiness and push. Where else in literature is there a mind, moving in so rare a medium, that gives one such a sense of tangible resistance and force ?

.   .   .   .

But after we have made all possible deductions from Emerson there remains the fact that he is a living force, and, tried by home standards, a master. Wherein does the secret of his power lie ? He is the prophet and philosopher of young men. The old man and the man of the world make little of him, but of the youth who is ripe for him he takes almost an unfair advantage. One secret of his charm I take to be the instant success with which he trans- fers our interest in the romantic, the chivalrous, the heroic, to the sphere of morals and the intellect. We are let into another realm unlooked for, where daring and imagination also lead. The secret and suppressed heart finds a champion. To the young man fed upon the penny precepts and staple Johnsonianism of English literature, and of what is generally doled out in the schools and colleges, it is a surprise; it is a revelation. A new world opens before him. The nebulæ of his spirit are resolved or shown to be irresolvable. The fixed stars of his inner firmament are brought immeasurably near. He drops all other books. . . . Emerson is the knight errant of the moral sentiment. He leads in our time and country, one illustrious division, at least, in the holy crusade of the affections and the intuitions against the usurpations of tradition and theological dogma.

.   .   .   .

Everything about a man like Emerson is important. I find his phrenology and physiognomy more than ordinarily typical and suggestive. Look at his picture there,—large, strong features on a small face and head,—no blank spaces; all given up to expression ; a high, predacious nose, a sinewy brow, a massive, benevolent chin. In most men there is more face than feature ; but here is vast deal more feature than face, and a corresponding alertness and emphasis of character. Indeed, the man is made after this fashion. He is all type. His mind has the hand's pronounced anatomy, its cords and sinews and multiform articulations and processes, its opposing and co-ordinating power. There may have been broader and more catholic natures, but few so towering and audacious in expression, and so rich in characteristic traits. Every scrap and shred of him is important and related. Like the strongly aromatic herbs and simples,— sage, mint, wintergreen, sassafras,—the least part carries the flavour of the whole. Is there one indifferent, or equivocal, or unsympathising drop of blood in him? Where he is at all he is entirely,—nothing extemporaneous ; his most casual word seems to have lain in pickle for a long time, and is saturated through and through with the Emersonian brine. Indeed, so pungent and penetrating is this quality, that his quotations seem more than half his own.

Mention has already been made of Emerson's sympathy with the Anti-Slavery Movement (*v.* p. 59), and the priceless service he rendered to that cause. His views on Free Trade were of the most advanced and far-reaching nature. "America," he said in one of his public addresses, "means opportunity, freedom, power. The genius of this country has marked out her true policy; opportunity—doors wide open— every port open. If I could I would have Free Trade with all the world, without toll or custom-house. Let us invite every nation, every race, every

skin; white man, black man, red man, yellow man.
Let us offer hospitality, a fair field, and equal laws
to all. The land is wide enough, the soil has food
enough for all." With regard to National Education he said :—"We should cling to the common
school, and enlarge and extend the opportunities it
offers. Let us educate every soul. Every native
child, and every foreign child that is cast on our
coast should be taught, at the public cost, first, the
rudiments of knowledge, and then, as far as may
be, the ripest results of art and science." An acute
writer in the "Spectator," of May 6th, 1882, speaking of the interest Emerson took in all public
events, makes this remark : "He sympathised
ardently with all the great practical movements of
his own day, while Carlyle held contemptuously
aloof. He was one of the first to strike a heavy
blow at the institution of slavery. He came forward to encourage his country in the good cause,
when slavery raised the flag of rebellion. He
had a genuine desire to see all men free, while
Carlyle only felt the desire to see all men strongly
governed—which they might be, without being
free at all. Emerson's spirit, moreover, was much
the saner, and more reverent, of the two, though
less rich in power and humour."

During the last three or four years his memory

frequently failed him, especially in reference to his recollection of more recent events. But he was himself perfectly conscious of this, and though it did not prevent his occasionally delivering lectures and taking part in public gatherings, from the time this defect became manifest he was always accompanied to the platform by his daughter, whose devotion and considerate tact invariably supplied the words and phrases which Mr. Emerson could not recall. To the last he continued to take great interest in the well-being of his neighbours and the intellectual and material progress of his native village. He had never lost his inherent love of dignified simplicity in domestic life, and his home was a model of refinement and unostentatious comfort. He was never more happy than in the company of his grandchildren, and all children loved him. His old age was serene, and the sweetness and gentleness of his character were more and more apparent as the years rolled on. To the last, even when the events of yesterday were occasionally obscured, his memory of the remote past was unclouded. He would talk about the friends of his early and middle life with unbroken vigour ; and those who ever had the good fortune to hear him, in the free intercourse of his own study, will not soon forget the charm of his conversation and the

graciousness of his demeanour. He would drive
with his visitors to the numerous interesting spots
in and about Concord, he would point out the old
home of his own family, the house of his friend,
Mr. Alcott, and the still more famous "old manse"
which Hawthorne has made immortal.

One who had the pleasure of visiting him within
the last two years has told how he saw the wise old
man whom he had first heard in Manchester more
than thirty years before, and again in the seclusion
of a friend's house during Mr. Emerson's last visit
to England, and at last in the home of his youth
and age. "Assuredly," says this privileged visitor,
"this great and good man was seldom seen to
rarer advantage. He drove me to the haunts of
the pilgrims who came to Concord to see the place
of so many noble and interesting associations; in
the public library of the town which he had helped
to establish, he showed me not a few literary
treasures which the greatest libraries in the world
might envy—he pointed out the famous tavern
where the British soldiers stopped on the day made
memorable by the first fight in the war of Independence. And on the battle-field itself, where the
beautiful Concord river still flows silently between
the low hills which almost entwine the little town,
he told the story of the famous struggle. It was a

perfect spring day; light breezes stirred the pine trees under which lay the remains of the nameless English soldiers; and hard by was the granite monument to the memory of the local militiamen who fell in that famous skirmish. The scenes and the associations were in themselves eloquent, but they were rendered immeasurably more so by the narrative of the sage whose verses, cut in stone on the monument before us, will tell to future generations how Concord's noblest son sang of the renown of his country's defenders. A few weeks afterwards I was present at one of the dinners of the famous Saturday Club. As the wits of the Restoration and Queen Anne's days met at Will's Coffee House to listen to Dryden or in the more select conclave of the October Club, so the poets, essayists, and humourists of Boston assembled at these dinners, held sometimes at the houses of the members, and sometimes, when the meetings were larger, in one of the hotels. This was a notable gathering; it was intended to do special honour to the distinguished Massachusetts lawyer, who had just returned from presiding at the Chicago Convention which had nominated General Garfield, Republican candidate, for the Presidency. Longfellow was in the chair; James T. Fields was near him. Dr. Oliver Wendell Holmes was as usual the

life and soul of the party, and the company included other scarcely less famous men. Emerson
had not recently been able to attend many of the
meetings, but the occasion was no ordinary one.
' Look at Emerson,' said Fields ; ' how happy he
appears ; was there ever such a sweet smile, and
yet how silent he is. In the early days of the
club, when Agassiz, its founder, was with us, he
and Emerson were the liveliest of us all.' It was
touching to see the marks of reverence and regard
which all displayed to him, and to notice his
appreciatory responses. He thoroughly enjoyed
the sparkling sallies of Wendell Holmes, and when
Longfellow, to whom speech-making was always a
punishment, in a few well-chosen words, referred
to the presence of their honoured fellow-member,
Emerson was constrained to reply, and he did not
forget to tell us that if he could not make them
a speech he was only following the example of his
friend the chairman. It was altogether a delightful
meeting, but already there are melancholy associations with it. Fields, whose ' Yesterdays with
Authors' has given us so many delightful sketches
of famous men, has followed his friends Thackeray
and Dickens. Longfellow, the sweetest, the most
genial, and gentle of poets and men, has also gone,
and now we mourn the departure of the greatest

of them, Emerson himself, a man in whom were combined the strength of the New England Puritan and the grace and beauty of the accomplished Greek."

The sense of beauty was so vital an element in the very constitution of Emerson's being, that it decorated everything it touched. The perception and sentiment of beauty is one of the great characteristics of his intellect. Beauty is the theme of some of his noblest utterances. " So strong is this," says his friend Mr. E. Whipple, " that he accepts nothing in life that is uncomely, haggard, or ghastly. The fact that an opinion depresses, instead of invigorates, is with him a sufficient reason for its rejection. His observation, his wit, his reason, his imagination, his style, all obey the controlling sense of beauty which is at the heart of his nature, and instinctively avoid the ugly and the base."

The native elevation of his mind and the general loftiness of his thinking have sometimes blinded his admirers to the fact that he was one of the shrewdest of practical observers, and was capable of meeting so-called practical men on the level of the facts and principles which they relied upon for success in life. " He always impressed me with the conviction," says the last-quoted writer, "that an idealist of the high type of Emerson was as good a judge of investments on earth as he was of investments in the heaven above the earth." His practical, unerring sagacity and power of observation show themselves throughout his writings, whatever be the subject. No better illustration of this quality can be given than in the few sentences in which he happens to speak of infancy and its real though unacknowledged influence over every member of the household—everything having to adapt itself to its wants, and moods, and caprices :—

Who knows not the beautiful group of babe and mother, sacred in nature, now sacred also in the religious associations of half the globe? Welcome to the parents is the puny struggler, strong in his weakness, his little arms more irresistible than the soldier's, his lips touched with persuasion which Chatham and Pericles in manhood had not. The small despot asks so little that all nature and reason are on his side. His ignorance is more charming than all knowledge, and his little sins more bewitching than any virtue. All day, between his three or four sleeps, he coos like a pigeon-house, sputters and spurns, and puts on his faces of importance ; and when he fasts, the little Pharisee fails not to sound his trumpet before him. Out of blocks, thread-spools, cards and chequers, he will build his pyramid with the gravity of Palladio. With an acoustic apparatus of whistle and rattle he explores the laws of sound. But chiefly, like his senior countrymen, the young American studies new and speedier modes of transportation. Mistrusting the cunning of his small legs, he wishes to ride on the necks and shoulders of all flesh. The small enchanter nothing can withstand,—no seniority of age, no gravity of character; uncles, aunts, cousins, grandsires, grandames,— all fall an easy prey : he conforms to nobody, all conform to him ; all caper and make mouths, and babble and chirrup to him. On the strongest shoulders he rides, and pulls the hair of laurelled heads.

It was a peculiarity in Emerson that the thing he most disliked was sickness, while disease he regarded with the strongest aversion. He himself said that during forty years he was never confined to bed for a single day. To him virtue was health, and he used to quote a saying of Dr. Johnson's that " every man is a rascal when he is sick." He believed that the outward complaint originates in some inward complaint, and that if we were perfectly obedient to the laws of the soul and of nature, there would be no sickness or disease. He believed that human suffering arose from disobedience to laws that may and ought to be obeyed. When obeyed, the sickness will cease, and the weakness will be gone. Among many practical rules laid down for the promotion of the happiness of social intercourse he considered this as one of prime importance :— " Never name sickness. Even if you could trust yourself on that perilous topic, beware of unmuzzling a valetudinarian, who will soon give you your fill of it."

With regard to Emerson's claims as a poet, something must here be said. The essence of true poetry is manifest in many of his utterances that take not the form of versification. He is emphatically a poet in his prose. His poems contain genuine inspiration of the very highest kind, but rhyme does not always aid its development.   In a single page he gives more of the spirit of poetry than would supply a dozen of ordinary rhymesters for the whole of their lives ; and yet there are poetasters who could at least equal him in the construction of passable verses.   When the world is wiser, Emerson will be owned as a great poet. There are single poems of his which for depth of feeling, tender regret, profound insight into the human soul, and an inimitable quaintness and simplicity (sometimes rivalling George Herbert himself) are not to be matched in the works of the acknowledged masters of the poetic art.   It has been said that " Some of his stanzas read like oracles. Their worth to our moral being is so close, that we are scarcely surprised that he gives them forth with the confident tone of the seer and the prophet. They rank with the loftiest utterances which have ever proceeded from the awakened heart, and conscience, and intellect of man."

It is worth while to observe the *consensus* of opinion regarding the intrinsic worth of his poetry, resulting from minds of the widest diversity of constitution and culture.   His friend, Dr. Hedge, says:—" In poetic art he does not excel. The verses often halt, the conclusion sometimes flags, and metrical propriety is recklessly violated.

But this defect is closely connected with the characteristic merit of the poet, and springs from the same root—his utter spontaneity. And this spontaneity is but a mode of his sincerity. More than those of any of his contemporaries, his poems, for the most part, are inspirations. They are not made, but given ; they come of themselves. They are not meditated, but burst from the soul with an irrepressible necessity of utterance—sometimes with a rush which defies the shaping intellect. It seems as if it were not the man himself that speaks, but a power behind—call it Daemon or Muse. Where the Muse flags, it is her fault, not his ; he is not going to help her out with wilful elaboration or emendation. There is no trace, as in most poetry, of joiner-work, and no mark of the file. . . . Wholly unique, and transcending all contemporary verse in grandeur of style, is the piece entitled 'The Problem.' When first it appeared in 'The Dial,' forty years ago, I said : 'There has been nothing done in English rhyme like this since Milton. All between it and Milton seemed tame in comparison.' "

Miss Elizabeth Peabody, Emerson's life-long friend, in the same letter to the present writer, quoted at p. 21, says, with reference to his poetry :—" He seems to me to have most fully expressed his

peculiar individuality *in his poetry*. He seems to
me a poet, *par eminence*—his Sphynx, his Uriel,
Bacchus, The Problem, the Ode to Beauty, Each
and All, his Threnody, his Dirge, his In Memoriam,
Love and Thought—where can be found higher
flights—more of the music of the spheres? He
once said to me, ' I am not a great poet—but whatever is of me, *is a poet !* ' "

Since the first edition of this memoir was published, the writer of it has received a letter from
Earl Lytton (July 18th, 1882), containing some
remarks on Emerson as a poet, from which he
takes the liberty of giving a few sentences :—" I
suppose there are few Englishmen of our generation who have not been more or less influenced at
some period of life by Emerson's genius. He is
the most far-reaching of all American writers. On
my own youth he made a deep and delightful
impression, and when I visited America in 1849,
he was of all eminent Americans the only one I
had an ardent desire to meet. Alas for me, of
those then living he is also the only one I did *not*
meet. . . .   I am glad you have spoken up for
his verse, which I admire greatly and think underrated by the majority of critics, who, like the
majority of administrators, never know how to
deal with a case for which they can find no prece-

dent upon the file. Neither creative nor passionate, and, therefore, not of the highest order of poetry, they must be judged, I think, in reference to the value of the thought that inspires them, and to the fitness of their service as its vehicles. From these points of view they seem to me perfect of their kind ; and the roughness of their rhythm a virtue— not a defect of art. They are not Hebrew Psalms uttered to the harp, but Delphic oracles, or sunny meditations of a serene Pan, delivered in broken snatches to faint sounds of sylvan flutes. . . . Emerson's work in its *ensemble* (prose and verse together) I take to be the loftiest, the largest, and the loveliest expression yet given to the philosophy of Democracy."

In a letter to the present writer, soon after Emerson's death, from Mr. Henry Larkin,* one of his most discriminating English admirers and critics, some remarks occur relating to his poems which are worthy of preservation :—

" I well recollect the wonder with which I first

* Mr. Larkin is the author of a remarkable book, entitled " Extra Physics, and The Mystery of Creation : including a Brief Examination of Professor Tyndall's Admission concerning the Human Soul ;" but he is better known as having contributed one of the most interesting articles on Carlyle that has yet appeared, under the title of "Carlyle and Mrs. Carlyle ; a Ten Years' Reminiscence." It extends to over fifty pages, and will be found in "The British Quarterly Review," for July, 1881.

became familiar with those crystal-clear perceptions of his,—visions as if from the very mountain top of the human intellect.   To me they were a distinct revelation of new intellectual possibilities, hitherto only dimly imagined.   We talk, naturally enough, of Emerson being one of the greatest of American writers ; to me he has always stood alone in the great history of literature—the clearest seer, the most dauntless speaker, the deftest and most subtle intellect ; uttering his convictions in words of light tinted only from the azure of infinity.   I know nothing more exquisitely dainty than some of his snatches of poetry.   Those who see no poetry in them, simply do not see them at all.   I can only compare them to exquisite snow-crystals, fresh gathered from some highest mountain peak, where the clouds of human infirmity never reach.   Human passion, in the Edgar Poe sense, they have none ; but for subtlety of insight and delicacy of utterance, I think they stand alone in literature."

Another critic says :—" The reason that such grand utterances as these thrill us with unwonted emotion is to be found in our instinctive belief that the poet's character was on a level with his lofty thinking.   He affirmed the supremacy of spiritual laws because he spoke from a height of spiritual experience to which he had mounted by the steps of spiritual growth. In reading him, we feel that we are in communion with an original person, as well as with an original poet,—one whose character is as brave as it is sweet, as strong as it is beautiful, as firm and resolute in will as it is keen and delicate in might,—one who has earned the right to authoritatively announce, without argument, great spiritual facts and principles, because his soul has come into direct contact with them. As a poet he often takes strange liberties with the established laws of rhyme and rhythm; even his images are occasionally enigmas; but he still contrives to pour through his verse a flood and rush of inspiration not often perceptible in the axiomatic sentences of his most splendid prose. In his verse he gives free, joyous, exulting expression to all the audacities of his thinking and feeling."

Mr. E. Whipple, whom we have already quoted, contributes an article on Emerson's poetry to a recent number of the "North American Review," from which the following extract is given:—

Perhaps it may be asserted that the finest, loftiest, and deepest thoughts of Emerson, being poetic in essence, would naturally have found vent in some of the forms of poetic expression, for they announce spiritual facts and principles, vividly and warmly perceived, which are commonly not content with being stated, but carry with them an impulse and demand to be sung or chanted. If his piercing insight had been accompanied by a sensibility corresponding to it, he would have given us more poems and fewer essays ; but there was a certain rigidity in his nature which could be made to melt and flow only when it was subjected to intense heat. Some persons were inclined to confound this rigidity with frigidity of character, and called him cold ; but the difference was as great as that between iron and ice. The fire in him, which would instantly have dissipated ice into vapour, made the iron in him run molten and white-hot into the mould of his thought, when he was stirred by a great sentiment or an inspiring insight. It is admitted that he is worthy to rank among the great masters of expression ; yet he was the least fluent of educated human beings. In a company of swift talkers he seemed utterly helpless, until he fixed upon the right word or phrase to embody his meaning, and then the word or phrase was like a gold coin, fresh and bright from the mint, and recognised as worth ten times as much as the small change of conversation which had been circulating so rapidly around the table, while he was mute or stammering. That wonderful compactness and condensation of statement, which surprise and charm the readers of his books, were due to the fact that he exerted every faculty of his mind in the act of verbal expression. A prodigal in respect to thoughts, he was still the most austere economist in the use of words. We detect this quality in his poetry as in his prose ; but, in his poetry, it is found to be compatible with the lyric rush, the unwithholding self-abandonment to the inspiration of the muse, which commonly characterizes poets who, in their enthusiasm, have lost their self-possession and self-command.

As regards Emerson's literary methods, Mr. Cooke thus speaks :—" It was his habit to spend the forenoon in his study, with constant regularity. He did not wait for moods, but caught them as they came, and used their results in each day's work. It was his wont to jot down his thoughts at all hours and places. The suggestions resulting from his readings, conversations, and meditations, were immediately transferred to the note-book he always carried with him. In his walks, many a gem of thought was in this way preserved. Even during the night he would get up and jot down some thought worth laying hold of. The story is told that his wife suddenly awoke in the night, before she knew his habits, and heard him moving about the room. She anxiously inquired if he were ill. 'Only an idea' was his reply, and proceeded to jot it down. All the results of his thinking were thus stored up, to be made use of when required. After his note-books were filled, he transcribed their contents in a large common-place book. When a fresh subject possessed his mind, he brought together the jottings he found he had written down concerning it, forming them into a connected whole, with additional material suggested at the time. His essays were thus very slowly elaborated, wrought out through days and months, and even years, of patient thought. They were all carefully revised, again and again ; corrected, wrought over, portions dropped, new matter added, or the paragraphs arranged in a new order. He was unsparing in his corrections, striking out sentence after sentence ; and whole paragraphs disappear from time to time. His manuscript was everywhere filled with erasures and emendations ; scarcely a page that was not covered with these evidences of his diligent revision."

A friend says that few authors have published less than Emerson in comparison with the great mass of papers which remain unprinted. "Scarcely any of his numerous sermons have ever been published ; most of his speeches on political and social occasions remain uncollected and unedited ; many verses exist only in manuscript, or have been withdrawn from publication ; and even of his lectures, from which he has printed freely for nearly forty years, a great many still remain in manuscript. Even those published omit much that was spoken,—the five lectures on History, on Love, and others, displaying so many omissions to those who heard them, that the author was at the time sorely complained of by his faithful hearers for leaving out so much that had delighted them. Few or none of the philosophical lectures read at Harvard University eight or nine years ago, and designed to make part of what he called 'The Natural History of the Intellect,' have ever been printed. This work, when completed, was to be the author's most systematic and connected treatise. It was to contain, what could not fail to be of interest to all readers, his observations on his own intellectual processes and methods, of which he has always been studiously watchful, and which, from his habit of writing, he has carefully noted down. From this work, which, even if not finished, will at some time be printed, and from his correspondence of these many years, portions of which will finally be printed, it will be possible to reconstruct hereafter a rare and remarkable episode in literary history."

Another American writer, speaking of Emerson's unwillingness to print anything but his best, says :— " He has always been extremely careful of what he put into print, regarding the covers of a book as a sacred temple into which only the purest and best of a writer should be permitted to enter. No American or European has been so superlatively fastidious as he respecting publication. He believed that a book should have every reason for being ; that nothing trivial, passing, or temporary should be introduced into it ; that the sole excuse for a book should be the presentation of fresh thought ; that its contents should be in some manner an addition to the common stock of knowledge. Most authors would have put all their lectures and essays between covers because they had written them, and because they could gain something thereby. Emerson was an illustrious example to his guild in this particular. If he had less vanity than members of his craft generally he had more pride, more regard for his reputation, more confident expectation of enduring fame. It is said that he had unwavering confidence in this, and that therefore he published what was universal and abiding in interest and influence, and compressed his utterances into the smallest space. Had all writers followed his example how immeasurably libraries would have been reduced! A hundred volumes would shrink to one, and there might be some hope of a tireless student in a long life gaining a slight smattering of the great authors with whom everybody is presumed to be wholly familiar. Emerson is a pattern to all mere book-makers present and to come. If he had done nothing else than to inculcate by example the economy of print he would deserve a separate niche in the temple of literary fame, and who shall say that he has not secured it? All the writings he has wished to be known by can be put into three small volumes, and in these is there not as much weighty and important matter as can be discovered in the same space in any language? The matter is not (as in the great majority of books) what can be found elsewhere—generally far better said—in the illimitable wilderness of type. It is, barring quotations, which always serve to illustrate his idea, actually Emerson's own, the fruit of his observation, study, and reflection—the action of an original individual mind upon life, history, and nature."

Emerson always declined controversy, and refused to enter into disputation with a view to bring people round to his way of thinking. This characteristic is well brought out in the following extract from a recent article by Mr. E. Whipple.*

It is impossible for those who only knew Emerson through his writings to understand the peculiar love and veneration felt for him by those who knew him personally. Only by intercourse with him could the singular force, sweetness, elevation, originality, and comprehensiveness of his nature be fully appreciated ; and the friend or acquaintance, however he might differ from him in opinion, felt the peculiar fascination of his character, and revolved around this solar mind, in obedience to the law of spiritual gravitation—the spiritual law operating, like the natural law, directly as the mean, and inversely as the square of the distance. The friends nearest to him loved and honoured him most ; but those who only met him occasionally felt the attraction of his spiritual turn, and could not mention him without a tribute of respect. There probably never was a man of the first class, with a general system of thought at variance with accredited opinions, who exercised so much gentle, persuasive power over the minds of his opponents. By declining all temptations to controversy he never realised the ferocious spirit which controversy engenders ; he went on year after year in affirming certain spiritual facts which had been revealed to him when his soul was on the heights of spiritual contemplation ; and if he differed from other

* " Some Recollections of Ralph Waldo Emerson," in " Harper's Monthly Magazine," September, 1822.

minds, he thought it ridiculous to attempt to convert them to his individual insight and experience by *arguments* against their individual insights and their individual experiences. To his readers in the closet, and his hearers on the lecture platform, he poured lavishly out from his intellectual treasury—from the seemingly exhaustless Fortunatus' purse of his mind—the silver and gold, the pearls, rubies, amethysts, opals, and diamonds of thought. If his readers and his audiences chose to pick them up, they were welcome to them ; but if they conceived that he was deceiving them with sham jewelry, he would not condescend to explain the laborious processes in the mines of meditation by which he had brought the hidden treasures to light. I never shall forget his curt answer to a superficial auditor of one of his lectures. The critic was the intellectual busybody of the place, dipping into everything, knowing nothing, but contriving by his immense loquacity to lead the opinion of the town. "Now, Mr. Emerson," he said, "I appreciated much of your lecture, but I should like to speak to you of certain things in it which did not commend my assent and approbation." Emerson turned to him, gave him one of his piercing looks, and replied, "Mr. —— if anything I have spoken this evening met your mood, it is well ; if it did not, I must tell you that I never argue on these high questions."

Professor Tyndall thus speaks of his reason for so often quoting Emerson :—" I do so mainly because in him we have a poet and a profoundly religious man, who is really and entirely undaunted by the discoveries of science—past, present, or prospective. In his case poetry, with the joy of a bacchanal, takes her graver brother science by the hand and cheers him with immortal laughter. By Emerson scientific conceptions are continually transmuted into the finer forms and warmer hues of an ideal world." " If anyone can be said to have given the impulse to my mind, it is Emerson ; whatever I have done, the world owes to him." It is said that on the fly-leaf of an odd volume of Emerson's works, accidentally picked up by the Professor at an old-book stall, and which first made him acquainted with his writings, are inscribed these words : " Purchased by inspiration."

Herman Grimm, an accomplished German critic of Emerson, says:—"I found in his works a sense of joy and beauty, such as is given by the greatest books. I found myself made captive by thoughts which it seemed as if I were hearing for the first time. When I again read his sentences, the enchanting breezes of hope and spiritual joy fills my soul anew. The old worn-out machinery of the world is re-created, and I feel as if I had never breathed so heavenly an atmosphere. I can indeed say that no author has had such an influence upon me as Emerson. The manner of writing of the man, whom I hold to be the greatest of all living authors, has revealed to me a new way of expressing thought."

The late Dean Stanley concludes a letter about him in these words :—" Long may Ralph Waldo Emerson enjoy the influence which superiority gives over mediocrity, and calm reason over fleeting pas-

sion." The impressions of Emerson, received by
Frederika Bremer, and the magic influence he exercised upon her, are recorded in her "Homes of the
New World," extracts from which will be found at
the end of this volume. Elsewhere she concluded
some remarks on him by saying :—" I believe myself to have become greater through his greatness,
stronger through his strength ; and I breathe the
air of a higher sphere in this world, which is indescribably refreshing to me." In Harriet Martineau's "Retrospect of Western Travel," 1838, will
be found many pages relating to Emerson, his influence on the thought of his time even at that early
date, and the expectations that were then entertained
regarding his career. Hawthorne said that his mind
acted on other minds with "wonderful magnetism."
"It was good to meet him in the wood-paths, or
sometimes in our avenue, with that pure intellectual
gleam diffusing about his presence like the garment
of a shining one ; and he, so quiet, so simple, so
without pretension, encountering each man alive as
if expecting to receive more than he would impart,
and, in truth, the heart of many an ordinary man
had, perchance, inscriptions which he could not
read. But it was impossible to dwell in his vicinity
without inhaling more or less the mountain atmosphere of his lofty thought."

Whatever verdict may be pronounced upon Emerson's opinions, he must be universally regarded as one who by his teaching and practical example has done more to make the life of the scholar beautiful, and the career of the man of letters a reproof to all low aims, and an inspiration to all high ones, than any other man in America—one might almost say, in either continent. His greatest service has been the inculcation of intellectual self-reliance, of fearless manliness, and absolute sincerity of thought,—that we should stand morally and intellectually alone ; no prop left but the trust in God. "We must suffer no fiction to exist for us ; we must realise all that we know ; in the high refinement of modern life, in arts, in sciences, in books, in men, we must exact good faith, reality and a purpose, and first, last, midst, and without end, we must honour every truth by use. . . . What I must do is all that concerns me, not what people think. This rule, equally arduous in actual and in intellectual life, may serve for the whole distinction between greatness and meanness. It is the harder, because you will always find those who think they know what is your duty better than you know it. It is easy in the world to live after the world's opinion ; it is easy in solitude to live after our own ; but the great man is he, who, in the midst of the crowd, keeps with perfect sweetness the independence of solitude."

In an oration delivered before the literary societies of Dartmouth College in July, 1838, will be found the highest expression of his opinion regarding the duty and aims of the scholar:—

If, with a high trust, he can thus submit himself to the supreme soul, he will find that ample returns are poured into his bosom, out of what seemed hours of obstruction and loss. Let him not grieve too much on account of unfit associates. When he sees how much thought he owes to the disagreeable antagonism of various persons who pass and cross him, he can easily think that in a society of perfect sympathy, no word, no act, no record, would be. He will learn that it is not much matter what he reads, what he does. Be a scholar, and he shall have the scholar's part of everything. As, in the counting room, the merchant cares little whether the cargo be hides or barilla ; the transaction, a letter of credit or a transfer of stocks ; be it what it may, his commission comes gently out of it ; so you shall get your lesson out of the hour, and the object, whether it be a concentrated or a wasteful employment, even in reading a dull book, or working off a stint of mechanical day labour, which your necessities or the necessities of others impose.   .   .   .

Be content with a little light, so it be your own. Explore, and explore, and explore. Be neither chided nor flattered out of your position of perpetual inquiry. Neither dogmatize yourself, nor accept another's dogmatism. Why should you renounce your right to traverse the star-lit deserts of truth, for the premature comforts of an acre, house, or barn? Truth also has its roof, and bed, and board. Make yourself necessary to the world, and mankind will give you bread, and if not store of it, yet such as shall not take away your property in all men's possessions, in all men's affections, in art, in nature, and in hope. You will not fear that I am enjoining too stern an asceticism. Ask not, Of what use is a scholarship that systematically retreats? or Who is the better for the philosopher who conceals his accomplishments, and hides his thoughts from the waiting world? Hides his thoughts! Hide the sun and moon. Thought is all light, and publishes itself to the universe. It will speak, though you were dumb, by its own miraculous organ. It will flow out of your actions, your manners, and your face. It will bring you friendships. It will impledge you to truth by the love and expectation of generous minds. By virtue of the laws of that Nature, which is one and perfect, it will yield every sincere good that is in the soul, to the scholar beloved of earth and heaven.

Emerson is also one of the consummate masters of the English tongue. "His style is in the purest harmony with the character of his thought. It is condensed almost to abruptness. There is a singular beauty and intense life and significance in his language, which combines the most austere economy of words, with the determination to load every word with vital meaning." "His sentences are often like diamonds. There is no thinker of our day who, for sentences that have the ring of oracles, can quite compare with him." "In no other writer are there so many sentences which complete the subject, and which will stand, unsupported and alone, as indications of the author's thought." "No writer is so quotable. Scarcely a page, especially of the earlier essays, but supplies some terse and pregnant saying, worthy to be inscribed in a golden treasury of portable wisdom." "His sentences score themselves on the brain.   Force of statement, the surprise of fitness, the hitting of the nail on the head—are the distinguishing characteristics of his writings."   " His pages are laden with aphorisms—his style of composition is eminently aphoristic—and they are so felicitously put, and on such a variety of themes, that the capturing memory declines to surrender them, and speedily claims them as its own.   Let him the fit audience find, though few, and he will illustrate what it is to speak golden words in that natural style of perfect sincerity, tenderness, and thoughtfulness, by which every syllable is conducted straight home to the faculty it was meant for.   For the enunciation of his own sentences we call him simply a perfect speaker.   The manner fits the matter as if cut out for it from eternity."

Theodore Parker, in one of the best critical papers on Emerson that has appeared, written in 1849, says :—" He is the most republican of republicans, the most protestant of dissenters.   His culture is cosmopolitan.   He trusts himself, trusts man, and trusts God.   He has confidence in all the attributes of Infinity.   Hence he is serene ; nothing disturbs the even poise of his character, and he walks erect.   Nothing impedes him in his search for the true, the lovely, and the good ; no private hope, no private fear, no love of wife or child or gold or ease or fame. He has not written a line which is not conceived in the interest of mankind. He never writes in the interest of a section, of a party, of a church, of a man, but always in the interest of mankind. No faithful man is too low for his approval and encouragement; no faithless man too high and popular for his rebuke. To no English writer, since Milton, can be assigned so high a place; even Milton himself, great genius though he was, and great architect of beauty, has not added so many thoughts to the treasury of the race; no, nor been the author of so much loveliness. Emerson is a man of genius such as does not often appear; such as has never appeared before in America, and but seldom in the world. He learns from all sorts of men; but no English writer, we think, is so original. His style is one of the rarest beauty. It is simple, without imitation, unique and robust. It is manly, pure, direct and thoroughly natural, and he has the remarkable power of saying precisely and exactly the thing he means."

Mr. J. B. Crozier, in "The Religion of the Future," thus ably summarises his opinion of Emerson :— " There is, perhaps, no writer of the nineteenth century who will better repay a careful and prolonged

perusal than Emerson. He enjoys the rare distinction of having ascended to the highest point to which
the human mind can climb,—to the point where, as
he says of Plato, the poles of thought are on a line
with the axis on which the frame of things revolves.
. . . We can turn to him, with the same delight
for the philosophical expression of the deep laws
of human life, as we do to Shakespeare for their
dramatic representation. For he is one of the profoundest of thinkers, and has that universality,
serenity, and cosmopolitan breadth of comprehension, that place him among the great of all ages.
He has swallowed all his predecessors, and converted them into nutriment for himself. He is as
subtle and delicate, too, as he is broad and massive,
and possesses a practical wisdom and keenness of
observation that hold his feet fast to the solid earth
when his head is striking the stars. His scientific
accuracy and freedom of speculation mark him out
as one of the representative men of the nineteenth
century."

It would be out of place in a biographical sketch
like the present to attempt to explain Emerson's
philosophy. He has, in fact, propounded no system.
Those who read his works in the hope of finding a
theological or philosophical system will be disap-
pointed. Strictly, he is not the founder of any

school, but has furnished the foundation stones of many schools. He beholds and reports all, be it secular or sacred. He trustingly accepts what comes "to the open sense and the waiting mind." If he has not discovered the secret of the universe, he tells frankly what he finds as a perceiver or observer, and constantly endeavours to place himself in harmony with the Most High. He seeks to solve the riddle of the universe for himself, and is content with no traditionary answer. He insists on man's individuality, and protests against the merging of our separate beings into indolent conformity with a majority. His faith in God, in spiritual laws, in the moral order of the universe, never leaves him. This faith saturates and vitalizes all that he has written. With him the spiritual is the *real.* His own words on this subject are full of deepest import. "That which is signified by the words moral and spiritual is a lasting essence, and, with whatever illusions we have loaded them, will certainly bring back the words age after age to their ancient meaning. I know no words that mean so much. In our definitions we grope after the spiritual by describing it as invisible. The true meaning of spiritual is *real,* that law which executes itself, which works without means, and which cannot be conceived as not existing."

Emerson has been called a Transcendentalist; but he never adopted the name. "In the sense that Socrates and Plato, and the fathers of the Stoic school, and Paul and the apostles, and Luther, and the saints and martyrs of the Christian Church, and all the great poets, painters, sculptors, and musicians, have been, and will be to the end of time, Transcendentalists,—Emerson, too, was one. For Transcendentalism is essentially neither more nor less than Idealism—Spiritualism—in its best and highest meaning. The Transcendentalist believes in what *transcends* the senses; he believes in inspiration, flowing ever fresh and pure from the Infinite Source of all wisdom and power; he believes in the human soul, its power, its divine lineage, and its high destiny. He values the past, but he values more the present, and, most of all, the future,—that great promised land of all our hopes. He does not believe that all truth is enshrined in any book, or any institution, for he holds that man is always greater than his achievements, and God infinitely greater than either our memory or our comprehension."* Emerson neither dogmatizes nor defines. His chief anxiety seems to be to avoid committing himself to opinions, to keep all questions open, to close no avenue in any direction to the free ingress

* "The Harvard Magazine," April, 1855.

of the mind. "He will not be questioned; not because he doubts, but because his convictions are so rich, so various and many-sided, that he is unwilling, by laying emphasis on any one of them, to do an apparent injustice to the others. He will be held to no definition; he will be seduced to no final statements. The mind must have free range. He dwells in principles, and will not be cabined in beliefs."* "Those who, amid declining creeds or institutions, can only repeat the plaintive parrot-cry, What is to be put in its place? will have to unlearn something before they can gain the secret of Emerson."

His own words will be the most fit conclusion to this fragmentary summary of his ideas of Truth and Duty: "Let a man know his worth, and keep things under his feet. Beneath opinions, habits, customs, is the spirit of a man. The one thing in the world of value is the soul,—free, sovereign, active. Man shall be true to himself, let the world say what it will. The truly religious mind will find beauty and necessary facts,—in the shop and the mill. Proceeding from a religious heart, it will raise to a divine use the railroad, the insurance office, the telegraph, the chemist's retort,—in which we now seek only an economic use. The end and aim of life is not to assert ourselves, but by indivi-

* O. B. Frothingham's "Transcendentalism in New England."

dual faithfulness to become fit recipients of the Divine Mind, so as to live in thoughts and act with energies which are immortal. The greatest philosopher is but the listener of simple faithfulness; and the loftiest wisdom is gained when self is forgotten in communion with God. Let man thus learn the revelation of all nature and all thought to his heart; this, namely, that the Highest dwelleth with him; and that the sources of Nature are in his own mind. Therefore, let it not be recorded, that in this moment of the Eternity, when we who were named by our names, flitted across the light, we were afraid of any fact, or disgraced the fair day by a pusillanimous preference of our bread to our freedom. What is the scholar, what is the man *for*, but for hospitality to every new thought of his time? Have you leisure, power, property, friends? you shall be the asylum and patron of every new thought, every unproven opinion, every untried project, which proceeds out of goodwill and honest seeking. All the newspapers, all the tongues of to-day will of course at first defame what is noble; but you who hold not of to-day, not of the times, but of the Everlasting, are to stand for it; and the highest compliment Man ever receives from Heaven, is the sending to him its disguised and discredited angels."

Those who have felt throughout their lives the purifying and elevating power of this great man's writings, and who have recognised in his inspiring career the perfect sanity of true genius, can never think of him without affectionate reverence. He now rests, in that deep repose which he has so well earned, and beneath laurels that will never fade.

THE FUNERAL.

The last rites over the remains of Ralph Waldo Emerson took place at Concord on the 30th of April. A special train from Boston carried a large number of people. Many persons were on the street, attracted by the services, but were unable to gain admission to the church where the public ceremonies were held. Almost every building in town bore over its entrance door a large black and white rosette with other sombre draperies. The public buildings were heavily draped, and even the homes of the very poor bore outward marks of grief at the loss of their friend and fellow-townsman.

The services at the house, which were strictly private, occurred at 2-30, and were conducted by Rev. W. H. Furness, of Philadelphia. They were simple in character, and only Mr. Furness took part. The body lay in the front north-east room, in which were gathered the family and close friends of the deceased. The only flowers were contained in three vases on the mantel, and were lilies of the valley, red and white roses, and arbutus. The adjoining room and hall were filled with friends and neighbours.

The poet's wife and daughter Ellen sat near the coffin. Dr. Furness occupied a position in the passage-way, and made a brief and touching address, saying that the peaceful face lying before them only indicated a like quiet of soul within, and reflected the peace and purity of the soul while it yet tenanted the body. He then recited Tennyson's " Deserted Home," and repeated from Longfellow words read at that poet's own funeral, a few weeks ago. Appropriate quotations from Scripture followed.

The procession was then formed for the public services at the Unitarian Church, which is but a short distance from the house. The Concord Social Circle led the way, then followed the hearse and pall-bearers :—his son, Dr. Edward Waldo Emerson; and his nephews, Charles Emerson and Haven Emerson; Wm. H. Forbes, his son-in-law; J. Eliott Cabot, his designated biographer; Prof. James B. Thayer, of Harvard Law School; Mr. Ralph Forbes, and Mr. W. Thayer, all relatives of the deceased, and following them were a few carriages with the family and intimate friends, among whom were Oliver Wendell Holmes, G. W. Curtis, President Eliot, of Harvard College; Professors Norton, Pierce, Horsford, and Hills, of Cambridge; Mrs. J. T. Fields, representatives of the Boston publishing houses, and many others.

At the church many hundreds of persons were awaiting the arrival of the procession, and all the space, except the reserved pews, was packed. In front of the pulpit were simple decorations, boughs of pine covered the desk, and in their centre was a harp of yellow jonquils, the gift of Miss Louisa M. Alcott. Other floral tributes were an open volume, upon one page on white ground the word "Finis" in blue flowers. This was from the teachers and scholars in the Emerson School. By the sides of the pulpit were white and scarlet geraniums and pine boughs, and high upon the wall a laurel wreath.

Before 3-30 the pall-bearers brought in the plain black walnut coffin, which was placed before the pulpit. The lid was turned back and upon it was put a cluster of richly coloured pansies and a small bouquet of roses. While the coffin was being carried in, "Pleyel's Hymn" was rendered on the organ by request of the family of the deceased. Dr. James Freeman Clarke then entered the pulpit. Judge E. Rockwood Hoar remained by the coffin below, and when the congregation became quiet made a brief and pathetic address, his voice many times trembling with emotion.

Mr. Hoar began his tribute with the words: "The beauty of Israel is fallen in its high place." He then spoke of the world-wide sorrow felt at the poet's death and of the special veneration and grief of the townspeople, who considered him their own. "There is nothing to mourn for. That brave and manly life was rounded out to the full length of days; that dying pillow was softened by the sweetest domestic affection, and as he lay down to the sleep which the Lord giveth His beloved, his face was as the face of a child and seemed to give a glimpse of the opening heavens. Wherever the English language is spoken throughout the world his fame is established and secured; from beyond the sea and throughout this great land will come innumerable voices of sorrow for this great public loss. But we, his neighbours and townsmen, feel that he was ours; he was descended from the founders of the town; he chose our village for the place in which his life-long work was to be done; it was to our fields and orchards that his presence gave such value; it was in our streets that children looked up to him with love, and the elders with reverence; he was our ornament and pride. The

lofty brow, the home of all wise thoughts and
aspirations; those lips of eloquent music; that
great soul, which, trusting in God, never lost its
hope of immortality; that great heart, to which
everything was welcome that belonged to man;
that impressible nature, loving and tender and
generous, having no repulsion or scorn for anything but meanness and baseness; our friend,
brother, father, lover, teacher, inspirer, guide, is
gone. There is no more that we can do now than
to give this our hail and farewell!"

Judge Hoar's remarks were followed by the
congregation singing the hymns "Thy will be
done," "I will not fear the fate provided by Thy
love." The Rev. Mr. Furness then read selections
from the Scriptures.

The Rev. James Freeman Clarke then delivered
the following address :—

This assembly has come together not only to testify its respect for
one of the greatest thinkers and writers of our time, but also it is
drawn to this place by gratitude for the strength, help, and inspiration which has been given to us through the mediation of this noble
soul.   It is not for me, it is not for this hour, to say what ought to
be said of the genius which has kindled the fires of thought in two
continents.   The present moments belong to reverential love.   We
thank God here for the influences which have made us all better.
The voice now hushed never spoke but to lift us to a higher plane
of generous sentiment.   The hand now still never wrote except to
take us out of " our dreary routine of sense, worldliness, and sin,"

into communion with whatever is noblest, purest, highest. By the
side of this revered form, we thank God that through all these years
we have been made better by his words and his life. He has been
a preacher of righteousness to this and other lands. When he left
the pulpit, he said, in his farewell sermon, that he did not relinquish
his profession,—that he hoped, whatever was his work, to be still a
teacher of God's truth. How well has he kept that promise ! No
one can say, till the day of judgment declares it, how large a part of
the genuine faith in the things not seen but eternal has come to us
from the depths of his spiritual insight. He was one of God's seers;
and he was sent to us at a time like the one of which it is written,
" The Word of the Lord was precious in those days : there was no
open vision." Men lived by past inspirations, with no faith in the
possibility of any new revelation to the soul of the divine will. No
doubt they did well to resort to the words of ancient prophets until
the day should dawn and the day-star arise in their own hearts.
That day dawned anew when the sight of the divine truth kindled a
light in the solemn eyes of Channing and created a new power
which spoke from the lips of Emerson. Yet the young and hopeful
listened with joy to this morning song, they looked gladly to this
auroral light. When the little book "Nature" was published, it
seemed to some of us a new revelation. Mr. Emerson then said
what has been the text of his life, " Let the single man plant himself on his instincts, and the great world will come round to him."
He did not reply to his critics. He went on his way. And to-day
we see that the world has come round to him. He is the preacher
of spiritual truth to our age. We understand through him what
Jesus meant when he said, " You must eat my flesh and drink my
blood." Our souls have been fed by his life. We have been
nourished by his *character* more than by his words. He has been
bread and wine to us—the bread of strength, the wine of joy.

The saying of the liturgy is true and wise, that "in the midst of
life we are in death." But it is still more true that "in the midst of
death we are in life." Do we ever believe so much in immortality
as when we look on such a dear and noble face, now so still, which
a few hours ago was radiant with thought and love? "He is not

here : he is risen." That power which we knew,—that soaring intelligence, that soul of fire, that ever-advancing spirit,—*that* cannot have been suddenly annihilated with the decay of these earthly organs. It has left its darkened dust behind. It has outsoared the shadow of our night. God does not trifle with his creatures by bringing to nothing the ripe fruit of the ages by the lesion of a cerebral cell or some bodily tissue. Life does not die, but matter dies off from it. The highest energy we know, the soul of man, the unit in which meet intelligence, imagination, memory, hope, love, purpose, insight,—this agent of immense resource and boundless power,—this has not been subdued by its instrument. When we think of such an one as he, we can only think of life, never of death.

Such was his own faith, as expressed in his paper on Immortality. But he himself was the best argument for immortality. Like the greatest thinkers, he did not rely on logical proof, but on the higher evidence of universal instincts,—the vast streams of belief which flow through human thought like currents in the ocean ; those shoreless rivers which for ever roll along their paths in the Atlantic and Pacific, not restrained by banks, but guided by the revolutions of the globe and the attractions of the sun.

Mr. Emerson stated such indications of immortality as these : That all great natures love stability and permanence. " Everything here," he says, " is prospective." " The mind delights in immense time." " We are not interested in anything which ends." " All I have seen teaches me to trust the Creator for what I have not seen." "All the ways of virtuous living lead upwards and not downwards."

In his "Threnody" he shows us how the Deep Heart said to him :—

> " When the scanty shores are full
> With Thought's perilous, whirling pool ;
> When frail Nature can be more,
> Then the spirit strikes the hour ;
> My servant Death, with solving rite,
> Pours finite into infinite."

There are few who remain who remember the beginnings of this long progress. The first time I saw him I went with Margaret

Fuller to hear him preach in the church on Hanover-street. Neither of us then knew him. We sat in the gallery, and felt that a new influence, sweet and strong, had come. Then I recall his kindness, after I came to have his acquaintance, and how he gave me to print in a Western magazine four of his early poems, the first ever printed. Next, I think of the group which always collected at his lectures, ever the same persons, those who came to be fed, and never went away hungry. After that were the days of the Transcendental Club, which we called the " Like-minded,"—I suppose because no two of us thought alike. One summer afternoon we came to Concord and had one meeting in his parlour. There was George Ripley, admirable talker, most genial of men; and Orestes A. Brownson, full of intelligence, courage, and industry, who soon went over into the Roman Catholic Church; and James Walker, of whom Mr. Emerson once said to me, "I have come to Boston to hear Dr. Walker thunder this evening;" Theodore Parker, and many others. Days of enthusiasm and youthful hope, when the world seemed so new and fair, life so precious, when new revelations were close at hand as we thought, and some new Plato or Shakespeare was about to appear. We dwelt in what Halleck calls "the dear charm of life's illusive dream;" and the man who had the largest hope of all, yet joined with the keenest eye to detect every fallacy, was Ralph Waldo Emerson. We looked to him as our master. And now *the world* calls him its master—in insight, judgment, charm of speech, unfailing courage, endless aspiration. We say of him as Goethe of Schiller:—" Lo, he went onward, ever onward, for all these years,— then, indeed, he had gone far enough for this earth. For care is taken that trees shall not grow up to heaven." His work, like that of the apostle, was accomplished by the quantity of soul that was in him,—not by mere power of intellect, but "by pureness, by knowledge, by long-suffering, by kindness, by the Holy Spirit, by love unfeigned, by the word of truth, by the armour of righteousness on the right hand and the left."

Let us then ponder his words:—

> "Wilt thou not ope thy heart to know
> What rainbows teach and sunsets show?

> Voice of earth to earth returned,
> Prayers of saints that inly burned,
> Saying, *What is excellent,*
> *As God lives, is permanent;*
> *Hearts are dust, hearts' loves remain;*
> *Hearts' love will meet thee again.*
>
> .   .   .   .
>
> House and tenant go to ground,
> Lost in God, in Godhead found."

After the above address a feeling prayer was
offered by Rev. Howard M. Brown, of Brook-
line, and the benediction closed the exercises in
the church.   Immediately before the benediction,
Mr. Alcott recited the following sonnet which he
had written for the occasion.

> His harp is silent : shall successors rise,
> Touching with venturous hand the trembling string,
> Kindle glad raptures, visions of surprise,
> And wake to ecstasy each slumbering thing?
> Shall life and thought flash new in wondering eyes,
> As when the seer transcendent, sweet, and wise,
> World-wide his native melodies did sing,
> Flushed with fair hopes and ancient memories?
> Ah, no !   That matchless lyre shall silent lie :
> None hath the vanished minstrel's wondrous skill
> To touch that instrument with art and will.
> With him, winged poesy doth droop and die ;
> While our dull age, left voiceless, must lament
> The bard high heaven had for its service sent.

Over an hour was occupied by the passing files
of neighbours, friends, and visitors looking for the
last time upon the face of the dead poet.   The

body was robed completely in white, and the face bore a natural and peaceful expression. From the church the procession took its way to the cemetery. The grave was made beneath a tall pine tree upon the hill top to the east of Sleepy Hollow, where lie the bodies of his friends Thoreau and Hawthorne, the upturned sod being concealed by strewings of pine boughs. A border of hemlock spray surrounded the grave and completely lined its sides. The services here were very brief and the casket was soon lowered to its final resting place.

The Rev. Dr. Haskins, a cousin of the family, an Episcopal clergyman, read the Episcopal burial service, and closed with the Lord's Prayer, ending at the words "and deliver us from evil." In this all the people joined. Dr. Haskins then pronounced the benediction. After it was over the grandchildren passed by the open grave and threw flowers into it.

RECOLLECTIONS

OF

EMERSON'S VISITS TO ENGLAND IN 1833, 1847-8, AND 1872-3.

It was in the month of August, 1833—nearly fifty years ago—that I had the singular good fortune to make the acquaintance of Mr. Emerson, and to enjoy the privilege of several days' intercourse with him. I was then residing in Edinburgh, my native city, and he was on his way home, after his first visit to Europe. He had with him a letter of introduction to a friend of mine, who, luckily for me, was then so much engaged in professional duties, that he was unable to spare even a few hours to do the honours of the old Scottish metropolis ; so the young American traveller was handed over to me, and I thus became "an entertainer of angels unawares." In those early days Mr. Emerson was about thirty years of age, and his name was then utterly unknown in the world of letters; for the period to which I refer was anterior, by several years, to his delivery of those remarkable addresses which took by surprise the most thoughtful of his countrymen, as well as of cultivated English readers. Neither had he published any of those addresses or essays which afterwards stamped him as the most original thinker in America.

On Sunday, the 18th of August, 1833, I heard him deliver a discourse in the Unitarian Chapel, Young Street, Edinburgh, and I remember distinctly the effect which it produced on his hearers. It is almost needless to say that nothing like it had ever been heard by them before, and many of them did not know what to make of it. The originality of his thoughts, the consummate beauty of the language in which they were clothed, the calm dignity of his bearing, the absence of all oratorical effort, and the singular directness and simplicity of his manner, free from the least shadow of dogmatic assumption, made a deep impression on me. Not long before this I had listened to a wonderful sermon by Dr. Chalmers, whose force, and energy, and vehement, but rather turgid eloquence carried, for the moment, all before them—his audience becoming like clay in the hands of the potter.* But I must confess that the pregnant thoughts and serene self-possession of the young Boston minister had a greater charm for me than all the rhetorical splendours of Chalmers. His voice was the sweetest, the most winning and penetrating of any I ever heard ; nothing like it have I listened to since.

> That music in our hearts we bore,
> Long after it was heard no more.

We visited together the courts of law and other places of interest to a stranger, and ascended Blackford Hill, which commands a fine view of the city from the south. There were thus good opportunities for conversation. He spoke on many subjects connected with life, society, and literature, and with an affluence of thought and fulness of knowledge which surprised and delighted me. I had never before met with any one of so fine and varied a culture and with such frank sincerity of speech. There was a graciousness and kind encouragement, too, in his manner, inexpressibly winning to one so much younger than himself ; and it was with a feeling almost akin to reverence that I listened to and drank in his high thoughts

---

* "His tones in preaching would rise to the piercingly pathetic— no preacher ever went so into one's heart. . . . I suppose there will never again be such a preacher in any Christian Chvrch."— "Carlyle's Reminiscences," Vol. I, p. 160.

and ripe wisdom. A refined and delicate courtesy, a kind of mental hospitality, so to speak,—the like of which, or anything approaching to which, I have never encountered,—seemed to be a part of his very nature, and inseparable from his "daily walk and conversation." It was not therefore extraordinary,—rather quite a natural result,—that the impression produced on me was intense and lasting.

It is with a feeling of something like pride that I find recorded, in a journal kept at the time, some memoranda of that brief intercourse, written in a strain of youthful, enthusiastic admiration, and of perfectly confident expectancy as to his future— a strain which might at that time have sounded unduly inflated, but which his subsequent career may be said to have rendered almost tame and inadequate. He spoke much about Coleridge, whom he had just visited at Highgate. I happened then to be reading the prose works of that writer, and these formed a fruitful topic of conversation. He spoke of his "Friend" and "Biographia Literaria" as containing many admirable passages for young thinkers, many valuable advices regarding the pursuit of truth and the right methods to be adopted in its investigation, and the importance of having precise and correct notions on moral and intellectual subjects. He considered that there were single sentences in these two works, which embodied clearer ideas of some of the most subtle of human speculations than are to be met with in the pages of any other thinker. " Let no one, however, expect in these books of Coleridge's anything strictly symmetrical. The works themselves are disjointed, inconsecutive, and totally destitute of all regularity and plan. As Hazlitt, with his usual acuteness, well said of them—'They are vast prefaces and projects preliminary to immense productions which he was always contemplating, but could never bring himself to execute.'" He spoke of Dr. Channing, Sir James Mackintosh, Goethe's "Wilhelm Meister," and Charles Cotton's translation of Montaigne's " Essays," which he regarded as matchless among translations. "After reading Cotton's racy English," he said, "Montaigne seems to lose, if you look into him in the original old French." He also spoke of the excellence of Sir Thos. Urquhart's translation of Rabelais.

I find that in an essay on " Books," published in 1860, he says that he prefers reading the ancients in translation. It was a tenet of Goethe's that whatever is really valuable in any work is translateable. "I should as soon think," says he, " of swimming across Charles River when I want to go to Boston, as of reading all my books in originals, when I have them rendered for me in my mother tongue." After Bohn's volumes of translations of the Classics made their appearance, he held that they had done for literature what railroads have done for international intercourse.

Some of Walter Savage Landor's "Imaginary Conversations" he greatly admired—particularly those between Bacon and Richard Hooker, Sir Isaac Newton and Isaac Barrow, and Diogenes and Plato. He had visited Landor in Florence some time before. Emerson, long afterwards, said that he had made Landor's "Imaginary Conversations" his companion for more than twenty years, and publicly expressed his gratitude to him for having afforded a resource that had never failed him in solitude. "I have but to recur to its rich and ample page to find always free and sustained thought, a keen and precise understanding, an affluent and ready memory familiar with all chosen books, an industrious observation in every department of life, an experience to which it might seem that nothing had occurred in vain, honour for every just and generous sentiment, and a scourge like that of the Furies for any oppressor whether public or private." He felt how dignified was that perpetual Censor in his curule chair, and he wished to thank so great a benefactor. "Mr.

Landor," he continued, "is one of the foremost of that small class who make good in the nineteenth century the claims of pure literature. In these days of avarice and ambition, when there is so little disposition to profound thought, or to any but the most superficial intellectual entertainment, a faithful scholar, receiving from past ages the treasures of wit, and enlarging them by his own love, is a friend and consoler of mankind. . . . His acquaintance with the English tongue is unsurpassed. . . . Of many of Mr. Landor's sentences we are fain to remember what was said of those of Socrates, that they are cubes which will stand firm, place them how or where you will."

Although not an admirer of the Utilitarian philosophy, he had met with Dr. Bowring in London, and had some of Jeremy Bentham's hair and a scrap of his handwriting. He asked me if I was in the habit of writing down my thoughts. I said I was not ; that reading was my greatest pleasure and solace— *laborum dulce lenimen.* "I advise you," said he, "and other young men, to write down your ideas. I have found my benefit in it. It fixes more firmly in your mind what you know, and what you have acquired, and reveals to you unerringly which of your ideas are vague, and which solid." Of De Quincey, Wordsworth, and Carlyle he spoke many times—especially Carlyle, of whom he expressed the warmest admiration. Some of his articles in the "Edinburgh Review" and "Foreign Quarterly Review" had much struck him—one particularly, entitled "Characteristics"—and the concluding passages of another on German Literature, regarding which he was desirous of speaking to the author. He wished much to meet both Carlyle and Wordsworth : "Am I, who have hung over their works in my chamber at home, not to see these men in the flesh, and thank them, and interchange some thoughts with them, when I am passing their very doors?" He spoke of Carlyle's "rich thoughts, and rare, noble glimpses of great truths, his struggles to reveal his deepest inspirations,—not all at once very apparent, but to be digged out, as it were, reverently and patiently from his writings." There was great and, I remember, almost insuperable difficulty in ascertaining where Mr. Carlyle then lived, and I well remember the pains Mr. Emerson took to get the information ; at last, it was obtained from the secretary to the University. "I will be sure to send you, before sailing, an account of my visit to Carlyle and Wordsworth, if I should be fortunate enough to see them." Accordingly, in faithful fulfilment of his promise, he wrote me a long and most interesting letter on the 30th of

August, 1833, from Liverpool, giving an account
of the interviews he had with both of them.   These
interviews he has described in his "English Traits,"
published twenty-three years afterwards, and they
must be well known to the readers of that best of
all books on England.

He found that Carlyle had heard of his purpose
to visit him from a friend, and, on his arrival, he
insisted on dismissing the gig which had been hired
to carry him from Dumfries to Craigenputtock—
a distance of sixteen or seventeen miles.   It was
therefore sent back, to return the next day, in
time for him to secure his seat in the evening coach
for the south.   So he spent nearly twenty-four hours
with Carlyle and his accomplished wife, who were
living in perfect solitude among some desolate hills
in the parish of Dunscore—not a person to speak
to within seven miles.   Here are his words, from
the letter referred to—" I found him one of the most
simple and frank of men, and became acquainted
with him at once.   We walked over several miles
of hills, and talked upon all the great questions that
interest us most.   The comfort of meeting a man
of genius is that he speaks sincerely ; that he feels
himself to be so rich, that he is above the meanness
of pretending to knowledge which he has not, and
Carlyle does not pretend to have solved the great

problems, but rather to be an observer of their solution as it goes forward in the world. I asked him at what religious development the concluding passage in his piece in the 'Edinburgh Review' upon German literature (say five years ago), and some passages in the piece called 'Characteristics,' pointed ? He replied that he was not competent to state it even to himself—he waited rather to see. My own feeling was that I had met with men of far less power who had got greater insight into religious truth.* He is, as you might guess from his papers, the most catholic of philosophers ; he forgives and loves everybody, and wishes each to struggle on in his own place and arrive at his own ends. But his respect for eminent men, or rather his scale of eminence, is about the reverse of the popular scale. Scott, Mackintosh, Jeffrey, Gibbon — even Bacon — are no heroes of his ; stranger yet, he hardly admires Socrates, the glory of the Greek world—but Burns, and Samuel Johnson, and Mirabeau, he said interested him, and I suppose whoever else has given himself with all his heart to a leading instinct, and has not *calculated* too much. But I cannot think of sketching

---

* Emerson, in his more elaborate account of this interview, published in his " English Traits " twenty-three years later, has no remark embodying the substance of this sentence.

even his opinions, or repeating his conversations here. I will cheerfully do it when you visit me in America. He talks finely, seems to love the broad Scotch, and I loved him very much at once. I am afraid he finds his entire solitude tedious, but I could not help congratulating him upon his treasure in his wife, and I hope he will not leave the moors ; 'tis so much better for a man of letters to nurse himself in seclusion than to be filed down to the common level by the compliances and imitations of city society. And you have found out the virtues of solitude, I remember, with much pleasure."

The third day afterwards, Mr. Emerson called on Wordsworth at Rydal Mount, and was cordially received, the poet reckoning up all his American acquaintance. Here is his description of the interview :—" He had very much to say about the evils of superficial education, both in this country and in mine. He thinks that the intellectual tuition of society is going on, out of all proportion, faster than its moral training, which last is essential to all *education.* He does not wish to hear of schools of tuition ; it is the education of circumstances which he values, and much more to this point. He says that he is not in haste to publish more poetry, for many reasons, but that what he has

written will be at some time given to the world.
He led me out into a walk in his grounds, where
he said many thousands of his lines were composed, and repeated to me three beautiful sonnets,
which he had just finished, upon the occasion of
his recent visit to Fingal's Cave, at Staffa. I hope
he will print them speedily. The third is a gem.
He was so benevolently anxious to impress upon
me my social duties as an American citizen, that
he accompanied me near a mile from his house,
talking vehemently, and ever and anon stopping
short to imprint his words. I noted down some
of these when I got to my inn, and you may see
them in Boston, Massachusetts, when you will. I
enjoyed both my visits highly, and shall always
esteem your Britain very highly in love for its
wise and good men's sake. I remember with
much pleasure my visit to Edinburgh, and my
short acquaintance with yourself and your good
parents. It will give me very great pleasure to
hear from you, to know your thoughts. Every
man that ever was born has some that are peculiar.
Present my respects to your father and family.—
Your friend and servant, R. WALDO EMERSON."

So much with regard to Mr. Emerson's first
visit to England. As every one knows, his name,
in a very few years, became celebrated in his own

country, exercising a remarkable influence on thoughtful minds.

Mr. Carlyle edited Emerson's first series of Essays published in this country in 1841, and in his preface* introduced him to English readers, speaking of him with high appreciation, as a "spiritual notability." "The name of Ralph Emerson is not entirely new in England ; distinguished travellers bring us tidings of such a man ; fractions of his writings have found their way into the hands of the curious here. . . . That an educated man, of good gifts and opportunities, after looking at the public arena, and even trying, not with ill success, what its tasks and its prizes might amount to, should retire for long years into rustic obscurity ; and amid the all-pervading jingle of dollars and loud chaffering of ambitions and promotions, should quietly, with cheerful deliberateness, sit down to spend *his* life, not in Mammon worship, or the hunt for reputation, influence, place, or any outward advantage whatsoever : this, when we get a notice of it, is a thing worth noting."

The publication, in England, of this and the second series of essays, which took place a year or two later, made his name widely known throughout

* The reader is referred to p. 39 of this volume for extracts from Carlyle's Preface.

Great Britain, and men of thought recognised in him an intellectual leader. Many of his friends were desirous that he should come to England, and deliver courses of lectures similar to those he had given with such signal success in various cities of the United States. In this desire I warmly shared. In the autumn of 1846, a very favourable opportunity presented itself of sending a message to him by a common friend—Mr. Lloyd Garrison— who was then sailing from Liverpool to Boston, and who promised to deliver it himself. I gladly availed myself of the occasion, and on the spur of the moment, just before the ship steamed out of the Mersey, I wrote a hasty note in pencil, urging him to entertain the project of a lengthened visit to England, and which should embrace the delivery of lectures in the chief towns of the kingdom. That he might be freed from all irksome correspon- dence in connection with such a project, I gladly offered to undertake all the necessary business arrangements. Before long I received a reply, which was more favourable than I expected. It was full of kind words and reminiscences. "Your suggestion is new and unlooked for, yet opens to me at once so many flattering possibilities, that I shall cheerfully entertain it, and perhaps we may both see it ripen one day to a fact.

Certainly it would be much more practicable and pleasing to me to answer an invitation than to come into your cities and challenge an audience." Some months later (28th February, 1847) he wrote :—" I owe you new thanks for your friendly and earnest attention to the affair of Lectures which you have put me on, but I had not anticipated so prompt an execution of the project as you suggest. Certainly I cannot think of it for April (1847). For September I will think of it, but cannot at present fix anything. I really have not the means of forming an opinion of the expediency of such an attempt. I feel no call to make a visit of literary propagandism in England. All my impulses to work of that kind would rather employ me at home. It would be still more unpleasing to me to put upon a few friends the office of collecting an audience for me, by much advertisement and coaxing. At the same time it would be very agreeable to me to accept any good invitation to read lectures from institutions, or from a number of friendly individuals who sympathised with my studies. But though I possess a good many decisive tokens of interest in my pursuits and way of thinking from sundry British men and women, they are widely sundered persons, and my belief is that in no one city, except perhaps in London, could I find any numerous company to whom my name was favourably known. If I were younger, it would give me great pleasure to come to England and collect my own audience, as I have done at home here ; and I have that confidence in my favourite topics and in my own habits, that I should undertake the affair without the least distrust. But perhaps my ambition does not give to a success of this kind that importance it has had for me. At all events, in England I incline rather to take than to give the challenge. So that you see my project requires great frankness on your part. You must not suffer your own friendly feelings to give the smallest encouragement to the design. . . . You inquire what are the rates of remuneration of lecturers here. . . . I am glad to hear what you tell me of your employments and position. I doubt not life has taught and is teaching us both one lesson. It would be strange, but most agreeable to me, to renew again our brief yet never-forgotten acquaintance of thirteen or fourteen years ago in Edinburgh.—With ever kindest regards."

It was quite characteristic of Mr. Emerson to under-estimate the extent to which his name was known and his writings appreciated in England. No sooner was it announced that he had decided to revisit this country and to read lectures, than (as has been stated at p. 48) applications from every part of the kingdom began to flow in, and in many cases it was found impossible to comply with the wishes of the requisitionists, from a fear of committing him to engagements which might have become burdensome to him. Speaking of the occasion of his second visit to England in "English Traits," he says:—"I did not go very willingly. I am not a good traveller, nor have I found that long journeys yield a fair share of reasonable hours. But the invitation was repeated and pressed at a moment of more leisure, and when I was a little spent by some unusual studies. I wanted a change and a tonic, and England was proposed to me. Besides, there were, at least, the dread attraction and salutary influences of the sea, so I took my berth in the packet ship, 'Washington Irving,' and sailed from Boston on Tuesday, 5th October, 1847."

His friend Carlyle was greatly delighted with the prospect of again seeing Mr. Emerson. A letter from the latter, announcing the probable time of his sailing, had, by accidental negligence at a country post-office, failed to reach Carlyle in due course, and only turned up near the time of Mr. Emerson's expected arrival, thus depriving his friend of the opportunity of responding. The only thing left to be done was to get the reply delivered to Mr. Emerson as soon as he should land. Knowing that I was in communication with him, and certain to be cognisant of the time of his arrival, Mr. Carlyle wrote me on the subject, and his letter is so delightfully characteristic of his high regard for Mr. Emerson, and his earnest desire to free himself from even the slightest appearance of a want of hospitality, that I must give an extract from it. It is dated Chelsea, 15th October, 1847, just ten days after Mr. Emerson had sailed :—" By a letter I had very lately from Emerson—which had lain, lost and never missed, for above a month in the treacherous post-office of Buxton, where it was called for and denied—I learn that Emerson intended to sail for this country ' about the 1st of October ;' and infer, therefore, that probably even now he is near Liverpool or some other of our ports. Treadmill, or other as emphatic admonition, to that scandalous post-master of Buxton! He has put me in extreme risk of doing one of the most unfriendly and every way unpardonable-looking things a man could do! Not knowing in the least to what port Emerson is tending, when he is expected, or what his first engagements are, I find no way of making my word audible to him in time, except that of entrusting it, with solemn charges, to you, as here. Pray do me the favour to contrive in some sure way that Emerson may get hold of that note the instant he lands in England. I shall be permanently grieved otherwise; shall have failed in a clear duty (were it nothing more) which will never, probably, in my life offer itself again. Do not neglect, I beg much of you; and, on the whole, if you can, get Emerson put safe into the express train, and shot up hither, as the first road he goes! That is the result we aim at. But the note itself, at all events, I pray you get that delivered duly, and so do me a very great favour, for which I depend on you." I need scarcely say that these solemn injunctions, so characteristic of Carlyle, were faithfully carried out to the very letter.

The ship reached Liverpool on the 22nd of October, 1847, and Mr. Emerson at once proceeded to Manchester, where I had the pleasure of receiving him at the Victoria Station. After spending a few hours together, he was "shot up," as Carlyle had desired, to Chelsea, and at the end of a week returned to Manchester to commence the first of a series of lecturing engagements which had been arranged for him. In a previous page (*v.* Memoir, pp. 53-4) I have endeavoured to give the reader some idea of Emerson's manner of reading in public. But I have felt it impossible to convey to those who never heard him an adequate impression of what to me was the most startling and unexpected revelation of the power of speech I ever listened to. It was absolutely unique.

In February, 1848, he went from Manchester to Edinburgh and lectured there (*v.* Memoir, p. 51), and, in returning, stopped at Ambleside to see Wordsworth and Miss Martineau, his first visit to the former having taken place in 1833. " I spent a valuable hour, and perhaps a half more, with Mr. Wordsworth, who is in sound health at seventy-seven years, and was full of talk. He would even have walked with me on my way towards Miss Martineau's, but it began to rain, and I would not suffer it." His four lectures created a great sensation in the Scottish metropolis, and stirred the hearts of many independent thinkers. The orthodox of that firm stronghold of religious formalism were grieved and shocked, although Emerson, knowing the tone of feeling there, had, with the utmost delicacy, avoided such subjects as might bring him into direct contact with it. One who heard these lectures said of him: "A lecturer in the common sense of the term, he is not ; call him rather a public monologist, talking rather to himself than to his audience ; and what a quiet, calm, commanding conversation it is ! It is not the seraph or burning one you see; it is the naked cherubic reason thinking aloud before you. It is a soul totally unsheathed you have to do with; and you ask, Is this a spirit's tongue sounding on its way? so solitary and severe seems its harmony. There is no betrayal of emotion, except now and then when a slight tremble in his voice proclaims that he has arrived at some spot of thought to him peculiarly sacred or dear. There is no emphasis often but what is given by the eye, and this is felt only by those who see him on the side-view. Neither standing behind him nor before can we form any conception of the rapt, living flash which breaks forth athwart the spectator. His eloquence is thus of that high kind which produces great effects at small expenditure of means, and without any effort or turbulence; still and strong as gravitation, it fixes, subdues, and turns us round."* A remarkable article on Emerson and his Edinburgh lectures was written by a young student, George Cupples, which appeared in Douglas Jerrold's "Shilling Magazine" under the title of "Emerson, and his Visit to Scotland," signed "A Student." Dr. Samuel Brown, the chemical philosopher (whose guest Emerson was during his Edinburgh visit), used to say that this was the best

* George Gilfillan's "Gallery of Literary Portraits." First series.

article he had ever seen on Emerson. I venture to give a few sentences from it,*

While in Edinburgh he sat to David Scott, the well-known Scottish artist, for his portrait. This is the best of the few paintings of this kind which Scott executed. On leaving London, Emerson thus wrote to him : " I carry with me a bright image of your house and studio, and all your immortal companions therein, and I wish to keep the ways open between us, natural and supernatural. If the Good Power had allowed me the opportunity of seeing you at more leisure and of com-

---

*"Of all men, Emerson is the most freely, fully, and longingly open to the Future; it is his element; without it he dies; the everlasting morning all but breathes on him. In this he is national; America is the land of the Future; she is vague and abundant in airy undefined possibilities, somewhat cold to the actual necessities, the old griefs of men; she has food and land in store, and can afford to look out for truth. . . . The reverse of a Mystic, he yet often appears one, from that mental clearness and marvellous expression by which he leads you into the unimagined depths, not of speculation, but of him and of yourself, dividing the light-beam of a consciousness, upon the invisible edge that is in it; not letting you conceive of an object. He is thus, at once the oldest and the newest of thinkers, the most Greek-like of all modern minds ; and, therefore, in his nationality free of all times and countries. . . . But, in fine, setting aside the intellect of Emerson and his doctrine, it is to be said that his most important aspect is that of his personal character, as a man, and as revealed secondarily through these writings of his. In this respect, I take leave to think that Emerson is the most mark-worthy, the loftiest and most heroic

paring notes of past years a little! And it may
yet be allowed in time ; but where and when ?"

During his stay in Manchester, and just before
going to London to pay a round of visits and
to lecture, he invited a number of friends from
various parts of the country to dine and spend
an evening with him at his lodgings in Lower
Broughton. His guests were principally young
men—ardent, hopeful, enthusiastic moral and religious reformers, and independent thinkers, gathered
together from Birmingham, Sheffield, Nottingham,
Liverpool, Huddersfield, Newcastle, and other

---

mere man that ever appeared. And just because Humanity itself,
at this epoch of its progress, needs such an individual, has he
arisen. Like all representative characters, he is the anticipative
product of a universal want, as Luther of Reformation. . . .
Nothing would disgust this man more than followers,—to have a
school : the whole of men and women can only be Emersonian
by being different from him and from each other. Till then, they
can no more join hands in brotherhood and sisterhood than you can
clasp the fingers of a shadow ; he would not have them do good or be
done good to, till they are *themselves:* did they mimic his voice and
attitude, he would turn from them as from a flock of apes. . . .
Well may tyrannies, superstitions, and authority tremble at the
steps of Emerson, for he heralds an epoch of humanity, the stage of
man self-conscious and free from within. Other forms after that
have to arise, no doubt, and higher stations to be won, but meantime *this* is sure as the nature of man. . . . With that inward
fortitude of his—that sunbright insight of intuition—that instinct to
feel and to divine—that power to express—and that perfect individual freedom—he forestalls centuries of general progress."

towns. One of them, a man of erratic genius, and of very straitened means (but nevertheless an inveterate smoker), who not many years ago died in a lunatic asylum in New York, trudged on foot all the way from Huddersfield to be present, and next day performed the same feat homeward. He has left behind him a detailed description of this gathering, written in a rather sarcastic spirit, but curious for its life-like sketches of his fellow-guests. One of the finest spirits assembled on that occasion—Henry Sutton, of Nottingham, whose little volume of Poems, in Emerson's opinion, contained pieces worthy of the genius of George Herbert— and who, happily, is still living amongst us, honoured and beloved by his friends—says that the impression left on his mind was that the affair went off admirably, and that all seemed delighted to have had such an opportunity of coming into closer contact with Emerson—that no one could but feel gratified by his kindliness and gentle dignity, and that his conduct and manner were perfect. " Any criticism to the contrary could only excite pity for the writer, if it did not too strongly call forth disgust." It was a memorable symposium. With his fine graciousness of manner and delicate courtesy, Emerson listened with serene amiability, and an ineffably sweet smile to everything his young guests had to say, and made them feel, as was his wont, that *he* was the favoured one of the party, and that *he* specially was imbibing much wisdom and benefit from their discourse. In the course of the evening, being urgently requested to do so, he read his lecture on Plato, then unpublished, but now printed in his " Representative Men."

Among the guests who were present at this motley gathering were two—no longer living—of whom I wish to say a few words. One of them was Dr. W. B. Hodgson, late Professor of Political Economy in the University of Edinburgh, who died unexpectedly in Brussels in 1880, lamented by a very large circle of friends. I had known him intimately almost from his boyhood. `At the time of Emerson's visit he was proprietor and conductor of the Chorlton High School, Manchester. He was a man of brilliant gifts, a classical scholar of no common mark, and master of several European languages. His kindly disposition, extensive know-ledge of literature, and conversational powers can never be forgotten by those who knew him. As an after-dinner talker he had few equals. His mar-vellous memory (for he never forgot anything he had ever read, or heard, or seen), supplied him with an inexhaustible store of witty and humorous stories and anecdotes, sparkling *bon mots*, and an unfailing affluence of apt quotation. No story, however good, could be told by another person in his presence which he was not able to cap on the instant by a better one. In this social field he was *facile princeps.* During his life he rendered most valuable services to the cause of education by his addresses, lectures, and other publications, and by his *vast* (for no other word can in this case be used) correspondence with Educational Reformers, Political Economists, and conductors of Schools and Colleges, in every part of the kingdom, as well as on the Continent and in the United States. I may advisedly say that, during forty years, he spent, on an average, two or three hours a day, at least, in correspondence.

The other guest to whom I wish to refer was Joseph Neuberg, whom I knew for more than twenty years, and whose memory I cherish for his many admirable qualities of head and heart. He was a highly-cultivated and thoughtful German, born at Würzburg. Mr. Emerson had made his acquaintance at Nottingham, when lecturing there— was, indeed, his guest, and while under his roof, met Mr. Henry Sutton, already referred to, who was a native of that town.* Neuberg was a success-

---

* Besides the volume of Poems referred to, Mr. Sutton was the author of "The Evangel of Love" (1847), with this motto from

ful merchant, and had recently sustained a severe domestic affliction in the death of his wife. At the time I speak of, he was living with a sister, as his companion, in a beautiful home, looking down upon the Trent and its green meadows. During this visit, he took Emerson to see Newstead Abbey. Neuberg had ardent literary tastes, was an enthusiastic admirer of Carlyle's writings, and had long wished to know him. The gratification of this desire was brought about by the friendly aid of Emerson, who spoke of him to Carlyle in terms of high commendation. In the spring of 1848 he went to London, by Emerson's invitation, to be introduced by him to Carlyle. In company with the former, he paid a visit to Oxford. He soon after this left Nottingham, after winding up his affairs there, and went to London, where he resided for a time, and then settled in Bonn, attending lectures at the University. In 1852, Carlyle visited him there, and they went together to the various battle-fields and places of historical interest

Emerson: "That which befits us, embosomed in beauty and wonder as we are, is cheerfulness and courage, and the endeavour to realize our aspirations." Some years later, he published a volume entitled "Quinquenergia ; or Proposals for a New Practical Theology." In this volume are included some thirty-five pages of verse, distinguished by deep religious feeling, and a certain quaintness characteristic of certain of our seventeenth century English poets.

afterwards described in the " Life of Friedrich." In
the autumn of the same year he returned to London, to be nearer Carlyle for a time, intending
ultimately to take up his permanent residence in
Bonn, but in the meantime, his sister becoming
engaged to a gentleman living in London, they
removed thither, and settled on its northern heights.
There he lived during the remainder of his days,
devoting himself, heart and soul, to Carlyle's service. From that period up to the time of his
death, about fifteen years ago, he was in almost
daily communication with him. His industry was
untiring. He made researches for him in all
quarters—often spending days and weeks in the
library of the British Museum, unearthing facts
and dates from hundreds of obscure and neglected
books, manuscripts, and maps, thus saving his
friend an endless amount of distasteful drudgery.
He would think nothing of spending a whole
day in verifying a single fact or date. During
the composition of " The Life of Friedrich,"
his services were of great value, and were fully
appreciated by Carlyle. He translated into
German the successive volumes of the " Life of
Friedrich." By this arrangement they appeared
simultaneously in London and Berlin. Neuberg
did not live to translate the last two volumes,

which were done by another hand. Carlyle was much grieved when death deprived him of this faithful friend and assistant. In no account of Carlyle which has yet appeared, has any notice been taken of Neuberg, nor any tribute paid to his memory. In Carlyle's "Reminiscences" his name once occurs in a parenthesis, but there is no note appended to tell the reader who he was—*Stat nominis umbra.* In "Shooting Niagara ; and after ?" Carlyle quotes a piece of information furnished to him by Neuberg. Without naming him, he speaks of his informant as "one of the wisest and faithfullest German friends I ever had, a correct observer, and much a lover both of his own country and of mine." In a letter from Carlyle to Mr. Neuberg's sister (Madame Frankau), written in April, 1867, he says:—"If the bust give you any satisfaction, surely I shall think it, all my days, to have been well worth while ! No kinder friend had I in this world ; no man of my day, I believe, had so faithful, loyal, and willing a helper as he generously was to me for the last twenty or more years. To look for his like again would be very vain indeed, were I even at the beginning of my course, instead of at the end ! A man of fine faculty, too ;—decidedly the most intelligent, swift, and skilful, at that kind of work, whom I have ever seen and known of. The memory of him will remain dear and noble to me ;—the sudden stroke that has cut away such a friend, in these my otherwise desolate days, may well be sad and heavy to me. But if so to me, what then is it to you and your dear little ones? Alas on this head I must *say* nothing. I will bid you be of courage, pious *courage*, and in all things try to do as you think he would have ordered and wished ; which I believe will daily be your best consolation in this sore trial."

During the fortnight in which Mr. Emerson delivered his course of lectures in London, at the Portman Square Literary and Scientific Institution, in the summer of 1848 (referred to at page 51 of the Memoir), I had the privilege of being his guest. He lived in the house of Mr. John Chapman, in the Strand—a well-known publisher of those days. As he had already been many weeks in London, he had met a considerable number of literary and social celebrities, including Rogers, Hallam, Milman, Barry Cornwall, Helps, Clough, Matthew Arnold, Faraday, Owen, Lyell, Carpenter, Mrs. Jameson, Henry Crabb Robinson, Mrs. Somerville, Dickens, Thackeray, Tennyson ("one of the most satisfying men of letters I have seen"), and Macaulay ("that Niagara of information," as Mrs.

Fanny Kemble called him).* He also received invitations from and visited several members of the
aristocracy, including the Duchess of Sutherland.
Notwithstanding his numerous social engagements,
he generally devoted many hours a day to study,
retiring to his room immediately after breakfast,
and extending the forenoon to three o'clock. The
lectures to which I have referred were prepared

---

* In his "English Traits," there is a short and contemptuous
criticism of Macaulay, in which he says :—"The brilliant Macaulay,
who expresses the tone of the English governing classes of the day,
explicitly teaches that *good* means good to eat, good to wear,
material commodity ; that the glory of modern philosophy is its
direction on 'fruit ;' to yield economical inventions ; and that its
merit is to avoid ideas, and avoid morals, &c." He witnessed one
of Macaulay's brilliant feats in conversation at a dinner, where
Hallam was one of the guests. The talk was on the question
whether the "additional letters" of Oliver Cromwell, lately published by Carlyle, were spurious or genuine. Emerson afterwards
described this conversation to a friend in the following terms :—
"For my part, the suspicious fact about them was this, that they all
seemed written to sustain Mr. Carlyle's view of Cromwell's character ;
but the discussion turned on the external evidences of their being
forgeries. Macaulay overcame everybody at the table, including
Hallam, by pouring out with victorious volubility instances of the
use of words in a different meaning from that they bore in Cromwell's time, or by citing words which were not in use at all until
half a century later. A question which might have been settled in
a few minutes by the consent of a few men of insight opened a tire-
some controversy which lasted during the whole dinner. Macaulay
seemed to have the best of it ; still, I did not like the arrogance with
which he paraded his minute information ; but then there was a fire,

with much care, as will be seen by his correspondence with myself, prior to my joining him in
London.

During this visit we went to some of the theatres
together—on one evening hearing Jenny Lind, who
was then achieving her first triumphs in London.
He was very desirous of calling upon Leigh Hunt,
and as I had known the latter for many years,
and was in the habit of spending an evening with

speed, fury, talent, and effrontery in the fellow which were very
taking."

Apropos of Macaulay's overwhelming power of talk, the two
following anecdotes are worth recording: "Hallam, whom Sidney
Smith called the 'bore contradictor,' was once sitting near
Macaulay at a dinner party, and they quarrelled so dreadfully about
something that happened in the Middle Ages that the wretched
unfortunate who sat between them could get no dinner." In
a printed letter of Lord Brougham's in the Macvey Napier Correspondence the following passage occurs :—"It is very provoking
when a man has such extraordinary abilities, and really some
powers of a first-rate order, to see the result of it all. He is
absolutely renowned in society as the greatest bore that ever yet
appeared. I have seen people come in from Holland House,
breathless and knocked up, and able to say nothing but 'Oh dear,
oh mercy!' What is the matter? being asked. 'Oh, Macaulay.'
Then every one said, 'That accounts for it, you're lucky to be
alive,' etc. Edinburgh is now celebrated for having given us the
two most perfect bores that have ever yet been known in London,
for Jack Campbell in the House of Lords is just what poor Tom
Macaulay is in private society."

Carlyle, in speaking of Macaulay, used sometimes to exclaim
"Flow on, thou Shining River!" following up with his accustomed
loud shout of laughter.

him when business carried me to London, it was proposed that I should take him to Hunt's house. The interview lasted more than a couple of hours, and evidently gave great pleasure to both. I have already mentioned that he thought the two finest-mannered literary men he had met in England were Leigh Hunt and De Quincey. Hunt charmed him by his sprightly, sparkling conversation, over-flowing with anecdote and quotation. His courteous and winning manner was on this occasion tem-pered by a certain delicate reverence, indicating how deeply he felt the honour of being thus sought out by his distinguished visitor. It is singular that Hunt produced a similar impression upon Hawthorne. I venture to give a portion of his description of him—one of the most touching sketches that Hawthorne has written :—"He was a beautiful old man. In truth, I never saw a finer countenance, either as to the mould of features or the expression, nor any that showed the play of feeling so perfectly. It was like a child's face in this respect. At my first glimpse of him, I discerned that he was old, his long hair being white, and his wrinkles many. It was an aged visage, in short such as I had not at all expected to see, in spite of dates, because his books talk to the reader with the tender vivacity of youth. But when he began to speak, and as he grew more earnest in conversation, I ceased to be sensible of his age ; sometimes, indeed, its dusky shadow darkened through the gleam which his sprightly thoughts diffused about his face, but then another flash of youth came out of his eyes, and made an illumination again. I never witnessed such a wonderfully illusive transformation, before or since ; and, to this day, trusting only to my recollection, I should find it difficult to decide which was his genuine and stable predicament—youth or age. I have met no Englishman whose manners seemed to me so agreeable—soft, rather than polished, wholly unconventional, the natural growth of a kindly and sensitive disposition, without any reference to rule, or else obedient to some rule so subtle that the nicest observer could not detect the application of it. I felt that no effect upon my mind of what he uttered, no emotion, however transitory, in myself, escaped his notice,—his faculty of observation was so penetrative and delicate. On matters of feeling, and within a certain depth, you might spare yourself the trouble of utterance, because he already knew what you wanted to say, and perhaps a little more than you would have spoken. There were abundant proofs throughout our interview of an unrepining spirit, resignation, quiet relinquishment of

the worldly benefits that were denied him, thankful
enjoyment of whatever he had to enjoy, and piety,
and hope shining onward into the dark,—all of
which gave a reverential cast to the feeling with
which we parted from him. I wish that he could
have had one full draught of prosperity before he
died. At our leave-taking he grasped me warmly
by both hands, and seemed as much interested in
our whole party as if he had known us for years.
All this was genuine feeling, a quick, luxuriant
growth out of his heart, which was a soil for flower-
seeds of rich and rare varieties, not acorns, but a
true heart, nevertheless."

The effect produced upon Emerson by his visit
to Leigh Hunt was in most respects the same as
in the case of Hawthorne, and could not be expressed in more true and touching words than
those I have just quoted. He often recurred to the
interview, and spoke of it as one of the most
delightful he had ever had with a man of letters.
Hunt's exquisite little poem, "Abou Ben Adhem,"
which must ever linger in the memory of anyone
who has once known it, was a great favourite
with him, and he has included it in his volume
of poetical selections, "Parnassus," with another of
Hunt's pieces, which he thought well worthy of
remembrance—"Song to Ceres"—a few stanzas

with a true classical flavour. Hunt's essays and critical works he admired for their delicate and subtle perception of the beautiful in life, nature, and literature—their tendency to sweeten and adorn daily existence—to encourage high aims and honest endeavour—and to teach the love of simple pleasures. He considered Hunt a true lover of letters and of mankind ; all that he has written being pervaded by the music of kindly thoughts, and breathing the spirit of the key-note motto to his "London Journal":—"To assist the Inquiring, animate the Struggling, and sympathise with all."

Many interesting places and persons we saw together in London. An evening spent at the house of John Minter Morgan, a wealthy social reformer and associationist, deserves special mention. This gentleman was an amiable, gentle, and sweet-mannered enthusiast, and had written several works well-known in his peculiar field of literature: "Hampden in the Nineteenth Century," "Colloquies on Religion," "The Christian Commonwealth," "Extinction of Pauperism," "The Revolt of the Bees," and other works on Reform and Progress in Society, in Religion, Morality, and Science. It is only necessary to read the titles of these works in order to know the views and opinions of this worthy moral reformer. He had met Emerson somewhere in London, and obtained the promise of an evening. Thereupon was gathered in his large drawing-room an extraordinary assembly, consisting of many of the leading socialists in London. The first part of the evening was spent in the contemplation of a huge coloured revolving view of a series of associated villages and homes, with the most enchanting representations of churches for the cultivation of universal religion, elegant lecture and concert rooms, and theatres, — of ladies and gentlemen walking about in the healthy costumes of the future, their children playing about them, and over all, a sky of unclouded blue. Mr. Morgan, with a long rod, explained to his audience the meaning and significance of all these beautiful objects, and answered many questions put to him by timid believers and admirers, chiefly ladies. After this entertainment the company adjourned to tea and coffee, and after a couple of hours spent in introductions and the conversations naturally flowing therefrom, the party broke up at eleven o'clock. Emerson confessed that he had never before met such a gathering of singular people, and often humorously alluded to it afterwards.

Prior to his departure from home, on the occasion of his last visit to Europe, towards the end of 1872, he attended a complimentary dinner in New York, in honour of Mr. Froude, the historian, and made a short address. He said that Mr. Froude had shown "at least two eminent faculties in his histories—the faculty of seeing wholes, and the faculty of seeing and seizing particulars. The one makes history valuable ; the other makes it readable and interesting. . . . The language, the style of his books, draws very much of its excellence from the habit of giving the very language of the times."

On the day which Mr. Emerson spent in Edinburgh, on his last visit to Europe (May 8th, 1873), he dined at the house of a friend, Dr. William Smith, the translator of many of Fichte's works, and President of the Edinburgh Philosophical Association, who heard him preach in Edinburgh in 1833, and who had listened to his lectures in 1848. At the dinner party he met Lord Neaves,*

* Lord Neaves was a distinguished member of the Scottish bench, and a man of fine culture, a recognised wit and humourist, and of the most genial disposition ; he was a general favourite in Edinburgh social circles. He was the author of many songs and verses, social and scientific, contributed to " Blackwood's Magazine." These have been collected, and have gone through several editions. Some of these verses had quite a renown at the time of their publication. Among them may be named " The Origin of Species," " The Permissive Bill," " I'm very fond of Water," " Hilli-onnee," " Stuart Mill on Mind and Matter," " Let us all be unhappy on Sunday," and others.

Dr. W. B. Hodgson,* and the widow of Dr. Samuel Brown, who had been his host in 1847-8, and a few other friends. He was greatly delighted with the brilliant fire of repartee and wit which was kept up between Lord Neaves and Dr. Hodgson, as well as with the songs of the former, who sang not a few ; and he frequently referred to this " wit combat " on his visit to me a few days later. In a scrapbook of the son of his Edinburgh host he inscribed this memorial of his visit. " After a happy evening with excellent company."—R. WALDO EMERSON. 8th May, 1873. On the evening of his arrival (7th May) he met a large party of notabilities in the house of Professor Fraser. A characteristic incident relating to this visit is worth recording. His host, Dr. Smith, thus relates it :—" On the 8th I drove him for some time about the city ; Miss Emerson, being rather indisposed, remained at the hotel. In the course of our drive we stopped at the shop of a worthy tradesman in Nicholson-street, who is an enthusiastic admirer of E. I had been informed that he had been making anxious inquiries about E.'s place of abode and the probable time of his departure, so that he might have a chance of getting a glimpse of his hero. I alighted, and entering the

---

* Late Professor of Political Economy in the University of Edinburgh, already referred to.

shop said, ' Mr. ——, Mr. Emerson is at the door, and will be glad to see you for a few minutes.' You may imagine his delight at this unexpected fulfilment of his wishes. The five minutes were well spent, and I have no doubt are a cherished memory."

During his stay in Oxford and London he was invited to give lectures, but declined. The only appearance he made was at Mr. Thomas Hughes's Working Men's College in London, where he made a short address.

He spent the last two days of this his final visit to England, under my roof, along with his devoted daughter, Ellen. This afforded an opportunity of bringing together many of his old friends and hearers of 1847-8, whom he was well pleased to meet. To every one he gave a few minutes, and the stream of conversation flowed on for several hours. After all the guests had departed, he indulged in a cigar, and expressed his gratification at having met so many " good people," as he called them. " Would that I could have held converse with each for half-an-hour!" A capital pun, related by him on this occasion, must here be recorded. It would have rejoiced the heart of Charles Lamb. Speaking of a convivial club, of which he was a member, having ceased and dispersed for many years, it was thought desirable that the survivors should once more assemble, and revive their old recollections. An interval of ten years had meanwhile elapsed. While the wine was circulating, someone proposed that the society should have a gathering every ten years. Mr. Appleton, one of the company, instantly said, " Then it should have the title of a Dutch picture, ' Boors Drinking' after Teniers" (ten years). His last hours in Liverpool, before sailing, were spent with Mr. R. C. Hall, an old friend and admirer.

It has often struck me that the "marble self-possession" of Emerson, his perfect reliance upon his own genius and intuitions, his grand self-dependence, which no passing excitement could disturb or shake for a moment; and his steadfast belief in the ultimate sovereignty of righteousness and truth, are well indicated in the following remarkable lines, written by an old English poet early in the seventeenth century—Samuel Daniel :—

> One who of such a height hath built his mind,
> And reared the dwelling of his thoughts so strong,
> As neither fear nor hope can shake the frame
> Of his resolvéd powers,   .   .   .
> .   .   .   .   nor pierce to wrong
> His settled peace, nor to disturb the same.
> .   .   .   .

And with how free an eye doth he look down
Upon these lower regions of turmoil,
Where all these storms of passion vainly beat
On flesh and blood ; where honour, power, renown,
Are only gay afflictions, golden toil ;
Where greatness stands upon as feeble feet
As frailty doth, and only great doth seem
To little minds, who do it so esteem.

  .   .   .   .   who hath prepared
A rest for his desires ; and sees all things
Beneath him ; and hath learned this book of man,
Full of the notes of frailty ; and compared
The best of glory with her sufferings :

  .   .   .   inured to any hue
The world can cast ; that cannot cast that mind
Out of its form of goodness ; that doth see
Both what the best and worst of earth can be ;

  .   .   .   .

Which makes, that whatsoever here befals,
He in the region of himself remains."

CORRESPONDENCE.

EMERSON TO CARLYLE ON "THE LIFE OF FRIEDRICH" AND THE AMERICAN CIVIL WAR.

"*Concord, 1st May, 1859.*

"The book [the first volume of 'The Life of Friedrich'] came, with its irresistible inscription, so that I am all tenderness and all but tears. The book, too, is sovereignly written. I think you the true inventor of the stereoscope, as having exhibited that art in style long before we had yet heard of it in drawing. The letter came also. Every child of mine knows from far that handwriting, and brings it home with speed. . . . You hug yourself on missing the illusion of children, and must be pitied as having one glittering toy the less. I am a victim all my days to certain graces of form and behaviour, and can never come into equilibrium. Now I am fooled by my own young people, and grow old contented. The heedless children suddenly take the keenest hold on life, and foolish papas cling to the world on their account, as never on their own. Out of sympathy, we *make believe* to value the prizes of their ambition and hope. My two girls, pupils once or now of Agassiz, are good, healthy, apprehensive, decided young people, who love life. My boy divides his time between Cicero and cricket,—knows his boat, the birds, and Walter Scott, verse and prose, through and through,—and will go to college next year. Sam Ward and I tickled each other the other day, in looking over a very good company of young people, by finding in the new comers a marked improvement on their parents. There, I flatter myself, I see some emerging of our people from the prison of their politics. . . . I am so glad to find myself speaking once more to you, that I mean to persist in the practice. Be as glad as you have been. You and I shall not know each other, on this platform, as long as we have known. A correspondent even of twenty-five years should not be disused unless through some fatal event. Life is too short, and with all our poetry and morals too indigent, to allow such sacrifices. Eyes so old and weary, and which have learned to look on so much, are gathering an hourly harvest; and I cannot spare what on noble terms is offered me. . . ."

"*Concord, 1861.*

" Here has come into the country, three or four months ago, another volume of your 'History of Friedrich,' infinitely the wittiest book that ever was written;—a book that one would think the English people would rise up in mass and thank the author for by cordial acclamation, and signify, by crowning him with oak leaves, their joy that such a head existed among them, and sympathising and much-reading America would make a new treaty, or send a Minister Extraordinary to offer congratulation of honouring delight to England in acknowledgment of this donation ;—a book holding so many memorable and heroic facts, working directly on practice, with new heroes, things unnoticed before—the German Plutarch (now that we have exhausted the Greek and Roman and the British Plutarchs),— with a range, too, of thought and wisdom, so large and so elastic, not so much applying as inculcating to every need and sensibility of man,—that we do not read a stereotype page,—rather we see the eyes of the writer looking into ours; mark his behaviour,

humming, chuckling,—with under tones and trumpet
tones, and long commanding glances, stereoscoping
every figure that passes, and every hill, river, road,
hummock, and pebble in the long perspective—with
its wonderful system of mnemonics, whereby great
and insignificant men are marked and modelled in
memory by what they were, had, and did.   .   .   .
And, withal, a book that is a Judgment Day for its
moral verdict on the men and nations and manners
of modern times.   And this book makes no noise.
I have hardly seen a notice of it in any newspaper
or journal, and you would think there was no such
book. I am not aware that Mr. Buchanan has sent
a special messenger to Cheyne Row, Chelsea, or
that Mr. Dallas had been instructed to assure Mr.
Carlyle of his distinguished consideration.   But the
secret wits and hearts of men take note of it, not
the less surely.   They have said nothing lately in
praise of the air, or of fire, or of the blooming of
love ; and yet, I suppose, they are sensible of these
and not less of this book, which is like these."

" *Concord, 8th December, 1862.*

"Long ago, as soon as swift steamers could
bring the new book across the sea, I received the
third volume of ' Friedrich' with your autograph
inscription, and read it with joy.   Not a word went

to the beloved author, for I do not write or think. I would wait perhaps for happier days, as our President Lincoln will not even emancipate slaves until on the heels of a victory, or the semblance of such.   But he waited in vain for his triumph, nor dare I in my heavy months expect bright days.

" The book was heartily grateful, and square to the author's imperial scale.   You have lighted the glooms, and engineered away the pits, whereof you poetically pleased yourself with complaining, in your sometime letter to me, clean out of it, and have let sunshine and pure air enfold the scene. First, I read it honestly through for the history ; then I pause and speculate on the muse that inspires, and the friend that reports it. 'Tis sovereignly written, above all literature. . . . I find, as ever in your books, that one man has deserved well of mankind for restoring the scholar's profession to its highest use and dignity.   I find also that you are very wilful, and have made a covenant with your eyes that they shall not see anything you do not wish they should.   But I was heartily glad to read somewhere that your book was nearly finished in the manuscript, for I would wish you to sit and taste your fame, if that were not contrary to the law of Olympus.   My joints ache to think of your rugged labour.   Now that

you have conquered to yourself such a huge kingdom among men, can you not give yourself breath,
and chat a little—an *Emeritus* in the Eternal
University—and write a gossiping letter to an old
American friend or so? Alas, I own that I have
no right to say this last, I who write never. Here
we read no books. The war is our sole and doleful
instructor. All our bright young men go into it,
to be misused and sacrificed by incapable leaders.
One lesson they all learn ; to hate slavery, *teterrima
causa !* But the issue does not yet appear. We
must get ourselves morally right. Nobody can
help us. 'Tis of no account what England or
France may do. Unless backed by our profligate
parties, their action would be nugatory, and, if so
backed, the worst. But even the war is better
than the degrading and descending politics that
preceded it for decades of years ; and our legisla-
tion has made great strides, and if we can stave
off that fury of trade which rushes to peace, at
the cost of replacing the South in the *status ante
bellum*, we can, with something more of courage,
leave the problem to another score of years—free
labour to fight with the beast, and see if bales,
barrels, and baskets cannot find out that thus they
pass more commodiously and surely to their ports,
through free hands than through barbarians."

" Concord, 26th Sept., 1864.

"I had received in July the fourth volume of 'Friedrich,' and it was my best reading in the summer, and for weeks my only reading. One fact was paramount in all the good I drew from it, that whomsoever many years had used and worn, they had not yet broken any fibre of your force;—a pure joy to me who abhor the inroads which time makes on me and my friends. . . . But this book will excuse you from any unseemly haste to make up your accounts, nay, holds you to fulfil your career with all amplitude and calmness. I found joy and pride in it, and discovered a golden chain of continuity not often seen in the works of men, apprising me that one good head and great heart remained in England immovable,— superior to his own eccentricities and perversities,—nay, wearing these, I can well believe, as a jaunty coat or red cockade to defy or mislead idlers, for the better securing his own peace and the very ends which the idlers fancy he resists. England's lease of power is good during his days. I have in these last years lamented that you had not made the visit to America, which in earlier years you projected or favoured. It would have made it impossible that your name should be cited for one moment on the side of the enemies of mankind. Ten days' residence in this country would have made you the organ of the sanity of England and Europe to us and to them, and have shown you the necessities and aspirations which struggle up in our free states, which, as yet, have no organ to others and are ill or unsteadily articulated here. In our to-day's division of Republican and Democrat it is certain that the American nationality lies in the Republican party (mixed and multiform though that party be), and I hold it not less certain that, viewing all the nationalities of the world, the battle of Humanity is at this hour in America. A few days here would show you the disgusting composition of the other party which within the Union resists the national action. Take from it the wild Irish element, imported in the last twenty-five years into this country, and led by Romish priests, who sympathise of course with despotism, and you would bereave it of all its numerical strength. A man intelligent and virtuous is not to be found on that side.

"Ah! how gladly I would enlist you with your thunderbolt on our part! How gladly enlist the wise, thoughtful, efficient pens and voices of England! We want England and Europe to hold our people staunch to their best tendency. Are English of this day incapable of a great sentiment? Can

they not leave cavilling at petty failures and bad
manners, and at the dunce part (always the largest
part in human affairs), and leap to the suggestions
and finger-pointing of the gods, which, above the
understanding, feed the hopes and guide the wills
of men? This war has been conducted over the
heads of all the actors in it, and the foolish terrors,—
'What shall we do with the negro?' 'the entire
black population is coming North to be fed,' &c.,
have strangely ended in the fact that the black
refuses to leave his climate; gets his living and the
living of his employer there, as he has always done;
is the natural ally and soldier of the Republic in
that climate; now takes the place of 200,000 white
soldiers; and will be, as the conquest of the country
proceeds, its garrison, till Peace without Slavery
returns. Slaveholders in London have filled English
ears with their wishes and perhaps beliefs; and our
people, generals and politicians, have carried the
like, at first, to the war, until corrected by irresistible
experience. . . . The dismal Malthus, the dismal De Bow, have had their night. Our Census
of 1860, and the war, are poems which will, in the
next age, inspire a genius like your own.

"I hate to write you a newspaper, but, in these
times, 'tis wonderful what sublime lessons I have
once and again read on the bulletin boards in the

streets. Everybody has been wrong in his guess, except good women, who never despair of the ideal right."

REMINISCENCES OF THE REV. EZRA RIPLEY, D.D.

[The subject of this letter was Pastor in the Church at Concord, Massachusetts, from 1778 until his death in 1841, in his 91st year. The letter was addressed to the Rev. Dr. Sprague, of Albany.]

" *Concord, Oct. 25, 1848.*

" My dear sir,—It will be easy, as it is grateful, to me to answer your inquiries in regard to Dr. Ripley, as I still have by me some sketches which I attempted of his character very soon after his decease. Indeed, he is still freshly remembered in all this neighbourhood. He was a man so kind and sympathetic, his character was so transparent, and his merits so intelligible to all observers, that he was very justly appreciated in this community: He was a natural gentleman ; no dandy, but courtly, hospitable, manly, and public-spirited ; his nature social, his house open to all men. I remember the remark made by an old farmer, who used to travel thither from Maine, that 'no horse from the eastern country would go by the doctor's gate.' Travellers from the west, and north, and south could bear like testimony. His brow was serene and open to his visitor, for he loved men, and he had no studies, no occupations which company could interrupt. His friends were his study, and to see them loosened his talents and his tongue. In his house dwelt order, and prudence, and plenty; there was no waste and no stint; he was open-handed, and just and generous. Ingratitude and meanness in his beneficiaries did not wear out his compassion; he bore the insult, and the next day his basket for the beggar, his horse and chaise for the cripple, were at their door. Though he knew the value of a dollar as well as another man, yet he loved to buy dearer and sell cheaper than others. He subscribed to all charities, and it is no reflection on others to say that he was the most public-spirited man in the town. The late Dr. Gardner, in a funeral sermon on a parishioner whose virtues did not come readily to mind, honestly said, 'He was good at fires.' Dr. Ripley had many virtues, and yet all will remember that even in his old age, if the fire bell was rung, he was instantly on horse-back, with his bucket and bag.

" He was never distinguished in the pulpit as a writer of sermons, but in his house his speech was form and pertinence itself. You felt, in his presence, that he belonged by nature to the clerical class.

He had a foresight, when he opened his mouth, of all that he would say, and he marched straight to the conclusion. In private discourse or in debate, in the vestry or lyceum, the structure of his sentences was admirable—so neat, so natural, so terse, his words fell like stones, and often, though quite unconscious of it, his speech was a satire on the loose, voluminous, patch-work periods of other speakers. He sat down when he had done. A man of anecdote, his talk in the parlour was chiefly narrative. I remember the remark of a gentleman, who listened with much delight to his conversation, at the time when the doctor was preparing to go to Baltimore and Washington, that 'a man who could tell a story so well was company for kings and John Quincey Adams.' With a very limited acquaintance with books, his knowledge was an external experience, an Indian wisdom, the observation of such facts as country life for nearly a century could supply. He watched with interest the garden, the field, the orchard, the house, and the barn, horse, cow, sheep, and dog, and all the common objects that engage the thought of the farmer. He kept his eye on the horizon, and knew the weather like a sea captain. The usual experience of men—birth, marriage, sickness, death, burial, the common temptations, the common ambitions, he studied them all and sympathised so well in these that he was excellent company and counsel to all, even the most humble and ignorant. With extraordinary states of mind, with states of enthusiasm or enlarged speculation he had no sympathy and pretended to none. He was very sincere, and kept to his point, and his mark was never remote. His conversation was strictly personal, and apt to the person and the occasion. An eminent skill he had in saying difficult and unspeakable things ; in delivering to a man or woman that which all other friends had abstained from saying ; in uncovering the bandage from a sore place, or applying the surgeon's knife with a truly surgical spirit. Was a man a sot, or a spendthrift, or too long time a bachelor, or suspected of some hidden crime, or had he quarrelled with his wife, or collared his father, or was there any cloud or suspicious circumstances in his behaviour, the good pastor knew his way straight to that point, believing himself entitled to a full explanation ; and whatever relief to the conscience of both parties plain speech could effect, was sure to be procured. In all such passages he justified himself to the conscience and commonly to the love of the persons concerned. Many instances in which he played a right manly part, and acquitted himself as a brave and wise man, will be long remembered. He was the more competent to these searching discourses from his knowledge of family history. He knew everybody's grandfather, and seemed to talk with each person rather as the representative of his house and name than as an individual. In him has perished more local and personal anecdote of this village and vicinity than is possessed by any survivor. This intimate knowledge of families, and this skill of speech, and still more his sympathy, made him incomparable in his parochial visits, and in his exhortations and prayers with sick and suffering persons. He gave himself up to his feeling, and said on the instant the best things in the world. Many and many a felicity he had in his prayer, now forever lost, which defied all the rules of all the rhetoricians. He did not know when he was good in prayer or sermon, for he had no literature and no art ; but he believed, and therefore he spoke.

" He was eminently loyal in his nature, and not fond of adventures or innovation. By education, and still more by temperament, he was engaged to the old forms of the New England Church. Not speculative, but affectionate ; devout, but with an extreme love of order, he adopted heartily, though in its mildest forms, the creed and catechism of the fathers, and appeared a modern Israelite in his

attachment to the Hebrew history and faith.   Thus he seemed, in his constitutional leaning to their religion, one of the rear-guard of the great camp and army of the Puritans ; and now, when all the old platforms and customs of the Church were losing their hold in the affections of men, it was fit that he should depart, fit that, in the fall of laws, a loyal man should die.—Yours with great respect,
                    "R. W. EMERSON."

LETTERS TO A. IRELAND.

"*Liverpool, 30th August, 1833*" (before sailing for America).—Extracts from this letter, describing his first interviews with Carlyle and Wordsworth, will be found at pp. 148-151 of "Recollections."

"*Concord, 28th Dec., 1846.*—I was very glad to be reminded by your concise note, written on shipboard and conveyed to me by Mr. Garrison, of our brief intercourse thirteen years ago, and which it seems has not yet quite ended.   Your affectionate expressions towards me and my friends are very grateful to me ; and, indeed, what better thing do men or angels know of than an enduring kindness ?   In regard to your inquiry whether I shall visit England now or soon, the suggestion is new and unlooked for, yet opens to me at once so many flattering possibilities that I shall cheerfully entertain it, and, perhaps, we may both see it ripen one day to a fact. Certainly it would be much more practicable and pleasant to me to answer an invitation, than to come into your cities and challenge an audience. You have been slower to visit Mr. Wordsworth than I was, but, according to all testimonies, he retains his vigour and his social accomplishments. He could not now remember me in my short and unconnected visit, or I might easily send him assurances, from me and many others also unknown to him, of a regard that could not fail to gratify him.—With the best wishes of these days, &c."

The next letter from him (*Concord, 28th February, 1847,*) will be found at page 154 of "Recollections."

"*Concord, 1st April, 1847.*—My townsman, E. Rockwood Hoar, Esq., is ordered by his physicians to quit his professional duties for a time, and to travel for his health. Mr. Hoar is an eminent practitioner at the Massachusetts Bar, and was lately a member of our State Senate. As he proposes to visit Manchester in his route, I use the opportunity to beg you to introduce him to

the Athenæum, and to give him any local information that you may think may be useful to him.—
Yours with great regard."

" *Concord, 31st July, 1847.*—I owe you hearty
thanks for your effective attention to my affair,
which was attractive enough to me in the first
proposition, and certainly assumes in your hands
a feasible shape.   I have a good deal of domestic
immoveableness—being fastened down by wife
and children, by books and studies, by pear
trees and apple trees—but after much hesitation
can find no sufficient resistance to this animating
invitation, and I decide to go to England in the
autumn.   I think to leave home about the 1st
October, perhaps in the steamer, but more probably
in the sailing packet which leaves Boston for Liverpool on the 5th of each month; and, at any rate,
shall expect to be in England before the 1st
November.   From the 1st November, I will take
your advice as to the best order of fulfilling those
engagements you offer me at Manchester, Sheffield, and Leeds.   In regard to the subjects of
my lectures, I hope to send you by the next
steamer some programme or sketch of programme
that may serve a general purpose.   I could more
easily furnish myself for so 'numerous' a course

as seems to offer itself if there were any means
of preventing your newspaper reporters from publishing such ample transcripts as I notice (in the
'Examiner' you were so good as to send me) of
Mr. Marston's lectures. But I will see what I have
to say. Meantime, I beg you not to give yourself
any further pains in this matter, which I fear has
already cost you much. It will give me pleasure
to speak to bodies of your English people, but I
am sure it will give me much more to meet with
yourself and other honoured individuals in private;
and I see well that, if there were no lecturing, I
should not fail to find a solid benefit in the visit.—
With great regard."

"*Concord, 30th Sept., 1847.*—I have decided,
after a little hesitation and advising with better
sailors than myself, to follow my inclination in
taking passage in a ship, and not in the steamer.
I have engaged a berth in the 'Washington
Irving,' which leaves Boston for Liverpool next
Tuesday, 5th October. The owners are confident
that, with ordinary fortune, we shall arrive in Liverpool in twenty days. But I shall not complain if
the voyage should be a little longer. . . . I
shall probably think it best to go directly to Manchester to meet yourself, and to settle with you

the plan of my little campaign.   I suppose that I
shall be ready to read lectures at once as soon as
the proper notices can be given ; or, if more time
is required by the institutes, I can go to London,
and make a short visit before I begin.   I know
that I ought to have sent you some synopsis long
ago, but it has never been quite certain to me what
I could promise, as I have been endeavouring to
complete some lectures not even yet quite finished.
I think I will now reserve my table of contents
until I see you.—Yours, with great regard."

"*Edinburgh, 17th February, 1848.*—Some friends
here wish me to read my lecture on Plato to the
Phil. Society, on Saturday night, at half-past eight
o'clock.   It lies in one of my bureau drawers at
Mrs. Massey's.   Now will you proceed with beneficent action at once to Fenny-street, demand a
candle, and open the various newspaper envelopes
in my drawers until you eliminate and extort
' Plato,' and send it by post immediately to me,
care of Dr. Brown, 1, Cuthbert's Glebe, Edinbro' ?
The good Misses Massey will assist your search,
and yourself will reward your pains.   I have seen
your father and mother, and Mr. Chambers, and
others your friends, and all your despatches and
benefits have safely arrived.—Ever yours."

"*Ambleside, 29th Feby., 1848.*—Here am I for
one day more at Miss Martineau's house. I had
fully intended to set out for Manchester this morning; but let myself be over-persuaded by some
hospitable friends yesterday, to stay to-day and
see the mountains. I had the best visit at Edinburgh, where I parted with your kindest mother
last Sunday p.m.; and on Monday, with Dr. Brown
and De Quincey, at the station on my way north-
ward. Yesterday I spent a valuable hour, and
perhaps a half more, with Mr. Wordsworth, who
is in sound health at seventy-seven years, and was
full of talk. He would even have walked on my
way with me towards Miss Martineau's, but it
began to rain, and I would not suffer it.—Ever,
with best wishes."

"*London, 142, Strand, 7th March, 1848.*—I am
well enough domiciliated here, and am awaiting
your visit. . . . I am beginning to see London
shows, but, as everywhere, find the morning too
precious to go abroad in, and am prone to lengthen
the morning till three o'clock. I have seen Carlyle
one good day, and, as you ask it, I will send you
some good token of him, of this day or a better.
But now for another change. . . .—Yours affectionately."

"*142, Strand, London, 9th March, 1848.*—I find him (Carlyle) full of strong discourse. He is in the best humour at the events in France. For the first time in his life he takes in a daily paper—the 'Times'—and yet I think he has not much confidence in the ability of the French to carry such great points as they have to carry. He interests himself a good deal in the Chartists, and in politics generally, though with abundant contempt for what is called *political.* He talks away on a variety of matters, on London, on the Universities, on Church and State, on all notable persons, on the delusion that is called Art, on the Sand novels, &c., &c. I think him a most valuable companion, and speaking the best opinions one is likely to hear in this nation. It is by no means easy to talk with him, but there is little need of that, as he enjoys his pictures and his indignations highly. The guiding genius of the man, and what constitutes his superiority over other men of letters, is his commanding sense of justice and incessant demand for sincerity. And I cannot help thinking that he has more books, or at least one more book to write, of more efficiency than any he has written. I expect your promised visit as soon as the hard work is over.—Yours ever."

"*London, 3rd April, 1848.*—I had hoped to

have seen you here ere this. My London adventures already make too long a story to write. I spend my time not quite unprofitably, but in a way that must soon have an end, or it would make an end of my comfort. Yet I cannot decline these valued opportunities of seeing men and things which are offered me here. Excepting Tennyson, I believe, I have seen all the literary and many of the political notabilities who interested me. On Thursday last, I went to Oxford, and spent two days and more, very agreeably there, and made the acquaintance of many good men. I have not quite yet decided how long to stay, or whither next to go, but soon must. I carried our good friend Neuberg, the other night, to Carlyle, who was in better mood than usual. I have a good chamber for you here, waiting your advent, and am ever yours. I doubt about Paris a little, being very impatient to be at home and at work."

"*142, Strand, 13th April, 1848.*—Some friends are taking steps here to find me an audience in London, if only I were ready—and if I do this thing, I must perhaps be too late for you in M. and L. Never ask such a tardy workman as I when his wares will be finished. Meantime I am very industrious, eat a great many dinners, hear a great many lectures, see many persons, many things, go to clubs, theatres, and soirees, receive good letters, through your hands, from home, and get on a line or two in my literary tasks every day. I have never gone to Bristol, Cheltenham, and Exeter, though reminded of my privilege. The London day is not long enough for its manifold deed, and I leave my letters long unanswered. I received with thanks the good 'Examiners.' The last is gone to Boston. I sent you a new 'Mass. Quarterly Review,' but it could not go by post, I found too late, because I had written your name on it.—With kindest remembrances to your friends, I remain, yours faithfully."

" *London, 142, Strand, 3rd May, 1848.*—I have stayed in London a great while, yet have not quite finished my visit. I am going to Paris, I think, on Saturday, and mean to stay there but a short time, as it is decided, almost against me, that I shall read lectures here three weeks hence. Ah, if I knew what to call those lectures ! they have grown from day to day and have not yet a name. But the indecision whilst I have been writing here, whether to read or not, and which I had once decided NO, has left me quite unable to send you any word to Manchester. . . . It will also be too late at Manchester for any of those private classes which hovered in your friendly imagination. Besides it is late in the year, and it will be high time for me to set my slow sail for the Capes of Massachusetts. In my short and crowded days here I have given you no account of myself, yet I have found London rich and great, quite equal to its old fame. I have seen a large number of interesting persons, and I suppose the best things—the Parliament, Oxford, the British Museum, Kew Gardens, the Scientific Societies, the Clubhouses, the Theatres, and so forth. I attend Mr. Owen's lectures at the Royal College of Surgeons ; Faraday, at the Royal Institution ; Lyell, Sedgwick, Buckland, Forbes, I hear at the Geologic Society ; and two nights ago I dined with the Antiquaries, and discussed Shakspeare with Mr. Collier. Dr. Carpenter has shown me his microscopes, Sir Henry Delabeche his geologic museum, and I have really owed many valuable hours to the scientific bodies. Now the Picture Galleries are open, and I have begun to see pictures and artists. It is very easy to see that London would last an inquisitive man a good while, and find him in new studies, but the miscellany is distracting, and quiet countrymen will soon have enough of dining out and of shilling-shows. Yet I value all my new experience, and doubtless shall not wish it less when

I am safe in my woods again. In Paris I shall remain three weeks to see the revolution, and to air my nouns and verbs. Mr. Bancroft, who has just returned, takes the most favourable views of their politics, and says the workmen have quite got through all scheme [*sic*] of asking Government to find them labour, repudiate the whole plan, &c. By the last steamer I had no letters from home ; if the letters of the due ship come to you, speed them to your ever obliged and grateful."

"*London, Tuesday, 11th July, 1848.*—It now appears certain that I cannot reach Manchester [on his way to Liverpool], do what I can, before 9-4 p.m. on Thursday. So you must give me tea and toast and a bed that night, and despatch me early next morning to Liverpool, where Mrs. Paulet has always been promised the homage of a day. I am very sorry that I am so late and crowded and speedy ; 'tis the inevitable fate of my nation. But I could not go without a call at Chatsworth, which I must report to some friends at home, and I stop at Coventry one night first. I have just got home from Stonehenge, whither I went with Carlyle, and Chapman has made out the plan of my new journey to you the best he could.— Yours ever."

" *Concord, 5th July, 1849.*—You will think I died
and was buried soon after I left Manchester. No,
I escaped the sea and survive until this day, but
with no studies or fortunes worth transmitting news
of so far ; yet not despairing, one of these days, to
send you something. But here is my friend, Rev.
James Freeman Clarke, an excellent and accomplished man, who can tell you of every good thing
in Boston and America, and whom you must furnish with good tidings to me of all your circle.—
Yours affectionately."

" *Concord, 12th May, 1850.*—I received many
weeks ago a note from you for which I found no
answer,—I am sorry for it,—and so sent none. I
am so disconnected from all the common systems
of lucrative work, that when I hear of an appli-
cant I inquire of other people if there is room.
Mr. Greeley (of N.Y.) said, 'None for literary
work; we refuse such applications in great numbers.'
Rev. Dr. Furness, of Philadelphia, said, 'I always
advise the Englishman to come ; I know of so
many instances of success.' My belief is that there
is, for all men of energy, much more room and
opportunity here than with you ; but almost no
more promise here than with you for any infirmity.
In the case of your friend, I should think it not

wise,—from my impressions of his tendencies and
turn of mind,—to make the adventure.   I saw him
but little, and learned something of him from his
friends, the Fishers,—I saw no writing, heard no
public speaking, and have no knowledge of what
public talent he possesses ; but he did not inspire
me with any confidence in his good sense, or in
his reasonable expectations from society.   So I
only praise the more your and Mr. Fisher's generous
fidelity to him.   I was very glad to see your hand
and name, and you must not fail to write me again
when you have the like application to make for
another person. 'Tis likely I may give you a much
better answer.   But mainly I look and shall not
cease to look for your own arrival, though late, yet
sure, it must be, on your tour of observation.   Mr.
Lawrence, I see, tells you once a month, in London,
that 'we are a great nation,' and my dear Carlyle
tells you that we are a very dull one ; but Nature
never disappoints, and our square miles and the
amount of human labour here are incontestable,
and will interest all your taste, intelligence, and
humanity.   Forgive me that I never write.   My
eyes are not good, and I write no letter that is not
imperative.   I remember you at all times with
kindest thankfulness.   .   .   .   I heard with joy
that E—— was well placed, to command his time

and studies. Of Mr. B——, too, his paper brought me good news. And Mr. Kell, of Huddersfield, gave me good tidings of others of your friends.— Yours affectionately."

" *Concord, April 26, 1869.*—Unless I knew your generosity . . . I should hesitate to write a line to you after such unpardonable intervals, lest, if you have not forgotten my handwriting, you should burn it unread. But now I have two commanding motives which break down even my chronic and constitutional reluctance to write a letter. In the first place, a pretty good acquaintance with the brave book you sent me,*—I dare not count how many months ago,—and whose examination even I was long forced to postpone, mainly on account of tasks which have closely succeeded each other ever since October until now, and partly, also, because you had forgotten how much twenty-one or two years have damaged my eyes since I saw you, so that they now refuse to read a type so fine and solid as that of this book, unless in the most favourable circumstances.

---

* Mr. Emerson here refers to a volume printed by me in 1868— a labour of love—a " Bibliographical List of the Writings of William Hazlitt and Leigh Hunt," chronologically arranged, including notes, opinions, &c., with an article on Charles Lamb and his works, Wm. Hazlitt, &c.

Polite friends assure me that it is only because I have darkened my house with a grove of trees, which allow easy reading in my library only in the brightest days. But, at last, I have read much in this pleasant book of justice and love, and can willingly join in the general thanks of scholars to you for this work of loyalty and good taste, so thoroughly and accurately performed, that it will be the *liber veritatis* and *liber studiorum* for all lovers of Lamb and Hazlitt and Hunt, now and hereafter. . . . My second motive for the pen to-day is that my friends, Mr. and Mrs. Fields, who know so many of your English friends, but have never seen yourself, are departing in a couple of days for England and France and Switzerland, and I desire to make it certain that you and they shall meet. You and they have many good qualities in common, and among them the singular eccentricity of an eminent goodwill and helpfulness to me. If it is possible, I hope that Mrs. Ireland and Mrs. Fields may meet, that I may have new information to add to all I drew from the valued photograph you sent me. Miss Mabel Lowell, Mr. J. R. Lowell's only daughter, is of the Fields' party in their tour. I should like well to see you and your Manchester again, you and your household, and to know the history of many of those who

surrounded you in 1847-8. Mr. Bright has been
at last placed as you anticipated and wished, and
the world thinks of Mr. Cobden as you and your
friends did.   With Mr. W. E. Forster and Mr.
Rawlins I have had some communication. . . .
All your political friends have been ours, and I
wish you will keep them so.   But one duty you
have left undone, which is to make your own visit
to these States, and I shall expect you till you
come.   Be assured you shall find a hearty welcome
in this house.—Yours ever affectionately."

"*Concord, 19th January, 1872.*—I wish that my
son-in-law, Col. W. H. Forbes, and my daughter
(Edith), his wife, should not fail to see you if they
reach Manchester in their passage through England
to the continent.   They know well your steadfast
goodwill and good action at one time, and at all
times to me and to my friends, and I have charged
them not to fail at seeing you on their way, or
else certainly on their return through England.
You must show them the specialties of your great
city, and you must make them acquainted with
Mrs. Ireland, whom I have never seen, though
I keep her photograph.   Tell them, I pray you,
all that I should hear from you, and believe me,
ever yours affectionately."

"*Oxford, 1st May, 1873, House of Professor Max Müller.*—It seems that I have been travelling too fast for your letters to catch me. To-day I have received yours of 29th April, and rush to say with thankfulness and regret that my day for reaching Manchester should be the 12th May, and that I will come to you then at Bowdon. Meantime, for Mr. Brown, of Selkirk, I think with gratitude to him that it will be safer for such swift travellers as my daughter and I must be, that it will be best not to trouble him with our swiftness, but to sit down at Kennedy's Hotel, in Edinburgh, and trust to the ordinary resources for our visit to the important points, and I will try to express our thanks to him for his kindest offices. I am sorry to be so tardy with my acknowledgments, and am just now waited for by my hospitable Professor Müller to go to the colleges.—In great haste, but greater love, I remain."

"*Edinburgh, Kennedy's Hotel, 8th May, 1873.*— My best thanks for your affectionate care for me and mine. Ellen tells me that the result of her arithmetic and dates is that we shall arrive at Manchester at 5-20 on Monday from the Lakes, and that I will stay till Wednesday with you, and Ellen will go to Liverpool on Tuesday noon, such are her necessities. Continue, I pray you, your loving-kindness to me and mine. With my greetings to Mrs. Ireland.—Yours ever faithfully."

MR. MONCURE D. CONWAY.

I consider it due to my friend, Mr. Moncure D. Conway, to give here the letter of introduction which he brought to me from Emerson in 1863. Through the study of his writings he had been led to abandon the creed in which he was reared, and to turn against the institution of slavery prevailing in Virginia. His father was a planter and slave-owner in that State, and the change which came over his son led to their alienation, and to his departure from the paternal home. By Emerson's advice he went to Cambridge University, and entered the "Divinity School," connected with Harvard University. His object was to be near his master, and to know more of the man through whom his life had been revolutionised. " Now and then he came at the solicitation of the students to pass an evening in conversation with them or to read an essay. On one occasion, when it was announced that he was to read a lecture at Concord, the Emersonians collected in some force and drove in sleighs by night over the twenty miles to hear him. The lecture had been postponed, but the philosopher took us to his house, and we found in his conversation ample compensation for our disappointment. He treated those present as the guests of his thoughts, with an imperial hospitality, and the questions and answers of the youthful inquirers must have convinced him that if the old circle of Concord had broken up, it was only into divers circles with other centres. Within the next few years his influence in the Divinity School had so increased that he might have been regarded as an ungowned professor; and it will not seem surprising to those who remember those days that he should since have been brought into official relations with the University. A great deal of my time was passed at Concord; Thoreau, Miss Peabody, Ellery Channing, and one or two others of the old fraternity were still there, and the society was very attractive. There were courses of lectures given in the village by eminent gentlemen, and Mr. Emerson's open evenings preserved the literary character of the society. The motley group described by Hawthorne were no longer seen crowding in the streets of Concord, but there were to be frequently met strange faces which, as they passed, the villagers were apt to note with the surmise that they might be famous men from far-off places."

Mr. Conway, after residing for some time in Cincinnati, ultimately settled as a minister in Boston. In 1863 he came to London, where he succeeded to the pastorate of Mr. W. J. Fox's congregation at South Place, Finsbury, a position which he still holds. Mr. Conway has contributed many valuable papers on Emerson and other subjects to " Fraser's Magazine," between 1864 and 1874, and he is a frequent writer in other periodicals. Several books from his pen have made their mark, and are well known and appreciated—" Republican Superstitions ; " " The Earthward Pilgrimage ; " " Sacred Anthology, being Selections from Oriental Scriptures;" an elaborate "History of Demonology," in two vols.; " Legend of the Wandering Jew ; " " Thomas Carlyle : Recollections of Seventeen Years' Intercourse ; " " Address on John Stuart Mill ; " &c., &c. Mr. Conway's abilities and acquirements have gradually secured for him and his admirable wife a very large circle of friends in London, which includes many of the most distinguished men and women of letters, and artists.

LETTER INTRODUCING MR. CONWAY.

" *Concord, 9th April, 1863.*

" Mr. Moncure D. Conway, a valued neighbour of mine, and a man full of public and private virtues, goes to England just now, having, as I understand, both inward and outward provocation to defend the cause of America there. I can assure you, out of much knowledge, that he is very competent to this duty, if it be one. He is a Virginian by birth and breeding; and now for many years a Northerner in residence and in sentiment. He is a man of excellent ability in speaking and writing, and I grudge to spare his usefulness at home even to a contingency so important as the correcting of opinion in England. In making you acquainted with Mr. Conway, I charge him to remind you that the first moment of American peace will be the best time for you to come over and pay us and me a long promised visit."

TRIBUTES TO EMERSON.

The regular monthly meeting of the Massachusetts Historical Society was held at Boston on Thursday, May 11, 1882. Dr. George E. Ellis occupied the chair.

REMARKS OF DR ELLIS.

Many of us who meet in this library to-day are doubtless recalling vividly the memory of the impressive scene here when, fifteen months ago, Mr. Emerson, appearing among us for the last time, read his characteristic paper upon Thomas Carlyle. It was the very hour on which the remains of that remarkable man were committed to his Scotch grave. There was much to give the occasion here a deep and tender interest. We could not but feel that it was the last utterance to which we should listen from our beloved and venerated associate, if not, as it proved to be, the last of his presence

among us.' So we listened greedily and fondly.
The paper had been lying in manuscript more
than thirty years, but it had kept its freshness and
fidelity. The matter of it, its tone and utterance,
were singularly suggestive. Not the least of the
crowding reflections with which we listened was
the puzzling wonder, to some of us, as to the tie of
sympathy and warm personal attachment, of nearly
half a century's continuance, between the serene
and gentle spirit of our poet-philosopher and the
stormy and aggressive spirit of Mr. Carlyle.

There are those immediately to follow me who,
with acute and appreciative minds, in closeness of
intercourse and sympathy with Mr. Emerson, will
interpret to you the form and significance of his
genius, the richness of his fine and rare endowments, and account to you for the admiring and
loving estimate of his power and influence and
world-wide fame in the lofty realms of thought,
with insight and vision and revealings of the cen-
tral mysteries of being. They must share largely
in those rare gifts of his who undertake to be the
channel of them from him to others. For it is
no secret, but a free confession, that the quality,
methods, and fruits of his genius are so peculiar,
unique, obscure, and remote from the appreciation
of a large class of those of logical, argumentative,

and prosaic minds, as to invest them with the ill-understood and the inexplicable. He was signally one of those, rare in our race, in the duality of our human elementary composition, in whom the dust of the ground contributed its least proportion, while the ethereal inspiration from above contributed the greatest.

The words which I would add, prompted as in keeping with this place and occasion, shall be in reminiscence of years long past. Those whose memories are clear and strong, and who forty-five years ago in their professional, literary, or social fellowships were intent upon all that quickened thought and converse in this peculiar centre of Boston and its neighbourhoods, will recall with what can hardly be other than pensive retrospects the charms and fervours, the surprises, and perhaps the shocks, certainly the bewilderment and the apprehension, which signalled the announcement here of what was called Transcendentalism. Though the word was from the first wrongfully applied, there was an aptness in its use, as in keeping with the mistiness and cloudiness of the dispensation to which it was attached. The excitement here was adjusted to the size, the composition, the tone and spirit, and the unassimilated elements of this community. The movement had the quickening zest of mystery. It was long before those who were not a part of it could reach to any intelligible idea of what it might signify, or promise, or portend. There were a score, a hundred, persons craving to have explained to them what it all meant, to each one who seemed ready or able in volunteering to throw light upon it. And this intended light was often but an adumbration. Mr. Emerson gained nothing from his interpreters. Nor does he now. The key which they offered did not fit the wards of the lock. The vagueness of the oracle seemed to be deepened when repeated by any other lips than those which gave it first utterance. In most of the recent references in the newspapers and magazines to the opening of Mr. Emerson's career in high philosophy, emphatic statements are made as to the ridicule and satire and banter evoked by the first utterances of this transcendentalism. It is not impressed upon my memory that any of this triviality was ever spent upon Mr. Emerson himself. The modest, serene, unaggressive attitude, and personal phenomena of bearing and utterance which were so winningly characteristic of his presence and speech, as he dropped the sparkles and nuggets of his fragmentary revelations, were his ample security against all such disrespect. The fun, as I remember, was spent upon the first circle of repeaters, and so-called disciples, a small but lively company of both sexes, who seemed to patent him as their oracle, as an inner fellowship who would be the medium between him and the un-illumined. Nor was it strange that explanations, or demonstrative and argumentative expositions of the Emersonian philosophy proffered by its inter-preters did not open it clearly to inquirers, inasmuch as he himself assured us that it was not to be learned or tested by old-fashioned familiar methods. I know of but one piece from his pen now in print, and dating from the first year of his publicity, in which he appears, not in self-defence under chal-lenge,—for he never did that,—but in attempted and baffled self-exposition. Nor have lines ever been written, by himself or by his interpreters, so apt, so characteristic, so exquisitely phrased and toned, so exhaustively descriptive of the style and spirit of his philosophy as those which I will quote.

The younger Henry Ware, whose colleague he had been during his brief pastorship of a church, disturbed by something in a discourse which Mr. Emerson, after leaving the pulpit, had delivered in Cambridge in 1838, had preached in the College chapel a sermon dealing in part with a position which had startled himself and others in his friend's address, and, in part, with a breeze of excitement

which it had raised in a tinderish community.   The
sermon being printed, Mr. Ware sent a copy of it
to Mr. Emerson, with a letter, which the latter says
" was right manly and noble."   The letter expressed
a little disturbance, puzzle, and anxiety of mind,
and put some questions hinting at desired explanations and arguments.

In reply Mr. Emerson interprets himself thus:—

[It is unnecessary to reprint the letter here
referred to, as the reader will find it already given
at pp. 27-8 of the Memoir.]

No one in comment, essay, or criticism upon
Mr. Emerson has improved upon his own revealing
of his philosophy of intuition, insight, eye, and
thought, as distinguished from that of logic and
argument.   It needed some considerable lapse of
time, with much wondering, questioning, and de-
bating in this community, to clear the understanding, that the new and hopeful message brought to
us was something like this,—that those who were
overfed, or starved, or wearied with didactic, prosaic
lessons of truth for life and conduct, through formal teaching, by reasoning, arguings and provings,
might turn to their own inner furnishings, to their
thinkings as processes, not results, and to the free
revealings and inspirings from without as interpreted
from within.

But whatever was the baffling secret of Mr. Emerson's philosophy, there was no mystery save that to the charm and power of which we all love to yield ourselves, in the poise and repose of his placid spirit, in the grace and felicity of his utterance, in the crowding of sense and suggestiveness into his short, terse sentences, in his high reachings for all truth as its disciple, and in the persuasiveness with which he communicated to others what was disclosed to him. He never answered to a challenge by apology or controversy.

At the conclusion of his address, Dr. Ellis read the following letter from Judge Hoar :—

Letter of The Hon. E. R. Hoar.

Concord, May 8, 1882.

My dear Dr. Ellis,—I find that it will be out of my power to attend the meeting of the Historical Society on Thursday next, and I am sorry to lose the opportunity of hearing the tributes which its members will pay to the memory of Mr. Emerson, than whose name none more worthy of honour is found on its roll. His place in literature, as poet, philosopher, seer, and thinker, will find much more adequate statement than any which I could offer. But there are two things which the Proceedings of our Society may appropriately record concerning him, one of them likely to be lost sight of in the lustre of his later and more famous achievements, and the other of a quality so evanescent as to be preserved only by contemporary evidence and tradition.

The first relates to his address in September, 1835, at the celebration of the two hundredth anniversary of the settlement of Concord ; which seems to me to contain the most complete and exquisite picture of the origin, history, and peculiar characteristics of a New England town that has ever been produced.

The second is his *power as an orator*, rare and peculiar, and in its way unequalled among our cotemporaries.   Many of us can recall instances of it, and there are several prominent in my recollection ; but perhaps the most striking was his address at the Burns centennial, in Boston, on the 25th of January, 1859.*

The company that he addressed was a queer mixture.   First, there were the Burns club,—grave, critical, and long-headed Scotchmen, jealous of the fame of their countryman, and doubtful of the capacity to appreciate him in men of other blood. There were the scholars and poets of Boston and its

* This speech is given near the end of the volume.

neighbourhood, and professors and undergraduates from Harvard College. Then there were state and city officials, aldermen and common councilmen, brokers and bank directors, ministers and deacons, doctors, lawyers, and "carnal self-seekers" of every grade.

I have had the good fortune to hear many of the chief orators of our time, among them Henry Clay, John Quincy Adams, Ogden Hoffman, S. S. Prentiss, William H. Seward, Charles Sumner, Wendell Phillips, George William Curtis, some of the great preachers, and Webster, Everett, Choate, and Winthrop at their best. But I never witnessed such an effort of speech upon men as Mr. Emerson apparently then attained. It reached at once to his own definition of eloquence,—" a taking sovereign possession of the audience." He had uttered but a few sentences before he seemed to have welded together the whole mass of discordant material and lifted them to the same height of sympathy and passion. He excited them to smiles, to tears, to the wildest enthusiasm. His tribute to Burns is beautiful to read, perhaps the best which the occasion produced on either side of the ocean. But the clear articulation, the ringing emphasis, the musical modulation of tone and voice, the loftiness of bearing, and the radiance of his face, all made a part of the consummate charm. When he closed, the company could hardly tolerate any other speaker, though good ones were to follow.

I am confident that every one who was present on that evening would agree with me as to the splendour of that eloquence.

Very truly yours,

E. R. HOAR.

Rev. GEORGE D. ELLIS, D.D.,
    Vice-President of the Massachusetts Historical Society.

ADDRESS OF DR. OLIVER WENDELL HOLMES.

Dr. Oliver Wendell Holmes then arose and addressed the Society as follows :—

It is a privilege which any of us may claim, as we pass each of these last and newly raised mounds, to throw our pebble upon the cairn. For our own sakes we must be indulged in the gratification of paying our slender tribute. So soon, alas, after bidding farewell to our cherished poet to lose the earthly presence of the loftiest, the divinest of our thinkers ! The language of eulogy seemed to have exhausted itself in celebrating him who was the darling of two English worlds, the singer of Acadian and Pilgrim and Indian story, of human affections and aspirations, of sweet, wholesome life from its lullaby to its requiem. And now we hardly know what measure to observe in our praises of him who was singularly averse to over-statement, who never listened approvingly to flattery when living, and whose memory asks only the white roses of truth for its funeral garlands.

The work of his life is before us all, and will have full justice done it by those who are worthy of the task and equal to its demands. But, as out of a score of photographs each gives us something of a friend's familiar face, though all taken together do not give us the whole of it, so each glimpse of reminiscence, each hint of momentary impression, may help to make a portrait which shall remind us of the original, though it is, at best, but an imperfect resemblance.

When a life so exceptional as that which has just left our earthly companionship appears in any group of our fellow-creatures, we naturally ask how such a well-recognised superiority came into being. We look for the reason of such an existence among its antecedents, some of which we can reach, as, for instance, the characteristics of the race, the tribe, the family. The forces of innumerable generations are represented in the individual, more especially those of the last century or two. Involved with these, inextricable, insoluble, is the mystery of mysteries, the mechanism of personality. No such personality as this which was lately present with us is the outcome of cheap paternity and shallow motherhood.

I may seem to utter an Hibernian absurdity ; I may recall a lively couplet which has often brought a smile at the expense of our good city ; I may—I hope I shall not—offend the guardians of ancient formulæ, vigilant still as watch-dogs over the bones of their fleshless symbols, but I must be permitted to say that I believe the second birth may precede that which we consider as the first. The divine renovation which changes the half-human animal, the cave-dweller, the cannibal, into the servant of God, the friend, the benefactor, the lawgiver of his kind, may, I believe, be wrought in the race before it is incarnated in the individual. It may take many generations of chosen births to work the transformation, but what the old chemists called *cohobation* is not without its meaning for vital chemistry ; life must pass through an alembic of gold or of silver many times before its current can possibly run quite clear.

A New Englander has a right to feel happy, if not proud, if he can quarter his coat-of-arms with the bands of an ancestry of clergymen. Eight generations of ministers preceded the advent of this prophet of our time. There is no better flint to

strike fire from than the old nodule of Puritanism.
Strike it against the steel of self-asserting civil freedom, and we get a flash and a flame such as showed
our three-hilled town to the lovers of liberty all
over the world. An ancestry of ministers, softened
out of their old-world dogmas by the same influences
which set free the colonies, is the true Brahminism
of New England.

Children of the same parentage, as we well know,
do not alike manifest the best qualities belonging
to the race. But those of the two brothers of
Ralph Waldo Emerson whom I can remember
were of exceptional and superior natural endowments. Edward, next to him in order of birth, was
of the highest promise, only one evidence of which
was his standing at the head of his college class at
graduation. I recall a tender and most impressive
tribute of Mr. Everett's to his memory, at one of
our annual Phi Beta Kappa meetings. He spoke
of the blow which had jarred the strings of his fine
intellect and made them return a sound

Like sweet bells jangled out of tune and harsh,

in the saddened tones of that rich sonorous voice
still thrilling in the ears of many whose hearing is
dulled for all the music, all the eloquence of to-day.

Of Charles Chauncy, the youngest brother, I
knew something in my college days. A beautiful,

high-souled, pure, exquisitely delicate nature in a
slight but finely wrought mortal frame, he was for
me the very ideal of an embodied celestial intelligence. I may venture to mention a trivial circum-
stance, because it points to the character of his
favourite reading, which was likely to be guided by
the same tastes as his brothers, and may have been
specially directed by him. Coming into my room
one day, he took up a copy of Hazlitt's British
Poets. He opened it to the poem of Andrew
Marvell's, entitled "The Nymph Complaining for
the Death of her Fawn," which he read to me with
delight irradiating his expressive features. The
lines remained with me, or many of them, from
that hour,—

> Had it lived long, it would have been
> Lilies without, roses within.

I felt as many have felt after being with his brother,
Ralph Waldo, that I had entertained an angel
visitant. The Fawn of Marvell's imagination survives in my memory as the fitting image to recall
this beautiful youth; a soul glowing like the rose
of morning with enthusiasm, a character white as
the lilies in its purity.

Such was the family nature lived out to its full
development in Ralph Waldo Emerson. Add to
this the special differentiating quality, indefinable

as the tone of a voice, which we should know not
the less, from that of every other of articulately
speaking mortals, and we have the Emerson of our
recollections.

A person who by force of natural gifts is entitled to be called a personage is always a surprise
in the order of appearances, sometimes, as in the
case of Shakespeare, of Goethe, a marvel, if not a
miracle. The new phenomenon has to be studied
like the young growth that sprang up between the
stones in the story of Picciola. Is it a common
weed, or a plant with virtues and beauties of its
own ? Is it a cryptogam that can never flower, or
shall we wait and see it blossom by and by ? Is it
an endogen or an exogen,—did the seed it springs
from drop from a neighbouring bough, or was it
wafted hither on the wings of the wind from some
far-off shore ?

Time taught us what to make of this human
growth. It was not an annual or a biennial, but a
perennial ; not an herbaceous plant, but a towering
tree ; not an oak or an elm like those around it,
but rather a lofty and spreading palm, which ac-
climated itself out of its latitude, as the little group
of Southern magnolias has done in the woods of
our northern county of Essex. For Emerson's was
an Asiatic mind, drawing its sustenance partly from

the hard soil of our New England, partly, too, from
the air that has known Himalaya and the Ganges.
So impressed with this character of his mind was
Mr. Burlingame, as I saw him, after his return from
his mission, that he said to me, in a freshet of
hyperbole, which was the overflow of a channel
with a thread of truth running in it, "There are
twenty thousand Ralph Waldo Emersons in China."

What could we do with this unexpected, un-
provided for, unclassified, half unwelcome new-
comer, who had been for a while potted, as it were,
in our Unitarian cold greenhouse, but had taken
to growing so fast that he was lifting off its glass
roof and letting in the hailstorms? Here was a
protest that outflanked the extreme left of liberalism,
yet so calm and serene that its radicalism had the
accents of the gospel of peace. Here was an icono-
clast without a hammer, who took down our idols
from their pedestals so tenderly that it seemed like
an act of worship.

The scribes and pharisees made light of his
oracular sayings. The lawyers could not find the
witnesses to subpœna and the documents to refer
to when his case came before them, and turned him
over to their wives and daughters. The ministers
denounced his heresies, and handled his writings
as if they were packages of dynamite, and the

grandmothers were as much afraid of his new teachings as old Mrs. Piozzi was of geology. We had had revolutionary orators, reformers, martyrs ; it was but a few years since Abner Kneeland had been sent to jail for expressing an opinion about the great First Cause ; but we had had nothing like this man, with his seraphic voice and countenance, his choice vocabulary, his refined utterance, his gentle courage, which, with a different manner, might have been called audacity, his temperate statement of opinions which threatened to shake the existing order of thought like an earthquake.

His peculiarities of style and of thinking became fertile parents of mannerisms, which were fair game for ridicule as they appeared in his imitators. For one who talks like Emerson or like Carlyle soon finds himself surrounded by a crowd of walking phonographs, who mechanically reproduce his mental and vocal accents. Emerson was before long talking in the midst of a babbling Simonetta of echoes, and not unnaturally was now and then himself a mark for the small shot of criticism. He had soon reached that height in the " cold thin atmosphere " of thought where

> Vainly the fowler's eye
> Might mark his distant flight to do him wrong.

I shall add a few words, of necessity almost

epigrammatic, upon his work and character. He
dealt with life, and life with him was not merely
this particular air-breathing phase of being, but the
spiritual existence which included it like a parenthesis between the two infinities. He wanted his
daily draughts of oxygen like his neighbours, and
was as thoroughly human as the plain people he
mentions who had successively owned or thought
they owned the house-lot on which he planted his
hearthstone. But he was at home no less in the
interstellar spaces outside of all the atmospheres.
The semi-materialistic idealism of Milton was a
gross and clumsy medium compared to the im-
ponderable ether of " The Oversoul " and the
unimaginable vacuum of " Brahma." He followed
in the shining and daring track of the *Graius homo*
of Lucretius :

> Vivida vis animi pervicit, et extra
> Processit longe flammantia mœnia mundi.

It always seemed to me as if he looked at this earth
very much as a visitor from another planet would
look upon it. He was interested, and to some
extent curious about it, but it was not the first
spheroid he had been acquainted with, by any
means. I have amused myself with comparing
his descriptions of natural objects with those of the
Angel Raphael in the seventh book of Paradise Lost.

Emerson talks of his titmouse as Raphael talks of his emmet. Angels and poets never deal with nature after the manner of those whom we call naturalists.

To judge of him as a thinker, Emerson should have been heard as a lecturer, for his manner was an illustration of his way of thinking. He would lose his place just as his mind would drop its thought and pick up another, twentieth cousin or no relation at all to it. This went so far at times that one could hardly tell whether he was putting together a mosaic of coloured fragments, or only turning a kaleidoscope where the pieces tumbled about as they best might. It was as if he had been looking in at a cosmic peep-show, and turning from it at brief intervals to tell us what he saw. But what fragments these coloured sentences were, and what pictures they often placed before us, as if we too saw them! Never has this city known such audiences as he gathered ; never was such an Olympian entertainment as that which he gave them.

It is very hard to speak of Mr. Emerson's poetry ; not to do it injustice, still more to do it justice. It seems to me like the robe of a monarch patched by a New England housewife. The royal tint and stuff are unmistakable, but here and there the gray worsted from the darning-needle crosses and ekes out the Tyrian purple.   Few poets who have written so little in verse have dropped so many of those "jewels five words long" which fall from their setting only to be more choicely treasured.   *E pluribus unum* is hardly more familiar to our ears than "He builded better than he knew," and Keats's "thing of beauty" is little better known than Emerson's "beauty is its own excuse for being." One may not like to read Emerson's poetry because it is sometimes careless, almost as if carefully so, though never undignified even when slipshod ; spotted with quaint archaisms and strange expressions that sound like the affectation of negligence, or with plain, homely phrases, such as the self-made scholar is always afraid of.   But if one likes Emerson's poetry he will be sure to love it ; if he loves it, its phrases will cling to him as hardly any others do.   It may not be for the multitude, but it finds its place like pollen-dust and penetrates to the consciousness it is to fertilize and bring to flower and fruit.

I have known something of Emerson as a talker, not nearly so much as many others who can speak and write of him.   It is unsafe to tell how a great thinker talks, for perhaps, like a city dealer with a village customer, he has not shown his best goods to the innocent reporter of his sayings.   However that may be in this case, let me contrast in a single glance the momentary effect in conversation of the two neighbours, Hawthorne and Emerson. Speech seemed like a kind of travail to Hawthorne. One must harpoon him like a cetacean with questions to make him talk at all. Then the words came from him at last, with bashful manifestations, like those of a young girl, almost,—words that gasped themselves forth, seeming to leave a great deal more behind them than they told, and died out, discontented with themselves, like the monologue of thunder in the sky, which always goes off mumbling and grumbling as if it had not said half it wanted to, and meant to, and ought to say.

Emerson was sparing of words, but used them with great precision and nicety. If he had been followed about by a short-hand writing Boswell, every sentence he ever uttered might have been preserved. To hear him talk was like watching one crossing a brook on stepping-stones. His noun had to wait for its verb or its adjective until he was ready; then his speech would come down upon the word he wanted, and not Worcester and Webster could better it from all the wealth of their huge vocabularies.

These are only slender rays of side-light on a personality which is interesting in every aspect and will be fully illustrated by those who knew him best. One glimpse of him as a listener may be worth recalling. He was always courteous and bland to a remarkable degree ; his smile was the well-remembered line of Terence written out in living features. But when anything said specially interested him he would lean toward the speaker with a look never to be forgotten, his head stretched forward, his shoulders raised like the wings of an eagle, and his eye watching the flight of the thought which had attracted his attention as if it were his prey to be seized in mid-air and carried up to his eyry.

To sum up briefly what would, as it seems to me, be the text to be unfolded in his biography, he was a man of excellent common-sense, with a genius so uncommon that he seemed like an exotic transplanted from some angelic nursery. His character was so blameless, so beautiful, that it was rather a standard to judge others by than to find a place for on the scale of comparison. Looking at life with the profoundest sense of its infinite significance, he was yet a cheerful optimist, almost too hopeful, peeping into every cradle to see if it did not hold a babe with the halo of a new Messiah about it. He enriched the treasure-house of literature, but, what was far more, he enlarged the boundaries of thought for the few that followed him and the many who never knew, and do not know to-day, what hand it was which took down their prison walls. He was a preacher who taught that the religion of humanity included both those of Palestine, nor those alone, and taught it with such consecrated lips that the narrowest bigot was ashamed to pray for him, as from a footstool nearer to the throne. "Hitch your wagon to a star;" this was his version of the divine lesson taught by that holy George Herbert whose words he loved. Give him whatever place belongs to him in our literature, in the literature of our language, of the world, but remember this : the end and aim of his being was to make truth lovely and manhood valorous, and to bring our daily life nearer and nearer to the eternal, immortal, invisible.

After the address of Dr. Holmes, the Rev. James Freeman Clarke, D.D., spoke of his long acquaintance with Mr. Emerson, and read several interesting extracts from letters which he had received from him at an early period of his career. At the close of his remarks, Dr. Clarke presented the following resolution, which was adopted by a rising vote.

Resolved,—That this Society unites in the widespread expression of esteem, gratitude, and affectionate reverence paid to the memory of our late associate, Ralph Waldo Emerson, and recognises the great influence exercised by his character and writings to elevate, purify, and quicken the thought of our time.

WILLIAM HENRY CHANNING ON EMERSON.

In a letter to the editor of the "Modern Review" for October, 1882, Mr. Channing regrets that ill-health has prevented him from bearing his promised testimony to Emerson in the "Review." He had written a voluminous heap of MSS. amidst recurring attacks of illness, but finds that neither strength nor time permit him to re-write or condense it fitly. "This disappointment causes regret, because my hope was to bring into brighter light the rare blending of the Spiritual with the Intellectual in Emerson's life and aims. For, though by common consent scholars of the Anglo-American race acknowledge him as the grandest 'Representative Man' of *Genius* of the Western Republic, by his embodiment in thought of her purest Ideal— apparently, they fail to see that, by his pre-eminent Virtue in character and life, he stood as a Real Type of that *Personal Greatness*, towards which he welcomed his compeers everywhere to aspire.

" How unique, in quickening influence and inspiring energy, his Genius and Personal Greatness
were, appears in this. As one reads with impartial
judgment the tributes of grateful love, which already
have been offered up in his honour—[Mr. Channing
then briefly refers to the various notices, addresses,
discourses, sermons, &c., relating to Emerson]—he
is cheered to find that, among these mirrored forms
of Emerson, there is scarcely one which has not
caught characteristic splendour from his glowing
beauty, translucent truthfulness, humane magnanimity, and symmetric manhood.

" Difficult would it be to add words of worth to
the manifold testimonials of our friend's transcending excellence, as exemplar, guide, inciter,
and illuminator. Indeed, it seems presumptuous to
describe Emerson at all! For has he not, throughout his works, imaged himself unconsciously, in
each alternate tendency, mood, attainment, aspiration, with such luminous fidelity, that it seems
irreverent to copy, with a blunt pencil, portraits
exquisitely perfected in characters of light? One
feels prompted, rather, to say to new students of
the Sage of Concord's writings : Would you know
aright this Prophet of the Soul, as he lived, read his
Orations, Addresses, Essays, Poems, and especially
the earlier ones, such as 'Nature,' 'The American

Scholar,', 'Literary Ethics,' 'The Method of
Nature,' &c., reading what is inscribed with sympathetic ink between the lines, and yielding to the
impressions made on heart and conscience, yet more
than on critical intellect, by these *Confessions*—and
you shall behold this beautiful Person as he was in
character, as in conduct he irradiated the scenes he
moved among, and as he was known inmostly to God
and guardian angels.   There he stands revealed!
For if man ever did, he wrote in hearts' blood,
according to Sidney's maxim, 'Look in your heart
and write.'   The very passage of Autobiography,
wherein this maxim is quoted — the Essay on
'Spiritual Laws '—is a transcript from his Diary :
'The way to speak and write what shall not go
out of fashion is to speak and write sincerely. The
argument which has not power to reach my own
practice, I may well doubt, will fail to reach yours.
He that writes to himself writes to an eternal
public.'

"A second difficulty, in attempting to sketch
Emerson, is that no two observers saw the same
man.   Unchangingly faithful to his own spirit, as
he was, he yet presented ever new phases to the
persons he met according to their quality.   And
each onlooker saw that side only which his own
vision was fitted to discern. So must it be with

his works. One is inclined, therefore, to whisper
in the ear of his critics : Beware how you judge
this whole-souled brother, for you go to judgment
yourself in the estimate you are enlightened and
just, humble and loving enough to form of one
who so earnestly listened to the 'Over Soul.'
This man was, in the best sense, a high-bred
Christian Gentleman ; but no Stoic was ever more
nobly proud, no Puritan more sternly upright.
He scorned pretension, had shrewd insight into
character, and, as he says of Nature, 'knew how,
without swell, brag, strain, or shock, to keep firm
common sense, " *Semper sibi similis.*" '

"Then a final hindrance to declaring what one's
heart prompts him to say of this singularly impersonal person is, that the friends who revered him
most highly, most scrupulously withheld the least
allusion which might be vitiated by praise, for the
reason that they knew how devoutly he referred all
goodness and wisdom to the ever-present Inspirer,
with whom he sought to dwell in calm communion,
unruffled by a breath of self-love. Well does his
confidential comrade, Alcott, write of the ' one sub-
traction from the pleasure of his books, his pains
to be impersonal or discrete, as if he feared any the
least intrusion of himself were an offence offered to
self-respect, the courtesy due to intercourse and

authorship.' And who can forget the passage in his essay on 'Friendship' where he writes : 'Let me be alone to the end of the world rather than that my friend should overstep, by a word or a look, his real sympathy. I am equally baulked by antagonism and by compliance. Let him not cease to be himself an instant. I hate, where I looked for a manly furtherance, or a manly resistance, to find a mush of concession. . . . Friendship demands religious treatment. Reverence is a great part of it. . . . Should not the society of my friend be to me poetic, pure, universal, as Nature itself?' "

" My conviction is firm, that hereafter Emerson will be recognised universally as a far *grander style of Person* than has been apprehended, as yet, except by the few drawn within the sphere of his close fellowship. To them he was peerless. Merely by living he opened new possibilities of personal being, of human society, of heavenly communion, of immortality begun on earth. But why present a blurred copy of his Ideal-Real when we have the original pictured with sunbeams, in this sublime outburst : 'I stand here to say :—Let us worship the mighty and transcendent Soul. The lovers of Goodness have been one class, the students of Wisdom another, as if either could exist in purity without the other. Truth is always holy, holiness always wise. I will that we keep terms with sin and a sinful literature and society no longer, but live a life of discovery and performance. Accept the intellect and it will accept us. Be the lowly ministers of that pure omniscience and deny it not before men. It will burn up all profane literature, all base, current opinions, all false powers of the world, as in a moment of time. I draw from Nature the lesson of Intimate Divinity. The sanity of man needs the poise of this immanent force. His nobility needs the assurance of this inexhaustible reserved power. . . . The doctrine of this Supreme presence is a cry of exultation and joy. . . . I praise with wonder this great Reality, which drowns all things in its deluge of Light. . . . The natural history of the Soul we cannot describe, but we know that *it* is Divine. . . . From this faith I draw courage and hope. Let those fear and fawn who will. The Soul is in her native realm, and it is wider than space, older than time, wide as hope, rich as love. Pusillanimity and fear she refuses with beautiful scorn ; they are not for her, who putteth on her coronation robes, and goes out through universal love to universal power.' "

MISCELLANEOUS RECORDS.

EMERSON'S HOUSE AND SURROUNDINGS.

"Emerson," says Mr. Cooke, "has been most fortunate in all his domestic relations; while the surroundings of his life have been such as he could desire, and they have been helpful to the life he has sought to live. His house has been well adapted to a scholar's wants, both as to its location and construction. About the house is a little farm; and he owns a wood-lot on the west shore of Walden Pond, where Thoreau's hut once stood." His home has been described in these words :—

A roomy barn stands near the house, and behind lies a little farm of nearly a dozen acres. The whole external appearance of the place suggests old-fashioned comfort and hospitality. Within the house the flavour of antiquity is still more noticeable. Old pictures look down from the walls; quaint blue and white china holds the simple dinner; old furniture brings to mind the generations of the past. Just at the right, as you enter, is Mr. Emerson's library, a large, square room, plainly furnished, but made pleasant by pictures and sunshine. The homely shelves which line the walls are well filled with books. There is a lack of showy covers or rich bindings, and each volume seems to have soberly grown old in constant service. Mr. Emerson's study is a quiet room up stairs, and there each day he is steadily at work, despite advancing years.

When Frederika Bremer called one day at his house, she did not find him at home. Going into his library, she thus describes it :—

I went for a moment into Emerson's study,—a large room, in which every thing was simple, orderly, unstudied, comfortable. No refined feeling of beauty has converted the room into a temple, in which stands the forms of the heroes of science and literature. Ornament is banished from the sanctuary of the stoic philosopher; the furniture is comfortable, but of a grave character, merely as implements of usefulness; one large picture only is in the room, but this hangs there with a commanding power; it is a large oil-painting, a copy of Michael Angelo's glorious Parcæ, the goddess of fate.

Some years ago, Mr. M. D. Conway called on him, and describes his visit, giving us a further glimpse of his study :—

My note of introduction was presented, and my welcome was cordial. Emerson was, apparently, yet young; he was tall, slender, of light complexion; his step was elastic, his manner easy and simple; and his voice at once relieved me of the trembling with which I stood before him,—the first great man I had ever seen. He proposed to take me on a walk; and whilst he was preparing, I had the opportunity of looking about the library. Over the mantel hung an excellent copy of Michael Angelo's Parcæ; on it there were two statuettes of Goethe, of whom also there were engraved copies on the walls. Afterwards Emerson showed me eight or ten portraits of Goethe which he had collected. The next in favour was Dante, of whom he had all the known likenesses, including various photographs of the mask of Dante, made at Ravenna. Besides portraits of Shakspere, Montaigne, and Swedenborg, I remember nothing else on the walls of the library. The book-shelves were well filled with select works; amongst which I was only struck with the many curious Oriental productions, some in Sanscrit. He had, too, many editions in Greek and English, of Plato, which had been carefully read and marked. The furniture of the room was antique and simple. There were, on one side of the room, four considerable shelves, completely occupied by his MSS. ; of which there were enough, one might suppose, to have furnished a hundred volumes instead of the seven which he has given to the world, though under perpetual pressure for more from the publishers and the public.

" Emerson's house is of the old New England sort, large and hospitable in its very construction. A long hall divides it through the middle. By the side of the entrance stands a table, over which is a picture of Diana. His book-shelves are very plain, and reach to the ceiling. A fire-place fills one end of the study, and has high brass andirons ; while on the antique mantel over it may now be found, among other articles, a small idol from the Nile. On the other end is a bronze lamp of antique pattern, such as is often pictured to represent the light of science. Back of this room is the large parlour, in which visitors are received, and where many a conversation party has been held. The gate always remains open. The path from the house to the road is lined with tall chestnut trees.

At the back of the house is a garden of half-an-acre, where both Emerson and his wife are wont to labour—he is passionately fond of flowers, and grows them in profusion. Great numbers of roses are in bloom here in June, while there is a bed of hollyhocks of many varieties. A small brook runs across his land and pours into the river."

In "Scribner's Monthly Magazine" for February, 1879, will be found an interesting descriptive article, entitled "The Homes and Haunts of Emerson," by his friend Mr. F. B. Sanborn. This article is enriched with views of Emerson's house and study, the Old Manse, a view of Concord from Lee's Hill, Walden Pond, The Alcott House, the graves of Hawthorne and Thoreau in Sleepy Hollow, &c.

EMERSON AT HOME.

George William Curtis, an accomplished author and orator, who at one time lived at Concord, thus spoke of Emerson's home :—"It is always morning within these doors. If you have nothing to say, if you are really not an envoy from some kingdom or colony of thought, and cannot cast a gem upon the heaped pile, you had better pass by upon the other side. For it is the peculiarity of Emerson's mind to be ever on the alert. He eats no lotus, but for ever quaffs the waters which engender immortal thirst. . . . The fame of the philosopher attracts admiring friends and enthusiasts from every quarter, and the scholarly grace and urbane hospitality of the gentleman send them charmed away. . . . It is not hazardous to say that the greatest questions of our day and of all days have been nowhere more amply discussed, with more poetic insight or more profound conviction, than in the comely square white house upon the edge of the Lexington turnpike. . . . 'I chide society, I embrace solitude,' he says, 'and yet I am not so ungrateful as not to see the wise, the lovely, and the noble-minded, as from time to time they pass my gate.' It is not difficult to understand his fondness for the spot. He has always been familiar with it, always more or less a resident of the village. Born in Boston upon the spot where Channery Place Church now stands, part of his youth was passed in the Old Manse, which was built by his grandfather, and in which his father was born ; and there he wrote 'Nature.' The imagination of the man who roams the solitary pastures of Concord, or floats dreaming down its river, will easily see its landscape upon Emerson's page. If there be something oriental in his philosophy and tropical in his imagination, they have yet a strong flavour of his mother earth—the underived sweetness of the open Concord sky,

and the spacious breadth of the Concord horizon."
In 1845 there was something like a club formed,
whose members met in Emerson's library on Monday evenings. This library is described by Mr.
Curtis. "It is a simple square room, not walled with
books like the den of a literary grub, nor merely
elegant like the ornamental retreat of a dilettante.
The books are arranged upon plain shelves, not
in architectural bookcases, and the room is hung
with a few choice engravings of the greatest men.
There was a fair copy of Michael Angelo's 'Fates,'
which, properly enough, imparted that grave serenity
to the ornament of the room which is always apparent in what is written there." Here the scholars
met at their symposium. " Plato " (Alcott) "was
perpetually putting apples of gold in pictures of
silver; for such was the rich ore of his thoughts,
coined by the deep melody of his voice. Orson "
(Thoreau) "charmed us with the secrets won from
his interviews with Pan in the Walden woods—
while Emerson, with the zeal of an engineer trying
to dam wild waters, sought to bind the wide-flying
embroidery of discourse into a web of clear sweet
sense. . . . Miles Coverdale " (Hawthorne), "a
statue of night and silence, sat, a little removed,
under a portrait of Dante, gazing imperturbably
upon the group; and as he sat in the shadow, his

dark hair and eyes and suit of sable made him, in that society, the black thread of mystery he weaves into his stories."

Mr. Alcott once wrote thus of Emerson :—
" Fortunate the visitor who is admitted of a morning for the high discourse, or permitted to join the poet in his afternoon walks to Walden, the Cliffs, or elsewhere,—hours to be remembered as unlike any others in the calendar of experiences. Shall I describe them as sallies oftenest into the cloudlands,—into scenes and intimacies ever new, none the less novel nor remote than when first experienced ?—interviews, however, bringing their own trail of perplexing thoughts,—costing some days' duties, several nights' sleep oftentimes, to restore one to his place and poise. Certainly safer not to venture without the sure credentials, unless one will have his pretensions pricked, his conceits reduced in their vague dimensions. But to the modest, the ingenuous, the gifted—welcome ! nor can any bearing be more poetic and polite to all such,—to youth and accomplished women especially. His is a faith approaching to superstition concerning admirable persons, the rumour of excellence of any sort being like the arrival of a new gift to mankind, and he the first to proffer his recognition and hope."

Concord was for many years a kind of Mecca to which many a devout and faithful pilgrim resorted. "Young visionaries (in the words of Hawthorne), to whom just so much of insight had been imparted as to make life all a labyrinth around them, came to seek the clew that should lead them out of their self-involved bewilderment. Grey-headed theorists—whose systems, at first air, had imprisoned them in an iron framework—travelled painfully to his door, not to ask deliverance, but to invite the free spirit into their own thraldom. People that had lighted on a new thought, or a thought that they fancied new, came to Emerson, as the finder of a glittering gem hastens to a lapidary to ascertain its value. For myself, there had been epochs in my life when it, too, might have asked of this prophet the master-word that should solve me the riddle of the universe ; but now, being happy, I felt as if there were no question to be put, and therefore admired Emerson as a poet of deep beauty and austere tenderness, but sought nothing from him as a philosopher."

A writer in the "Chicago Times," a few years ago, thus wrote from his own knowledge of Emerson :—" Although one of the severest of students and most abstract of philosophers, he always emerges from his library to the family

circle with evident satisfaction.   Notwithstanding
a certain gravity of manner, he is full of geniality
and *bonhomie*, and is never more eloquent and
charming than when away from his books and
manuscripts.   He is very fond of children and
young people; loves to talk and walk with them,
and listens to them as if they were revealing the
oracles of the gods.   No man in Concord is more
popular or accessible than he.   He is fully in sympathy with the old town ; he reveres and honours
it, and says he would not exchange it for New
York, Athens, Rome, or Paris.   To get a clear and
adequate conception of Emerson, one must see
him at home, in undress, so to speak, if he may be
considered as ever in uniform, who is the soul of
simplicity and sincerity.   He is the kindest of
husbands, the most considerate of fathers.   It is
related of him that when any thought strikes him,
when any suggestion occurs, or any pat quotation
is recalled, he invariably stops the thing he is doing
and jots down the thought or suggestion for future
use or reference.   Even in the middle of the night
he observes this habit, knowing that a good thing
may be lost forever unless recorded.   .   .   .
Nobody has ever seen him out of temper, or even
ruffled.   He is the embodiment of calm courtesy, of
placid refinement—the very reverse of the supremely

nervous, irritable being an author is believed to be, and often is, in truth."

EMERSON AS A LISTENER.—HIS CONVERSATION.

"He is one of the best of listeners," says Mr. Cooke, "whoever may be speaking, seeming to drink in all that is said, and giving the approval of his gracious smile to whatever attracts his attention. He is even more ready to listen than to speak. What he says is to the point, clearly stated, and in a serious, earnest tone; but his conversation is not brilliant in those ways which gave to Margaret Fuller's marvellous conversational powers a place of their own. It is not his to fascinate and attract by the ceaseless monologue of a versatile talker; for he would make conversation an act of friendship, and finds its charm broken by the presence of more than two. Yet he always speaks wisely, and with a charm and interest all his own. He does not talk easily or much, and needs the stimulus of a sympathetic and vigorous mind to draw out his best treasures of thought. In the midst of a company of bright minds he is not exuberant, never bubbles over; but what he says is marked by a keen wit, and a full wisdom, rich, appropriate, and remarkable. His conversation, when his mind is stimulated by a great theme and a sympathetic friend, is inspiring even beyond his lectures ; and then he pours forth his thought in the purest strain of noble words.   In this way, his influence over his friends has been very great ; and to many a mind his conversation has been an inspiration."

Mr. M. D. Conway, in an article in " Fraser's Magazine" for August, 1867, gives the following account of Emerson's conversation.   The latter took his visitor to Walden Pond, where they rowed, bathed, and talked :—

Having bathed, we sat down on the shore ; and then Walden and her beautiful woods began to utter their pæans through his lips. Emerson's conversation was different from that of any person I have ever met with, and unequalled by that of any one, unless it be that of Thomas Carlyle.   Of course there is no comparison of the two possible, but the contrasts between them are very striking and significant.   In speaking of that which he conceives to be ignorant error, Mr. Carlyle is vehement ; and when he suspects an admixture of falsehood and hypocrisy, his tone is that of rage ; and although his indignation is noble and the utterances always thrilling, yet when one recurs to the little man or thing at which they are often levelled, it seems to be like the bombardment of a sparrow's nest with shot and shell.   On such Emerson merely darts a spare beam of his wit, beneath which a lie is sure to shrivel ; but if he breaks any one on his wheel, it must be some one who has been admitted at the banquet of the gods, and violated their laws.   Every one who has witnessed the imperial dignity, or felt the weight of authentic knowledge, which characterize Mr. Carlyle's conversation, to such an extent that even his light utterances seem to stand out like the pillars of Hercules, must also have felt the earth tremble before the thunders and lightnings of his wrath ; but with Emerson, though the same falsehood is fatally smitten, it is by the invisible, inaudible sun-stroke, which has left the sky as bright and blue as before. For the rest, and when abstract truths and principles are discussed, whilst Carlyle astonishes us by the range of his sifted knowledge, he does not convey an equal impression of having originally thought out the various problems in other departments than those which are plainly his own ; but there is scarcely a realm of science or art in which Emerson could not be to some extent the instructor of the Academies. Agassiz, as I have heard him say, prefers his conversation on scientific questions to that of any other. I remember him on that day at Walden as Bunyan's Pilgrim might have remembered the Interpreter. The growths around, the arrow-head, and the orchis, were intimations of that mystic unity in nature, which is the fountain of poetry to him ; either of these, or of many others of the remarkably rich fauna of that region, excited emotions much more solemn than the æsthetic in him. He fully felt that if we only knew how to look around, we would not have need to look above.

Frederika Bremer's Visit to Emerson.

In her "Homes of the New World," Miss Bremer gives the following account of a visit she paid to Mr. Emerson at his home in Concord, in 1849 :—"During the four days that I remained in Emerson's house I had a real enjoyment in the study of this strong, noble, eagle-like nature. Any near approximation was, as it were, imperfect, because our characters and views are fundamentally dissimilar, and that secret antagonism which exists in me towards him, spite of my admiration, would at times awake, and this easily called forth his icy-alp nature, repulsive and chilly.

But this is not the original nature of the man—he does not rightly thrive in it, and he gladly throws it off if he can, and is much happier, as one can see, in a mild and sunny atmosphere where the natural beauty of his being may breathe freely and expand into blossom, touched by that of others as by a living breeze.

"I enjoyed the contemplation of him in his demeanour, his expression, his mode of talking, and his every-day life, as I enjoy contemplating the calm flow of a river bearing along and between flowery shores large and small vessels, as I love to see the eagle circling in the clouds, resting upon them and its pinions. In this calm elevation Emerson allows nothing to reach him, neither great nor small, neither prosperity nor adversity.

"Pantheistic as Emerson is in his Philosophy, in the moral view with which he regards the world and life, he is in a high degree pure, noble, and severe, demanding as much from himself as he demands from others. His words are severe, his judgment often keen and merciless, but his demeanour is alike noble and pleasing and his voice beautiful.

"One may quarrel with Emerson's thoughts, with his judgment, but not with himself. That which struck me most, as distinguishing him from most other human beings, is nobility. He is a born nobleman. I have seen before two other men born with this stamp upon them—his excellency W———r, in Sweden, and ——— is the second, Emerson the third which has it, and perhaps in a yet higher degree ; and added thereto that deep intonation of voice, that expression so mild yet so elevated at the same time. I could not but think of Maria Lowell's words, 'If he merely mention my name, I feel myself ennobled.'

" I enjoyed Emerson's conversation, which flowed as calmly and easily as a deep and placid river. It was animating to me both when I agreed and when I dissented ; there is always a something important in what he says, and he listens well and comprehends and replies well also. But whether it was the weariness of the spirit or whether a feeling of esteem for his peace and freedom, I know not, but I did not invite his conversation. When it came it was good, when it did not come it was good also, especially if he were in the room. His presence was agreeable to me. He was amiable in his attention to me and in his mode of entertaining me as a stranger and guest in his house.

" This is what I wished to say to Emerson, what I endeavoured to say, but I know not how

I did it. I cannot usually express myself either easily or successfully until I become warm and get beyond or through the first thoughts; and Emerson's cool, and as it were circumspect, manner prevented me from getting into my own natural region. I like to be with him, but when with him I am never fully myself. I do not believe that I now expressed myself intelligibly to him. He listened calmly, and said nothing decidedly against it, nor yet seemed inclined to give his views as definite. He seemed to me principally to be opposed to blind or hypocritical faith. 'I do not wish,' said he, 'that people should pretend to know or to believe more than they really do know and believe. The resurrection, the continuance of our being, is granted,' said he also; 'we carry the pledges of this in our own breast. I maintain merely that we cannot say in what form or in what manner our existence will be continued.' If my conversation with Emerson did not lead to anything very satisfactory, it led, nevertheless, to my still more firm conviction of his nobility and love of truth. He is faithful to the law in his own breast, and speaks out the truth which he inwardly recognises. He does right. By this means he will prepare the way for a more true comprehension of religion and of life. For when once this keen glance, seeing into the innermost of everything, once becomes aware of the concealed human form in the tree of life—like Napoleon's in the tree of St. Helena—then will he teach others to see it too, will point it out by such strong, new, and glorious words that a fresh light will spring up before many, and people will believe because they see."

The Young Preacher.

Mr. Charles T. Congdon, a veteran American journalist, in a series of papers in the New York "Tribune" in 1879, entitled "Reminiscences of a Journalist," gives some recollections of Emerson before he had abandoned his ministerial connection with the Unitarian body :—"It is curious that I should first have heard the lovable voice of Ralph Waldo Emerson, when he was the Rev. Waldo Emerson. One day there came into our pulpit the most gracious of mortals, with a face all benignity, who gave out the first hymn and made the first prayer as an angel might have read and prayed. Our choir was a pretty good one, but its best was coarse and discordant after Emerson's voice. I remember of the sermon only that it had an indefinite charm of simplicity, quaintness, and wisdom, with occasional illustrations from nature, which were about the most delicate and dainty things of the kind which I had ever heard. I could understand them, if not the fresh philosophical novelty of the discourse. Mr. Emerson preached for us for a good many Sundays, lodging in the home of a Quaker lady, just below ours. Seated at my own door, I saw him often go by, and once in the exuberance of my childish admiration I ventured to nod to him and to say 'Good morning!' To my astonishment, he also nodded and smilingly said 'Good morning!' and that is all the conversation I ever had with the sage of Concord—not enough, decidedly, for a reminiscent volume about him after he has left a world, which he has made wiser and happier. He gave us afterward two lectures based upon his travels abroad, and was at a great deal of trouble to hang up prints, by way of illustration. There was a picture of the tribune in the Uffizi Gallery in Florence, painted by one of our townsmen, and I recall Mr. Emerson's great anxiety that it should have a good light, and his lamentation when a good light was found to be impossible. The lectures themselves were so fine—enchanting we found them—that I have hungered to see them in print, and have thought of the evenings upon which they were delivered as 'true Arabian nights.'"

Emerson Hissed while Speaking Against "The Fugitive Slave Law."

In all Emerson's experience as a lecturer there was only one occasion when he received that tribute to a radical orator's timely eloquence which is expressed in hisses. The passage of the Fugitive Slave Law stirred him into unwonted moral passion and righteous wrath. He accepted an invitation to deliver a lecture in Cambridgeport, called for the purpose of protesting against that infamous anomaly in jurisprudence and insult to justice which had the impudence to call itself a law. Those who sympathised with him were there in force; but a score or two of foolish Harvard students came down from the college to the hall where the lecture was delivered determined to assert "the rights of the South," and to preserve the threatened Union of the States. They were the rowdiest, noisiest, most brainless set of young gentlemen that ever pretended to be engaged in studying "the humanities" at the chief university of the country. Their only arguments were hisses and groans whenever the most illustrious of American men of letters uttered an opinion which expressed the general opinion of the civilised world. If he quoted Coke, Holt, Blackstone, Mansfield, they hissed all these sages

of the law because their judgments came from the
illegal lips of Emerson. It was curious to watch
him as, at each point he made, he paused to let the
storm of hisses subside. The noise was something
he had never heard before; there was a queer,
quizzical squirrel-like or bird-like expression in his
eye as he calmly looked round to see what strange
human animals were present to make such sounds;
and when he proceeded to utter another indisputable
truth, and it was responded to by another chorus
of hisses, he seemed absolutely to enjoy the new
sensation he experienced, and waited for these
signs of disapprobation to stop altogether before
he resumed his discourse. The experience was
novel; still there was not the slightest tremor
in his voice, not even a trace of the passionate
resentment which a speaker under such circumstances and impediments usually feels, and which
urges him into the cheap retort about serpents, but
a quiet waiting for the time when he should be
allowed to go on with the next sentence. During
the whole evening he never uttered a word which
was not written down in the manuscript from which
he read. Many of us at the time urged Emerson
to publish the lecture; ten or fifteen years after,
when he was selecting material for a new volume
of essays, I entreated him to include in it the old

lecture at Cambridgeport; but he, after deliberation, refused, feeling probably that being written under the impulse of the passion of the day, it was no fit and fair summary of the characters of the statesmen he assailed. Of one passage in the lecture I preserve a vivid remembrance. After affirming that the eternal law of righteousness, which rules all created things, nullified the enactment of Congress, and after citing the opinions of several magnates of jurisprudence, that immoral laws are void and of no effect, he slowly added, in a scorching and biting irony of tone which no words can describe, "but still a little Episcopalian clergyman assured me yesterday that the Fugitive Slave Law must be obeyed and enforced." After the lapse of thirty years, the immense humour of bringing all the forces of nature, all the principles of religion, and all the decisions of jurists to bear with their Atlas weight on the shoulders of one poor little conceited clergyman to crush him to atoms, and he in his innocence not conscious of it, makes me laugh now as all the audience laughed then, the belligerent Harvard students included. — *Some Recollections of Emerson*, by Edwin P. Whipple, in "Harper's Monthly Magazine," September, 1882.

A Mother's Conversation with Emerson
in a Railway Car.

Many years ago, I was one day journeying from
Brattleboro to Boston, alone. As the train went
on from station to station, it gradually filled, until
there was no seat left unoccupied in the car excepting the one by my side. At Concord, the door of
the car opened, and Mr. Emerson entered. He
advanced a few steps into the car, looked down the
aisle, turned, and was about to go out, believing
the car to be entirely full. With one of those sudden impulses which are acted upon almost before
they are consciously realised, I sprang up, and said,
" Oh, Mr. Emerson, here is a seat."

As he came towards me, with his serene smile
slowly spreading over his face, my courage faltered.
I saw that he expected to meet in me an acquaintance, and as he looked inquiringly and hesitatingly
in my face I made haste to say, "You do not know
me, Mr. Emerson ; I never had the pleasure of
seeing you before. But I know your face, and I
could not resist the temptation of the opportunity
to speak with you. You know that so many
people, who are strangers to you, know you very
well."

" Perhaps there should not be the word stranger

in any language," he answered slowly, in a tone
and with a kindly look which at once set my
timidity at ease, " I do not know any good reason
for it."

In a short time, with that rare faculty which he
had for drawing out of each his inmost thought, he
had led me into speaking to him, with half-familiar
freedom, of my own personal history, and of my
experience as a mother. Hardly by question so
much as by tone and expression, he made me feel
at liberty to confide to him some of the many
perplexities and doubts with which every young
mother's heart is burdened.

His replies were more in the form of suggestions
than of solutions to the doubts, or direct meeting
of the perplexities. He told me much of his own
theories, somewhat of his own experience. Many
of his words remained vividly present with me for
years, and more than once recurred to my mind in
situations when they bore the weight and came in
with the appropriateness of specific advice, in im-
mediate emergencies. One point I recollect, as
most earnestly dwelt upon, was the unspeakable
value of simplicity of life and surroundings as an
agency in the formation of character. Of this he
spoke at length, and with great fervour. He said
that the children of rich men were born at such

disadvantage in this respect that it was a question if all their other advantages, such as educational faculties, travel, etc., could make up for it.

"This is the true meaning," he said, half humorously, "of a scripture which is much misquoted,—that it is easier for a camel to go through the eye of a needle than for a rich man to enter into the kingdom of heaven. It does not mean that the rich man must necessarily find it harder not to sin than another man ; on the contrary, he is removed from some of the deadliest forms of temptation to sin. But the kingdom of heaven, which the creative worker knows, is shut against him. Into that heaven we have to be driven, either by need or by the narrowing of the ministering horizons of our lives."

One sentence which he spoke in connection with this was said with such lingering emphasis that it stamped itself indelibly on my memory. He said, " When I think how I am sparing my boy all that made me,—the barefooted chambers and the stern denials of poverty,—I know I am making a mistake. But," he added after a pause," " I cannot help it."

In later years I had the privilege and pleasure of seeing Mr. Emerson frequently. At one time I spent a few days with him in a friend's house at

Newport, Rhode Island. There was something in the dreamy serenity of the bay upon which my friend's house stood that greatly charmed Mr. Emerson, and his remark at first looking out over the water was a characteristic one. It was from the dining-room windows that he looked. We had given him a seat from which he could see the bay. As we took our places for breakfast he gazed across the shining silver surface, and said half dreamily, "And are there any clocks in Newport?" It was some minutes before anyone perceived the precise drift of this question, and during the brief interval of our bewilderment the smile on Mr. Emerson's face deepened and spread until his whole countenance beamed with humorous enjoyment of our perplexity.

How precious is every memory of those days! The tender, yet beneficent, way in which Mr. Emerson listened for replies to the searching questions he sometimes put had in it a certain expression of unconscious royalty that no words could convey; and it kindled in one's breast that mingled sentiment of affection and incentive to all possible effort, for which allegiance is the only fitting name. As time goes on it will be more and more sure that he is the one truest representative our republic has borne, his thought and his words the truest rendering of the republic's idea, and ᴜᴜs life and character the truest fulfilling of the republic's ideal.—"Atlantic Monthly," September, 1882.

AWKWARD POSITION WHILE ON A LECTURING TOUR.

Many of Emerson's friends and acquaintances thought that his sense of humour was almost as keen as his sense of Beauty and his sense of Right. I do not remember an instance in my conversations with him, when the question came up of his being not understood, or, what is worse, misunderstood by the public, that he did not treat the matter in an exquisitely humorous way, telling the story of his defeats in making himself comprehended by the audience or the readers he addressed as if the misapprehensions of his meaning were properly subjects of mirth, in which he could heartily join. This is the test of the humourist, that he can laugh *with* those who laugh *at* him. For example, on one occasion I recollect saying that of all his college addresses I thought the best was that on "The Method of Nature," delivered before the Society of the Adelphi, in Waterville College, Maine, August 11, 1841. He then gave me a most amusing account of the circumstances under which the oration was delivered. It seems that after conceiving the general idea of the address, he banished himself to Nantasket Beach, secluded himself for a fortnight in a room in the public-house, the windows of which looked out on the ocean, moving from his chamber and writing-desk only to take early morning and late evening walks on the beach ; and thought, at the end, he had produced something which was worthy of being listened to even by the Society of the Adelphi. At that time a considerable portion of the journey to Waterville had to be made by stage. He arrived late in the evening, travel-worn and tired out, when almost all the sober inhabitants of Waterville had gone to bed. It appeared that there was some doubt as to the particular citizen's house at which he was to pass the night. "The stage-driver," said Emerson, "stopped at one door ; rapped loudly ; a window was opened ; something in a night-gown asked what he wanted ; the stage-driver replied that he had inside a man who *said* he was to deliver the lit-ra-rye oration to-morrow, and thought he was to stop there ; but the night-gown disappeared, with the chilling remark that he was not to stay at *his* house. Then we went to another, and still another dwelling, rapped, saw similar night-gowns and heard similar voices at similar raised windows ; and it was only after repeated disturbances of the peace of the place that the right house was hit, where I found a hospitable reception. The next day I delivered my oration, which was heard with cold, silent, unresponsive attention, in which there seemed to be a continuous unuttered rebuke and protest. The services were closed by prayer, and the good man who prayed, prayed for the orator, but also warned his hearers against heresies and wild notions, which appeared to me of that kind for which I was held responsible. The address was really written in the heat and happiness of what I thought a real inspiration ; but all the warmth was extinguished in that lake of iced water." The conversation occurred so long ago that I do not pretend to give Emerson's exact words, but this was the substance of his ludicrous statement of the rapture with which he had written what was so frigidly received. He seemed intensely to enjoy the fun of his material discomforts and his spiritual discomfiture.—*Some Recollections of Emerson*, by Edwin P. Whipple, in " Harper's Monthly Magazine," September, 1882.

MR. ALCOTT AND HIS DAUGHTERS.

The following account of the venerable Mr. A. Bronson Alcott, Emerson's life-long friend, still living, in his eighty-third year, will be read with interest. His name is inseparably associated with that of his distinguished fellow-townsman. It is from a paper in the New York "Home Journal," entitled "Literati at Concord," November, 1874 :—

"Not far from Mr. Emerson's hemlock grove—writes a pilgrim of the Inter-Ocean—is the picturesque home of the Alcotts. It is the queerest little cottage in the world. It stands at the foot of the hill which the British soldiers crossed the morning, nearly a hundred years ago, when they marched up from Lexington. The house is a dull brown colour, with peaked roof and many a gable end, in one of which, hooded by the jutting roof and festooned by some airy sprays of woodbine, is the window whence 'Aunt Joe' looks out on the sunny meadows. On each side of the front walk there is a huge elm with rustic seat built around its roots, and among the branches tame squirrels hold high revelry. Yonder a hammock swings under some apple trees, and around the whole runs a rustic fence, built by Mr. Alcott himself. It is made entirely of pine boughs, knotted, gnarled, and twisted into every conceivable shape. No two pieces are alike ; the gates are wonderful, and they alone would make credible the story that he spent years collecting the branches.

"Mr. Alcott, the 'Orphic Alcott,' as Curtis calls

him, is one of the Concord philosophers, and has
his ' ism,' of course.   Vegetables and conversation
are his *forte*, and he reared his family on a diet of
both, apparently with great success, judging from
appearances.   He ate weeds and talked and built
summer-houses, whose chief use was to be targets
for George William Curtis' wit.   Once he kept a
young ladies' school in Boston, where books were
discarded and teaching done entirely by conversation.*   He was also a member of those extraordinary assemblages, practicable in Boston
alone, over which Margaret Fuller presided, and it
must have been a rare sight to see how these two
inexhaustible talkers managed to tolerate each
other.   For it is said that Mr. Alcott's conversations are very much like the Irishman's treaty—the
reciprocity is all on one side ; or, as a Western host
described him once in his invitations to some friends,
' Come up this evening.   I have a philosopher on
tap.'

   " It is all well enough to joke about Mr. Alcott
till you see him.   Then to come face to face with
this white-haired, benign, gracious old man, makes
levity seem irreverent.   He is over six feet tall, but
a good deal stooped.   His long, grey hair falls
scantily around a face beautified by the placidity

---

* The school was a mixed one, for young scholars.—A. I.

and dignity of old age ; he is a perfect counterpart of the pictures of venerable *curés* one sees in French story books. His manners are very simple and un-affected, and it is his great delight to gather some of his daughters' young friends in his cosy, crimson-lined study and chat with them. Mr. Emerson esteems him highly, but his books seem to be less appreciated by his own people than they are abroad, a fate common to prophets if not philo-sophers. His most valuable work is a journal faithfully kept for fifty years, carefully bound, in-dexed, and with letters and other valuable papers ranged on his library shelves. This taste for minute detail, his orderly arrangement, his dis-tinguished associates, and the number of years covered by the record will make these volumes priceless to historians or biographers. If in Emer-son's study perpetual twilight reigns, in Alcott's it is always noon. The sun shines in it all day long, the great fireplace roars, and the warm crimson hangings temper the sunlight and reflect the fire-light. Quaint mottoes and pictures hang on the walls. The most noticeable picture is a photograph of Carlyle. It is what is called a ' Cameron photo-graph.' An English woman of rank takes these photographs of distinguished men just for her own amusement. The camera is set out of focus, the

heads nearly life-size, and the general effect is
singular—interesting, if nothing else.   All you
can see against a black background is the indistinct outlines of a shaggy white head and beard
and sharp features.   With all deference to Mr.
Carlyle, we must say that he looks like an old
beggar.

"Miss May Alcott, a fine-looking, stylish woman,
is an artist whom the critic of critics, Ruskin, has
declared to be the only successful copyist of
Turner.   She surely has one attribute not usually
allied to her profession—the most generous interest
in other artists—not only by word of mouth, but
with substantial endeavour.   She brought home
with her several English water colours, for whose
artists she is trying to find American patrons.
She herself paints in oil and water colours, and
sketches in crayons, charcoal, sepia, ink, and pencil,
and is one of the most popular Boston teachers.
Her studio at home, a most cobwebby, disorderly,
fascinating little den, is frescoed with profiles of
her acquaintances—that is the toll cheerfully paid
by her visitors—they must be drawn on the wall.
She is known to the general reading public through
her illustrations of ' Little Women,' in which she
fell far short of her usual ability.   She and Louisa
planned subsequently a charming little book called

' Concord Sketches,' which it is a great pity was never made public. Beside painting, Miss May models in clay sometimes. A head of Mercury and all sorts of pretty little sketches from her hands adorn her home, which is made a still sunnier remembrance to all visitors by her brightness and cordiality.*

"Louisa Alcott, the elder of the two, the darling of all American nurseries, is something of an invalid. She is amiable and interesting, and, like her sister, sociable, unless you unluckily approach her in her character of author, and then the porcupine bristles. There is no favour to be curried with her or Gail Hamilton by talking 'shop,' ' Little Women ' is drawn chiefly from Miss Alcott's own home life. Amy the golden-haired, is May, Hemmie and Demmie are her two little nephews, Mr. and Mrs. Marsh her father and mother ; she herself is Jo, of course. When the book was first published, children used to come by the dozen from all parts of the country to see ' Jo.' To the calls of these little pilgrims she always presented herself cheerfully, though she used to be infinitely amused at the unmistakable disappointment of her young admirers when they

---

* This lady married a French nobleman, named Nierecker. She died in January, 1880.—A. I.

saw this delicate, practical-looking lady, slightly stooped, for their rollicking, romping, nimble Jo. Miss Alcott struck a rich vein of popularity and more substantial reward in her juvenile books, though she herself considers 'Hospital Sketches' the best of her writings.

"Some four or five years ago she went into a Boston book-store to leave an order, which the clerk told her could not be attended to, 'because,' said he, not knowing to whom he spoke, 'we shall be busy all day packing books for a Western firm. Two weeks ago we sent ten thousand copies of "Little Women" out there, and to-day comes an order for twenty thousand more.' As soon as they got out of the store her companion turned to her with some congratulatory expression.

"'Ah!' said Miss Alcott, drawing a long breath, 'I have waited fifteen years for this day.'

"Mrs. Alcott is a beautiful old lady, herself something of a writer, or, as one of her daughters lovingly says, 'the brightest one of the family.'"

EMERSON AND HIS DAUGHTER.

A correspondent of the "Cincinnati Commercial," giving an account of a lecture delivered at Washington, in July, 1876, thus speaks of the beautiful

relation between Mr. Emerson and his daughter:—
" Into the Congressional library walked Emerson,
one of the immortals, and smiled his celestial smile,
as if two such things as mercury and the thermo-
meter were not. His daughter Ellen by his side,
and as she is the incarnation of common sense, she
also was sublimely indifferent to the weather. When
this rare spirit (far be the day) passes forever from
mortal sight we shall hear more from this daughter
Ellen. For she, in all likelihood, will be the
executor of his papers and the delineator of that
deep, still, inward life. It is memorable that the
men who have achieved the most in letters and in
science have always had a woman standing close
beside them within the veil, as Carl Schurz says
in homely phrase : 'Handing them the bricks while
they build,' and holding up their hands when they
were weary. It has just come to light how much
Sir William Herschel owed to the tender and tireless sister who, through a lifetime of nights, stood
by his side while others slept; who polished till
her hands grew numb the mirrors which were to
reflect back for him immensity ; who had no ambition in life but to be his servant ; who underrated
her own achievements that she might exalt his,
and, as her clear vision swept the paths of the
spheres, shrank from her own discoveries of worlds,

lest it might prove a shadow on his fame. So the great American seer has a woman walking close by his side, taking the very thoughts from his mind and translating them for the world, and this woman is his daughter."

"MONDAY CONVERSATIONS" AT CONCORD.

A writer in the "Boston Journal" (April 27, 1872,) gives an account of Emerson's "Monday Conversations" and "Literary Meetings" at the Mechanics' Hall, Concord :—" A venerable gentleman, well preserved, serene and elegant in manner, takes his seat upon the platform of a cosy and comfortable hall, at three o'clock on a Monday afternoon, when the rush and roar of business in practical Boston is at its height, and, gently arranging his papers before him, looks calmly around him upon the large audience gathered to hear him. It is the *causerie* which he has undertaken—the familiar and delicate enunciation of his ideas in the form invented by our sprightly yet thoughtful French friends—and the ladies throng to hear him in greater numbers even than when he appears in the attitude of the lecturer. A red curtain hangs behind him, setting off in sharp relief the keen and noble outline of his features—the head thrown

forward with the poise of daring assertion—and
the face now animated with all the warmth and
enthusiasm of a genuine poetic admiration, now
saddened and reserved with the diffidence of the
habitual student and the man of reverie. Side-
lights from each wing of the stage throw a sharp
light upon the ample manuscript on the reading-
desk, for the philosopher and poet is now rapidly
nearing seventy years of age, and the fatigues of
the lecture-room are easier felt than thirty years
ago. Yet the same consummate magnetism lingers
around and upon every word and phrase ; there is
the same thrilling earnestness of antithesis, the same
delight and gloating over poetry and excellence of
expression, as of old. There is no other man in
America who can, by the mere force of what he
says, enthrall and dominate an audience. Breathless
attention is given, although now and then his voice
falls away so that those seated farthest off have to
strain every nerve to catch the words. The grand
condensation, the unfaltering and almost cynical
brevity of expression are at first startling and
vexatious; but presently one yields to the charm,
and finds his mind in the proper assenting mood.
The conversations attract more women than men,
but they are of the more intellectual and reflective
class of our New England women, who find in

the intensity and wonderful precision of Mr. Emerson's mind something inexpressibly pleasing. Nor are they blind worshippers merely at a shrine before which they kneel in wonder ; but the large majority appreciate and enjoy to the uttermost the continual, unresting surging of thought thrust upon them. . . . Mr. Emerson is greeted by a class of people who are rarely seen together on any other public occasion in Boston. Aside from the large number of professed admirers and disciples, and the literati, who are present each time that he speaks or reads in Boston or vicinity, the men who go to hear him are mainly of the desire-to-be-dazzled-and-shocked order, who seem disagreeably surprised when they do comprehend what he says. Mr. Emerson's terse and vivid sentences cling in the memory, and will not be effaced. The *causerie* of yesterday afternoon gave an hundred ideas upon poetry, and the relations of nature to man, which will be henceforth grafted inseparably upon the common mind. The emphatic New Englander listens, incredulously at first, but finishes by saying, ' That's so ! ' Ideals and heretofore far-remote abstractions are brought down to the sphere of daily life—admirably illustrated—made plain, and tethered where even the humblest can appreciate them as realities. And in all cases it seems to the listener as if the phrases uttered were sculptured in the thought of the speaker—as if they had been so from the beginning, and could never be otherwise."

CONCORD AND ITS SCENERY.

The following letter, dated December, 1875, from an American lady to a relative in England, gives an account of a visit to Concord in the Autumn of 1875—that season of the year when the foliage assumes its most brilliant colouring and tints. In this letter we have a pleasant glimpse of Emerson and his home, and the local surroundings :—

. . . I have been in Concord, that quaint and lovely New England village, near Boston, where Emerson lives, and where Hawthorne and Thoreau did live, and many other minor literary celebrities drawn there perhaps by the great names of Emerson and Hawthorne, making a society of their own. . . . After a short ride in the twilight of a soft October evening, we reached our destination. It was just light enough to see how goldenly the drooping branches of the elms hung above us, and how brilliant were the scarlet hues of the maples. All day we had had a feast of colour, for our train had come from Albany through the

Berkshire-hill country, and every hillside and valley on that lovely sunny day, was like a blaze of glory, and now we were to live in it for awhile in this lovely village.

And then next day was *such a day*—indescribable—such as only *October* can produce—and we have them *only once a year!* soft warmth, and dreamy sunshine, and a large party wandering about under these beautiful trees, gathering the bright-hued branches exclaiming in ecstasy over the colours, and the children shouting with glee, Every step seemed to bring us to new and brighter colours. . . . And then when tired with one long ramble, we returned with our bright boughs through the village streets—the early sunset had begun, and was lighting up the grand old elms and brilliant maples, with such radiant hues, that we seemed to be colour-bearers walking under triumphal arches—brightened with the glory of another world than ours. Thoreau somewhere says—" October is the sunset of the year—November its later twilight." For three weeks I stayed in this lovely village, the *oldest* about Boston, and interesting in so many ways—*rich* for *this country*—with historical recollections, and full of revolutionary mementoes.

It was there they had the Centennial Celebration,

last spring, of the first battle of the Revolution.
A pleasant walk under an arch of elm trees all
the way leads you to the battlefield—so long long
since covered with softest turf—and we crossed
the pretty bridge over the quiet Concord, and
stood by the statue of the Minute Man—with one
verse of Emerson's famous ode engraved upon the
pedestal :—

> By the rude bridge that arched the flood,
>   Their flag to April's breeze unfurled,
> Here once the embattled farmers stood,
>   And fired the shot heard round the world.

It was a lovely place to see the sunsets—the bright
clouds reflected in the placid water, and the bright
o'erhanging trees also, colouring its dark depths.
In this walk we always passed by the "Old Manse,"
which stood just as it does now in those days, owned
by the same family—the "Ripleys." The grand-
mother held the baby in her arms and looked out
upon the battle where her husband was fighting.
They showed us the window one day, when a friend
who knew the family took us to see the house.
They keep it as nearly as possible as it was then,
and it is as quaint and interesting as it can be.
Hawthorne lived there a little while when he was
first married, and wrote the "Mosses from an Old
Manse" there, and he gives a description of the old

house in the preface to that book. There is something in one of the little panes of glass of the windows written by him with his wife's diamond, and their two names. And one Sunday afternoon we wandered all over Sleepy Hollow, the village cemetery—such a lovely place for sleep—and found Hawthorne's grave. He lies alone, as he loved to be in life—alone on a hill top, with the solemn pines above him, and the simplest headstone to mark his grave. His wife, you know, died, and was buried near London. We covered the grave with our beautiful October leaf blossoms. And then not far off we found a tablet with " Henry Thoreau " upon it, and we could not but drop our garlands of leaves there ; for how he loved and wrote of their " autumnal tints," that make the world so beautiful ! You know he lived in the woods for two years, and wrote from his heart about them. A strange, eccentric being he must have been. Emerson wrote the most beautiful " Biographical Sketch " of him.

I mustn't forget to tell you too that often in our rambles we met the *great man* of the village—and that he always stopped and smiled, and talked as simply and kindly as if he was not high as the stars above us common folk. He came to see us too, and asked us to take tea at his house (his wife is an invalid and never makes calls) ; of course we went and were delighted ; it was like going into the holy of holies. The *atmosphere* of the house was so pure and unworldly somehow ; everthing so simple and yet so refined. Miss Ellen Emerson, the unmarried daughter, has a beautiful head ; the brow and eyes of a saint, and the rarest smile. She is her father's *right hand* now ; they seem to work and think together. They were getting ready a new book of his for the press. He said he could do nothing without Ellen.

Well, I stayed in that dear little *New* England village three weeks. We saw the elms and maples scatter their bright treasures to the winds ; saw the lovely colours glow and gleam for a little while upon the ground, and then fade into brown dry leaves that rustled and cracked under our feet as we walked. But that wasn't the last of the colour; "the later twilight," you remember—for now came flaming into rich, darker brilliancy, the scarlet and crimson *oaks* that till now had been dark green, and *they* were relieved and set off by the deep yellow-like pure gold of the white-stemmed birch trees. If you could only have seen *Walden Pond* on one of those late warm days, when the sun was very brilliant, bringing out the colours wonderfully. The oaks were like flames, even in shady places, giving out such colour that the light seemed to come from them, and then lower down on the beautiful shores of the tiny lake came the delicate little yellow birch leaves, always quivering upon their silver-white stems, and reflected again—white stems and golden and crimson leaves—in that crystal clean water! It was unreal and fairy-like ; a picture of beauty that has haunted me ever since, but I can't describe it to bring it before you as it was to us that day. Perhaps Thoreau could have done so, but no one else.

The " School of Philosophy " at Concord, 1880.

The Concord Correspondent of the "Chicago Tribune" (September, 1880) gives the following sketch of Emerson at the age of seventy-seven:—
"An old man with large eyes, prominent nose, and awkward carriage, may often be seen shyly stealing into the 'School of Philosophy,' just after the beginning of the lecture. Passing through the aisle on tiptoe, he seats himself in a huge ear-lap chair at the left of the platform. The lips of the Sphinx are sealed, and their peaceful expression and the far-away look in the eyes would seem to indicate that the discussion going on has not sufficient interest to draw him from the calm joy of reverie. But the way in which he leans forward now and then

to catch the tones of an indistinct speaker, and the promptitude with which certain little red spots appear on his cheeks whenever a personal allusion or quotation is made, show that, after all, he is listening with respectful attention. Emerson has a noble propensity to overrate the works of his contemporaries. He has such a sublime faith that the coming man will eventually arrive that he is always on the look out for him, and finds his John the Baptists in eccentric Thoreau and uncouth Whitman, in whom so many see only insanity. And especially does his unaffected humility place an exaggerated estimate upon the works and words of his personal friends. Thoreau was an original genius, and his mother used to say : ' Why, how much Mr. Emerson talks like Henry !' Some people are unkind enough to say that the boot was squarely on the other foot, and that Thoreau was only a parody of his great friend. While such statements are grossly unjust, it remains true that the fame of the poet naturalist owes much to the friendship of Emerson. His house was thrown open last Sunday evening, and parlour and study and hall were filled with friends from the town and the School of Philosophy. Mr. and Mrs. Emerson (whose quaint, sweet face and simple, old-fashioned attire suggested to one lady that ' She might have just stepped off the *Mayflower*') bustled around, shaking hands and arranging chairs for the guests. Then Mr. Emerson rapped upon a door-jamb and said : 'Some of our friends have something to say to us, and we shall be glad to have them begin.' Mr. Channing, Mr. Alcott, Miss Peabody and Professor Harris did most of the talking. Mrs. Emerson made a single remark, but the host took no part whatever. The seventy-seventh birthday of Mr. Emerson occurred recently. He feels the weight of years, and though he walks about briskly, his memory is failing, and he is often thrown into pathetic confusion by his treacherous faculty. It seems very difficult for him to grasp a new name. Joseph Cooke called upon him just after Moody and Sankey had been in Boston, and he inquired of his visitor if he had been attending the 'Mosely and Sukey meetings !' He never appeared in public without his faithful maiden daughter Ellen, who has the face of a saint and the garb of a Quakeress. She has charge of his manuscripts, and when asked, a few days ago, what lecture her father proposed to read before the school, replied that 'she had not decided.' She intimated, furthermore, that she might put a veto on his lecturing at all."

A Touching Conversation.

A visitor at Concord, in August, 1881, records the following touching conversation with Emerson. "Just on the outskirts of the village, a little way back from the street, stands the old-fashioned country-seat which is sacred as being the home of the Jove of the Concord Immortals, Emerson. Mr. Emerson himself came to the door to greet me with a still active step, and with his placid, inscrutable countenance unchanged in the eight years since I had seen him last. A vein of sadness ran through his striking words as we conversed, which now and then deepened into indescribable pathos as he spoke of himself:—

"'I am visiting the Summer School, and called to pay my respects to you,' I said.

"'I thank you,' he replied, and a slight difficulty in articulation was noticeable as he spoke. 'I am glad to see you ; yet I fear I can do little. I can only disappoint those who come to see me. I find that I am losing myself, and I wander away from the matter that I have in mind.' There was little to be said, but I made some remark, and he continued :

"'I cannot say much. When I begin I lose myself. And so when my friends come to see me

I run away, instead of going to meet them, that I may not make them suffer.'

"I spoke of an examining committee on which he had served at Cambridge, and his face lightened for an instant. 'Yes, yes,' he said, and made some personal enquiry of me. 'But I see no one now,' he added.

"'Your general health is good, I trust?' I asked.

"'Yes, my health is good enough,' he replied indifferently. Then he said slowly, with a wonderful pathos in his voice: 'But when one's wits begin to fail, it is time for the heavens to open and take him away.'

"He turned sadly aside, and I left him. More keenly than anyone else can do, the philosopher realises that age is casting a shadow upon his memory and slowly chilling his faculties."

G. J. HOLYOAKE'S VISIT.

Mr. George Jacob Holyoake, in the latest chapter of his recent American tour in the "Co-operative News," describes a visit he paid to Emerson:—"Though tall, he is still erect, and has the bright eye and calm grace of manner we knew when he was in England long years ago. In European eyes, his position among men of letters in America is as that of Carlyle among English writers ; with the added quality, as I think, of greater braveness of thought and clearness of sympathy. . . . Friends had told me that age seemed now a little to impair Mr. Emerson's memory, but I found his recollection of England accurate and full of detail. Englishmen told me with pride that in the dark days of the war, when American audiences were indignant at England, Emerson would put in his lectures some generous passage concerning this country, and raising himself erect, pronounce it in a defiant tone, as though he threw the words at his audience. More than any other writer Emerson gives me the impression of one who sees facts alive and knows their ways, and who writes nothing that is mean or poor."

LITERARY OPINIONS.

A few years ago, an English literary gentleman visited Emerson at his home in Concord, and brought away many of his opinions on literary and other subjects. A few of these are here recorded :—
" Wordsworth's ode on Immortality touches the high water mark of modern literature. . . . Walter Savage Landor will always be read by the select few. Matthew Arnold is growing too diffusive. His 'sweetness and light' have become as heavy as lead with too much repetition. He

liked Arnold's critical essays very much, but was
not partial to his poetry. Sainte-Beuve he considered the great French writer. He said ' I don't
meddle with Auguste Comte,' in reply to the
question whether he was interested in the positive
philosophy. . . . 'Thoreau was a true genius,
and so great was his mastery of the phenomena
of nature that it would need another Linnæus, as
well as a poet, properly to edit his writings.' . . .
Of Buckle he spoke with admiration, comparing
his erudition with Gibbon's fulness of learning,
and cited his chapters on France in particular as
a splendid contribution to history. . . . Carlyle
being mentioned, Emerson defended him from
Margaret Fuller's criticism in her letters, and said
that 'Carlyle purposely made exaggerated statements, merely to astonish his listeners. His attitude
toward America during our war was unfortunate,
but no more than could be expected.'" Mr. Emerson's visitor records what Carlyle is reported to have
said regarding a distinguished English poet of the
" fleshly school," but his *pronunciamento* is too
scathing and hideous to be given in print.

HARMONY BETWEEN HIS LIFE AND TEACHINGS.

" Emerson's is one of those radiant lives scattered
at wide intervals through history, which become the

fixed stars of humanity. A youth of purest, fiery aspiration, a manhood devoted to the eloquent exposition in word and act of moral truths, an old age of serene benevolence—in his case the traditional fourscore years allotted to our kind were literally passed upon the heights, in daily familiarity with ideas and emotions which are generally associated only with moments of exaltation. His uncompromising devotion to Truth never hardened into dogmatism, his audacious rejection of all formalism never soured into intolerance, his hatred of sham never degenerated into a lip-protest and a literary trick, his inflexible moral purpose went hand in hand with unbounded charity. In him the intellectual keenness and profundity of a philosopher, and the imagination of a poet, were combined with that child-like simplicity and almost divine humility which made him the idol of his fellow-townsmen and the easily accessible friend of the ignorant and the poor. No discrepancy exists between his written words and the record of his life. He fought his battle against error and vice, not with the usual weapons of denunciation and invective, but by proclaiming in speech and deed the beauty of truth and virtue. He has founded no school, he has formulated no theory, he has abstained from uttering a single dogma, and yet his moral and intellectual influence has made itself felt as an active and growing power for highest good over the whole breadth of the continent."—"Emerson's Personality," by Emma Lazarus, " The Century," July, 1882.

LATEST GLIMPSES OF EMERSON.

One of the latest glimpses we have of Emerson, in his home surroundings, is from the journal of Walt Whitman, the American poet, who paid a visit to Concord in the Autumn of last year (1881). He dined with Emerson and his family, and on two successive days spent several hours in their company. The following sentences I cull from Whitman's journal, now before me :—

" *Camden, N. J., Dec. 1, 1881.*—During my last three or four months' jaunt to Boston and through New England, I spent such good days at Concord, and with Emerson, seeing him under such pro- pitious circumstances, in the calm, peaceful, but most radiant, twilight of his old age (nothing in the height of his literary action and expression so becoming and impressive), that I must give a few impromptu notes of it all. So I devote this cluster entirely to the man, to the place, the past, and all leading up to, and forming, that memorable and peculiar Personality, now near his 8oth year—as I

have just seen him there, in his home,—silent,
sunny, surrounded by a beautiful family."

" *Concord, Mass., Sept. 17.*—Never had I a better
piece of better luck befall me : a long and blessed
evening with Emerson, in a way I couldn't have
wished better or different. For nearly two hours he
has been placidly sitting where I could see his face
in the best light near me. Mrs. S.'s back parlour
well fill'd with people, neighbours, many fresh and
charming faces, women, mostly young, but some
old. My friend A. B. Alcott and his daughter
Louisa were there early. A good deal of talk,
the subject Henry Thoreau—some new glints of
his life and fortunes, with letters to and from him—
one of the best by Margaret Fuller, others by
Horace Greeley, W. H. Channing, etc.—one from
Thoreau himself, most quaint and interesting. My
seat and the relative arrangement were such that,
without being rude or anything of the kind, I could
just look squarely at E., which I did a good part of
the two hours. On entering he had spoken very
briefly, easily and politely to several of the company, then settled himself in his chair, a trifle
pushed back, and, though a listener and apparently
an alert one, remained silent through the whole
talk and discussion. And so, there Emerson sat,
and I looking at him. A good colour in his face,

eyes clear, with the well-known expression of sweetness, and the old clear-peering aspect quite the
same."

"*Next Day.*—Several hours at E.'s house, and
dinner there. An old familiar house (he has been
in it thirty-five years), with the surrounding fur-
nishment, roominess, and plain elegance and fulness,
signifying democratic ease, sufficient opulence, and
an admirable old-fashioned simplicity — modern
luxury, with its mere sumptuousness and affectation, either touched lightly upon, or ignored altogether. Of course the best of the present occasion
(Sunday, September 18th, 1881) was the sight of E.
himself. As just said, a healthy colour in the cheeks,
and good light in the eyes, cheery expression, and
just the amount of talking that best suited, namely,
a word or short phrase only where needed, and
almost always with a smile. Besides Emerson
himself, Mrs. E., with their daughter Ellen, the son
Edward and his wife, with my friend F. S. and Mrs.
S., and others, relatives and intimates. Mrs. Emerson, resuming the subject of the evening before (I
sat next to her), gave me further and fuller information about Thoreau, who years ago, during Mr.
E.'s absence in Europe in 1848, had lived for some
time in the family, by invitation.

" Let me conclude by the thought, after all the

rest is said, that most impresses me about Emerson. Amid the utter delirium-disease called book-making, its feverish cohorts filling our world with every form of dislocation, morbidity, and special type of anemia or exceptionalism (with the propelling idea of getting the most possible money, first of all), how comforting to know of an author who has, through a long life, and in spirit, written as honestly, spontaneously, and innocently, as the sun shines or the wheat grows — the truest, sanest, most moral, sweetest literary man on record — unsoiled by pecuniary or any other warp — ever teaching the law within — ever loyally outcropping his own self only — his own poetic and devout soul! If there be a Spirit above that looks down and scans authors, here is one at least in whom it might be well pleased."

CHARACTERISTIC ANECDOTES.

Some twenty years ago Emerson addressed a literary society, during Commencement, at Middlebury, Vermont, and when he ended, the President called upon a clergyman to conclude the service with prayer. Then arose a Massachusetts minister, who stepped into the pulpit Mr. Emerson had just left, and uttered a remarkable prayer, of which this was one sentence: "We beseech Thee, O Lord, to

deliver us from ever hearing any more such transcendental nonsense as we have just listened to
from this sacred desk." After the benediction, Mr.
Emerson asked his next neighbour the name of
the officiating clergyman, and when falteringly
answered, with gentle simplicity remarked : " He
seemed a very conscientious, plain-spoken man,"
and went on his peaceful way.*

———

Mr. Giles, the Irish essayist, tells a story of
Emerson. " We had a rich old merchant, who was
a tireless talker, with whom our lecturers sometimes lodged. The good-hearted gentleman caught
me one evening and kept me a complaisant but
dreadfully weary listener, morally button-holed, so
to speak, until nearly sunrise. Then, as we parted
for the night, or rather for the morning, the garru-
lous and gratified monologist said : ' I like you,
Mr. Giles ; you are willing to hear what I have
to say ; Mr. Emerson was here the other night,

* In a review of the first edition of this Memoir in the "Nation,"
a New York paper, the above anecdote was quoted. In a succeeding
number, the Editor received from a correspondent, J. D. B., the following communication :—" The prayer at the close of the Middlebury
address, spoken of as by ' a Massachusetts minister,' was in fact
offered by the Reverend Stephen Martindale, the Congregationalist
minister of Wallingford, Vermont. By two or three witnesses let
every word be established. My wife and I were both there, heard
the prayer, knew the maker of it, and agree in our testimony."

after he had lectured, and he said he did not wish to hear me talk—that he had rather go to bed.' Not that the kindest of men meant to be uncivil—he merely spoke with the simplicity and directness of a Greek philosopher."

———

The congregation of a church in East Lexington were anxious to have Emerson as their pastor, but he did not wish to enter again upon the duties of a clergyman, considering that the Lyceum platform had now become his platform. He therefore urged the congregation to call to their pulpit one of his friends. When a lady of the society was asked why they did not settle this friend her *naïve* reply was :—" We are a very simple people, and can understand no one but Mr. Emerson."

———

Emerson's good sense was so strong that it always seemed to be specially awakened in the company of those who were most in sympathy with his loftiest thinking. Thus, when " the radical philosophers" were gathered one evening at his house, the conversation naturally turned on the various schemes of benevolent people to reform the world. Each person present had a panacea to cure all the distempers of society. For hours the talk ran on, and before bed-time came, all the sin and misery of the world had been apparently expelled from it, and our planet was reformed and transformed into an abode of human angels, and virtue and happiness were the lot of each human being. Emerson listened, but was sparing of speech. Probably he felt, with Lamennais, that if facts did not resist thoughts, the earth would in a short time become uninhabitable.　At any rate, he closed the *séance* with the remark: " A few of us old codgers meet at the fireside on a pleasant evening, and in thought and hope career, balloon-like, over the whole universe of matter and mind, finding no resistance to our theories, because we have, in the sweet delirium of our thinking, none of those obstructive facts which face the practical reformer the moment he takes a single forward step ; then we go to bed ; and the pity of it is we wake up in the morning feeling that we are the same poor old imbeciles we were before!"—*Some Recollections of Emerson*, by Edwin P. Whipple, in "Harper's Monthly Magazine," September, 1882.

———

Walt Whitman, in the New York " Critic," December 3rd, 1881, gives the following recollection of a long argument with Emerson on Boston Common in 1860 :—" Oct. 10-13, '81.—I spend a good deal of time on the Common, these delicious days and nights—every mid-day from 11-30 to about 1—

and almost every sunset another hour. I know all the big trees, especially the old elms along Tremont and Beacon Streets, and have come to a sociable-silent understanding with most of them, in the sunlit air (yet crispy-cool enough), as I saunter along the wide unpaved walks. Up and down this breadth by Beacon Street, between these same old elms, I walked for two hours, of a bright sharp February mid-day twenty-one years ago, with Emerson, then in his prime, keen, physically and morally magnetic, armed at every point, and when he chose, wielding the emotional just as well as the intellectual. During those two hours, he was the talker and I the listener. It was an argument-statement, reconnoitering, review, attack, and pressing home (like an army corps, in order, artillery, cavalry, infantry), of all that could be said against that part (and a main part) in the construction of my poems, 'Children of Adam.' More precious than gold to me that dissertation—(I only wish I had it now, verbatim). It afforded me, ever after, this strange and paradoxical lesson ; each point of E.'s statement was unanswerable, no judge's charge ever more complete or convincing, I could never hear the points better put—and then I felt down in my soul the clear and unmistakable conviction to disobey all, and pursue my own way. ' What have you to say then to such things ?' said E., pausing in conclusion. 'Only that while I can't answer them at all, I feel more settled than ever to adhere to my own theory, and exemplify it,' was my candid response. Whereupon we went and had a good dinner at the American House. And thenceforward I never wavered or was touched with qualms (as I confess I had been two or three times before).

———

Dr. Ellis, of Boston, reports that in a visit to the poet Whittier, Emerson's last words as he left his friend's house in the morning were, " I cannot conceive of a greater soul than Jesus Christ." Dr. Bartol, an old friend of Emerson's, instituted a comparison between the Concord philosopher and Darwin, declaring that the one was the complement of the other—Darwin the explorer of structure, Emerson of the organising power. He also contrasted Emerson and Carlyle, much to the advantage of the former, who felt no less strongly than the Chelsea sage the defects of humanity, and who longed more earnestly for the millennial days, but who was yet " content with God's world, on good terms with its inhabitants, in love with his home, with peace in his heart, full of respect, and with due deference to his inferiors, never pouring out

Carlyle's torrent of volcanic flame, stones, and mud." Emerson and Darwin, according to Dr. Bartol, were very similar " in their candour, absence of grudge, freedom from vindictiveness and from disposition to reply or quarrel, manners of splendid culture and simplicity." Dr. Bartol relates how, on a visit to Emerson's house, the philosopher requested him in the morning to conduct family devotions. As they rose from their knees their eyes met. " There was in his a singular and surprising lustre which I never forgot ; not a surface glitter, but a soft unfathomable transparency, which made his looks to me like an embodied supplication." Dr. Bartol once prevailed on Emerson to meet at his house with Father Taylor, the eccentric Methodist evangelist of Boston, who has been sketched by Charles Dickens. Taylor was delighted with the philosopher. " Should Emerson go to hell," he declared, " it would change the climate, and the emigration would be that way." The evangelist added, " I have laid my ear close to his heart and never detected any jar in the machinery. He has more of the spirit of Jesus than anybody else I have known."

With regard to the humour in some passages of his lectures, Mr. M. D. Conway says, in an article on Emerson in "The Fortnightly Review" (June, 1882):

Emerson's humour as read has lost some of the flavour it possessed when spoken. Indeed, now and then I have noted the omission from a printed essay of some sally which when it was spoken elicited much mirth. He was inclined to suspect any passage which excited much laughter. There was omitted from his lecture on "Superlatives," when recently printed in "The Century," a remark about oaths. The oath, he said, could only be used by a thinking man in some great moral emergency: in such rare case it might be the solemn verdict of the universe; but—he presently added in a low tone, as if thinking to himself as he turned his page—"but sham damns disgust." I remember, too, how quietly a little drama was mounted on his face when he described a pedant pedagogue questioning a little maid about Fabius,—whether he was victorious or defeated in a certain battle. Susan, in distress, says he was defeated, and is reproved for her mistake before the school and the visitors. "Fabius was victorious. But Fabius is of no importance: Susan's feelings are of a great deal of importance. Fabius, if he had a particle of the gentleman about him, would rather be defeated a hundred times than that Susan's feelings should be hurt." These humorous passages came from Emerson gently, little wayside surprises, and without any air of an intention to cause laughter. On one occasion he was lecturing on the French,—a lecture, by the way, full of racy anecdotes derived from his sojourn in Paris,—and he instituted a comparison of the theatrical habit of that people with English love of reality. "A Frenchman and an Englishman fought a duel in the dark; they were to be let out of the room after two pistol-reports had been heard. The Englishman, to avoid wounding his antagonist, crept round to the fire-place; he fired up the chimney, and brought down the Frenchman." After the mirth that followed this was over, and Emerson had passed on to grave discourse, some individual tardily caught the joke about the duel, and his solitary explosion set the house in a roar that made the lecturer pause.

" His manner toward strangers, while extremely simple, was marked by an exquisite suavity and dignity which peremptorily, albeit tacitly, prohibited undue familiarity or conventional compliment. Sought after as he was, particularly during recent years, by literary novices who saluted him as master, and pestered, like all prominent persons, by visits and letters from the ordinary notoriety-mongers, he found no occasion to resort to inveterate exclusiveness or repelling harshness. . . . On one occasion, only a few years ago, a friend consulted him for advice in regard to the poems of a then unknown writer, who has since won high recognition. The manuscript was read to him in the presence of two or three persons of culture and intelligence ; the poems were crude, rugged, and strongly individual. So strange and uncouth did they seem that, when the reader ceased, no one else present had been able to form the vaguest opinion as to their artistic value ; but Mr. Emerson himself, without pause or hesitancy, gave utterance to a criticism so incisive and comprehensive as to supply in the briefest compass all the advice and encouragement which the young poet needed at the time. 'No discouragement must damp his ardour,' concluded Mr. Emerson, 'no rebuff be sufficient to quell this impulse which urges him to write. A single voice in his favour should be enough to support him till he attain the mastery of style and taste which shall complete and perfect his gift. Indeed, a single voice is more than I had myself as a beginner,' he added with his wise, subtle smile. 'My friends used to laugh at my poetry, and tell me I was no poet.' "—" Emerson's Personality," by Emma Lazarus, " The Century," July, 1882.

THE BROOK FARM COMMUNITY EXPERIMENT.

As has been already stated (Memoir, p. 42), the Brook Farm Community was one of the products of that quickening and fermentation of thought respecting social, religious, and educational reform which made its appearance, in New England especially, in the years preceding 1840. Many earnest men and women—some of them of the highest culture—dissatisfied with the tyranny and benumbing influence of usage and conventional-ism, aspired to make life richer and truer to first principles, " by lifting men to a higher platform, restoring to them the religious sentiment, bringing them worthy aims and pure pleasures, purging the inward eye, making life less desultory, and, through raising man to the level of nature, taking away its melancholy from the landscape, and reconciling the practical with the speculative powers." From this state of thought and feeling sprang "The Dial," in 1840. The spirit of the time is described by Emerson in the opening address of that periodical, with a rare felicity of phrase. "No one can converse much with different classes of society in New England without remarking the progress of a revolution. Those who share in it have no external organization, no badge, no creed, no name. They do not vote, or print, or even meet together. They do not know each other's faces or names. They are united only in a common love of truth, and love of its work. They are of all conditions and constitutions. Of these acolytes, if some are happily born and well bred, many are no doubt ill dressed, ill placed, ill made, with as many scars of hereditary vice as other men. Without pomp, without trumpet, in lonely and obscure places, in solitude, in servitude, in compunctions and privations, trudging beside the team in the dusty road, or drudging a hireling in other men's cornfields, schoolmasters who teach a few children rudiments for a pittance, ministers of small parishes of the obscurer sects, lone women in dependent condition, matrons and young maidens, rich and poor, beautiful and hard-favoured, without concert or proclamation of any kind, they have silently given in their several adherence to a new hope, and in all companies do signify a greater trust in the nature and resources of man than the laws or the popular opinions will well allow. This spirit of the time is felt by every individual with some difference,—to each one casting its light upon the objects nearest to his temper and habits of thought ;—to one, coming in the shape of special reforms in the state ; to another, in modifications of the various callings of men, and the customs of business; to a third, opening a new scope for literature and art ; to a fourth, in philosophical insight ; to a fifth, in the vast solitudes of prayer. It is in every form a protest against usage, and a search for principles. In all its movements it is peaceable, and in the very lowest marked with a triumphant success. Of course, it rouses the opposition of all which it judges and condemns, but it is too confident in its tone to comprehend an objection, and so builds no outworks for possible defence against contingent enemies. It has the step of Fate, and goes on existing like an oak or a river, because it must."

In Mr. O. B. Frothingham's "Transcendentalism in New England" will be found an interesting account of that singular social experiment. The Constitution of the Brook Farm Community given by him explains the project, and expresses the spirit in which it was undertaken. The jealous regard for the rights of the individual is not the least characteristic feature of this remarkable document. Every provision was made to guard against the infringement of individual independence. It was open to all sects, and admitted and welcomed all kinds and degrees of intellectual culture. Agriculture was made the basis of the life, as bringing man into direct and simple relations with nature, and restoring labour to honest conditions.

Provisions were either raised on the farm or purchased at wholesale. Meals were eaten in "commons." It was the rule that all should labour—choosing their occupations, and the number of hours, and receiving wages according to the hours. No labour was hired that could be supplied within the community; and all labour was rewarded alike, on the principle that physical labour is more irksome than mental, more absorbing and exacting, less improving and delightful. Moreover, to recognize practically the nobility of labour in and of itself, none were appointed to special kinds of work. All took their turn at the several branches of employment. None were drudges or menials. The intellectual gave a portion of their time to tasks such as servants and handmaidens usually discharge. The unintellectual were allowed a portion of their time for mental cultivation. The benefits of social intercourse were thrown open to all. The aim was to secure as many hours as practicable from the necessary toil of providing for the wants of the body, that there might be more leisure to provide for the deeper wants of the soul. The acquisition of wealth was no object. No more thought was given to this than the exigencies of existence demanded. To live, expand, enjoy as rational beings, was the never-forgotten aim.

The community trafficked by way of exchange and barter with the outside world ; sold its surplus produce ; sold its culture to as many as came or sent children to be taught. It was hoped that from the accumulated results of all this labour, the appliances for intellectual and spiritual health might be obtained ; that books might be bought, works of art, scientific collections and apparatus, means of decoration and refinement, all of which should be open on the same terms to every member of the association. The principle of coöperation was substituted for the principle of competition ; self development for selfishness. The faith was avowed in every arrangement that the soul of humanity was in each man and woman.

The reputation for genius, accomplishment and wit, which the founders of the Brook Farm enterprise enjoyed in society, attracted towards it the attention of the public, and awakened expectation of something much more than ordinary in the way of literary advantages. The settlement became a resort for cultivated men and women who had experience as teachers and wished to employ their talent to the best effect ; and for others who were tired of the conventionalities, and sighed for honest relations with their fellow-beings. Some took advantage of the easy hospitality of the association, and came there to live mainly at its expense—their unskilled and incidental labour being no compensation for their entertainment. The most successful department was the school. Pupils came thither in considerable numbers and from considerable distances. Distinguished visitors gave charm and reputation to the place.

The members were never numerous ; the number varied considerably from year to year. Seventy was a fair average ; of these, fewer than half were young persons sent thither to be educated. Several adults came for intellectual assistance. Of married people there were, in 1844, but four pairs. A great deal was taught and learned at Brook Farm. Classics, mathematics, general literature, æsthetics, occupied the busy hours. The most productive work was done in these ideal fields, and the best result of it was a harvest in the ideal world, a new sense of life's elasticity and joy, the delight of freedom, the innocent satisfaction of spontaneous relations.

The details above given convey no adequate idea of the Brook Farm fraternity. In one sense it was much less than they imply; in another sense it was much more. It was less, because its plan was not materially successful; the intention was defeated by circumstances; the hope turned out to be a dream. Yet, from another aspect, the experiment fully justified itself. Its moral tone was high; its moral influence sweet and sunny. Had Brook Farm been a community in the accepted sense, had it insisted on absolute community of goods, the resignation of opinions, of personal aims interests or sympathies; had the principle of renunciation, sacrifice of the individual to the common weal, been accepted and maintained, its existence might have been continued and its pecuniary basis made sure. But asceticism was no feature of the original scheme. On the contrary, the projectors of it were believers in the capacities of the soul, in the safety, wisdom and imperative necessity of developing those capacities, and in the benign effect of liberty. Had the spirit of rivalry and antagonism been called in, the sectarian or party spirit, however generously interpreted, the result would probably have been different. But the law of sympathy being accepted as the law of life, exclusion was out of the question; inquisition into beliefs was inadmissible; motives even could not be closely scanned; so while some were enthusiastic friends of the principle of association, and some were ardent devotees to liberty, others thought chiefly of their private education and development; and others still were attracted by a desire of improving their social condition, or attaining comfort on easy terms. The idea, however noble, true, and lovely, was unable to grapple with elements so discordant. Yet the fact that these discordant elements did not, even in the brief period of the fraternity's existence, utterly rend and abolish the idea; that to the last, no principle was compromised, no rule broken, no aspiration bedraggled, is a confession of the purity and vitality of the creative thought. That a mere aggregation of persons, without written compact, formal understanding, or unity of purpose, men, women, and children, should have lived together, four or five years, without scandal or reproach from dissension or evil whisper, should have separated without rancour or bitterness, and should have left none but the pleasantest savour behind them—is a tribute to the Transcendental Faith. . . .

The full history of that movement can be written only by one who belonged to it, and shared its secret : and it would doubtless have been written before this, had the materials for a history been more solid. Aspirations have no history. It is pleasant to hear the survivors of the pastoral experiment talk over their experiences, merrily recall the passages in work or play, revive the impressions of country rambles, conversations, discussions, social festivities, recount the comical mishaps, summon the shadows of friends dead, but unforgotten, and describe the hours spent in study or recreation, unspoiled by carefulness. But it is in private alone that these confidences are imparted. To the public very little has been, or will be, or can be told.

Mr. Hawthorne was one of the first to take up the scheme. He was there a little while at the beginning in 1841, and his note-books contain passages that are of interest. But Hawthorne's temperament was not congenial with such an atmosphere, nor was his faith clear or steadfast enough to rest contented on its idea. His, however, were observing eyes ; and his notes, being soliloquies, confessions made to himself, convey his honest impressions.

"It already looks like a dream behind me. The real Me was never an associate of the community ; there had been a spectral Appearance there, sounding the horn at day break, and milking the cows, and hoeing the potatoes, and raking hay, toiling in the sun, and doing me the honour to assume my name. But this spectre was not myself."

A friend of Emerson, George William Curtis,— of whom Hawthorne speaks as the one who could best write the real history of this very interesting experiment, which the inimitable and weird pencil of the latter has immortalized in that saddest of

romances, "The Blithedale Romance" thus speaks
of it:—" It was indescribably ludicrous to observe reverend doctors and other dons coming
out to gaze upon the extraordinary spectacle, and
going about as dainty ladies hold their skirts and
daintily step from stone to stone in a muddy street,
lest they be soiled. The dons seemed to doubt
whether the mere contact had not smirched them.
But, droll in itself, it was a thousandfold droller
when Theodore Parker came through the woods
and described it. With his head set low upon his
gladiatorial shoulders, and his nasal voice in subtle
and exquisite mimicry reproducing what was
truly laughable, yet all with infinite *bonhomie*
and with a genuine superiority to small malice,
he was as humorous as he was learned, and as
excellent a man as he was noble and fervent and
humane a preacher. On Sundays a party always
went from the Farm to Mr. Parker's little country
church. He was there exactly what he was
afterwards when he preached to thousands of
eager people in the Boston Music Hall ; the same
plain, simple, rustic, racy man. His congregation
were his personal friends. They loved him and
admired him and were proud of him ; and his
geniality and tender sympathy, his ample knowledge of things as well as of books, his jovial

manliness and sturdy independence, drew to him all ages and sexes and conditions.

"The society at Brook Farm was composed of every kind of person. There were the ripest scholars, men and women of the most æsthetic culture and accomplishment, young farmers, seamstresses, mechanics, preachers—the industrious, the lazy, the conceited, the sentimental. But they were associated in such a spirit and under such conditions that, with some extravagance, the best of everybody appeared, and there was a kind of *esprit de corps*, at least in the earlier or golden age of the colony. There was plenty of steady, essential hard work; for the founding of an earthly Paradise upon a rough New England farm is no pastime. But with the best intention, and much practical knowledge and industry and devotion, there was in the nature of the case an inevitable lack of method, and the economical failure was almost a foregone conclusion. But there were never such witty potato patches and such sparkling corn-fields before or since. The weeds were scratched out of the ground to the music of Tennyson or Browning, and the nooning was an hour as gay and bright as any brilliant midnight at Ambrose's. But in the midst of all was one figure, the practical farmer, an honest neighbour who was not drawn to the enterprise by any spiritual attraction, but was hired at good wages to superintend the work, and who always seemed to be regarding the whole affair with the most good-natured wonder as a prodigious masquerade. Indeed, the description which Hawthorne gives of him at a real masquerade of the farmers in the woods depicts his attitude toward Brook Farm itself: 'And apart, with a shrewd Yankee observation of the scene, stands our friend Orange, a thick-set, sturdy figure, enjoying the fun well enough, yet rather laughing with a perception of its nonsensicalness than at all entering into the spirit of the thing.' That, indeed, was very much the attitude of Hawthorne himself toward Brook Farm and many other aspects of human life.

" But beneath all the glancing colours, the lights and shadows of its surface, it was a simple, honest, practical effort for wiser forms of life than those in which we find ourselves. The criticism of science, the sneer of literature, the complaint of experience, is that man is a miserably half-developed being, the proof of which is the condition of human society, in which the few enjoy and the many toil. But the enjoyment cloys and disappoints, and the very want of labour poisons the enjoyment. Man is made body and soul. The health of each requires

reasonable exercise. If every man did his share of
the muscular work of the world, no other man
would be overwhelmed by it. The man who does
not work imposes harder toil upon him who does.
Thereby the first steals from the last the opportunity of mental culture, and at last we reach a
world of pariahs and patricians, with all the incon-
ceivable sorrow and suffering that surround us.
Bound fast by the brazen age, we can see that the
way back to the age of gold lies through justice,
which will substitute co-operation for competition.
. . . The spirit that was concentrated at Brook
Farm is diffused, but it is not lost. As an organised
effort, after many downward changes, it failed ;
but those who remember the Hive, the Eyrie, the
Cottage—when Margaret Fuller came and talked,
radiant with bright humour ; when Emerson and
Parker and Hedge joined the circle for a night or
a day ; when those who may not be publicly named
brought beauty and wit and social sympathy to the
feast ; when the practical possibilities of life seemed
fairer, and life and character were touched inef-
faceably with good influence—cherish a pleasant
vision which no fate can harm, and remember
with ceaseless gratitude the blithe days at Brook
Farm."

EMERSON'S RESIGNATION OF HIS PASTORAL CHARGE IN 1832.

EXTRACTS FROM HIS FAREWELL SERMON AND LETTER.

As has been stated in this Memoir, p. 12, Emerson felt compelled to resign his pastorate in Boston, on account of scruples in connection with the commemoration of the Lord's Supper in the sense generally entertained. "He had come," says Mr. Guernsey,* "to more than doubt the authority, and even the usefulness, of this Christian rite. His objections to it did not rest at all upon the mysterious doctrines of Transubstantiation and Consubstantiation, for which so many men have been sent to the stake, and have sent others to the state. . . . His own objections to the present practice of the ordinance lay far deeper than any mere question as to the form of administering it. In his view the rite was never instituted by Jesus as a permanent one for his followers through the ages ; and whatever of usefulness it may have had in the olden time, it was an outworn garment to be thrown aside. The sacerdotal blessing of the bread and wine was a ceremony in which he could no longer take part.

* "Ralph Waldo Emerson : Philosopher and Poet," by Alfred H. Guernsey.

From the remarkable sermon delivered to his congregation, setting forth his reasons for his resignation, described by Mr. Frothingham (Memoir, p. 14), the following passages are given :

Passing other objections, I come to this, that the *use of the elements*, however suitable to the people and the modes of thought in the East, where it originated, is foreign and unsuited to affect us. Whatever long usage and strong association may have done in some individuals to deaden this repulsion, I apprehend that their use is rather tolerated than loved by any of us. We are not accustomed to express our thoughts or emotions by symbolical actions. Most men find the bread and wine no aid to devotion, and to some it is a painful impediment. To eat bread is one thing ; to love the precepts of Christ and resolve to obey them is quite another.

The statement of this objection leads me to say that I think this difficulty, wherever it is felt, to be entitled to the greatest weight. It is alone a sufficient objection to the ordinance. It is my own objection. This mode of commemorating Christ is not suitable to me. That is reason enough why I should abandon it. If I believed that it was enjoined by Jesus on his disciples, and that he even contemplated making permanent this mode of commemoration, every way agreeable to an eastern mind, and yet, on trial, it was disagreeable to my own feelings, I should not adopt it. I should choose other ways which, as more effectual upon me, he would approve more. For I choose that my remembrances of him should be pleasing, affecting, religious. I will love him as a glorified friend, after the free way of friendship, and not pay him a stiff sign of respect, as men do to those whom they fear. A passage read from his discourses, a moving provocation to works like his, any act or meeting which tends to awaken a pure thought, a flow of love, an original design of virtue, I call a worthy, a true commemoration.

I am not so foolish as to declaim against forms. Forms are as essential as bodies ; but to exalt particular forms, to adhere to one form a moment after it is out-grown, is unreasonable, and it is alien to the spirit of Christ. If I understand the distinction of Christianity, the reason why it is to be preferred over all other systems and is divine is this, that it is a moral system; that it presents men with truths which are their own reason, and enjoins practices that are their own justification; that if miracles may be said to have been its evidence to the first Christians, they are not its evidence to us, but the doctrines themselves; that every practice is Christian which praises itself, and every practice unchristian which condemns itself. I am not engaged to Christianity by decent forms, or saving ordinances; it is not usage, it is not what I do not understand, that binds me to it—let these be the sandy foundations of falsehoods. What I revere and obey in it is its reality, its boundless charity, its deep interior life, the rest it gives to my mind, the echo it returns to my thoughts, the perfect accord it makes with my reason through all its representation of God and His Providence; and the persuasion and courage that come out thence to lead me upward and onward. Freedom is the essence of this faith. It has for its object simply to make men good and wise. Its institutions, then, should be as flexible as the wants of men. That form out of which the life and suitableness have departed, should be as worthless in its eyes as the dead leaves that are falling around us.

And therefore, although for the satisfaction of others, I have laboured to show by the history that this rite was not intended to be perpetual; although I have gone back to weigh the expressions of Paul, I feel that here is the true point of view. In the midst of considerations as to what Paul thought, and why he so thought, I cannot help feeling that it is time misspent to argue to or from his convictions, or those of Luke and John, respecting any form. I seem to lose the substance in seeking the shadow. That for which Paul lived and died so gloriously; that for which Jesus gave himself to be crucified; the end that animated the thousand martyrs and heroes who have followed his steps, was to redeem us from a formal religion, and teach us to seek our well-being in the formation of the soul. The whole world was full of idols and ordinances. The Jewish was a religion of forms. The Pagan was a religion of forms;

it was all body—it had no life—and the Almighty God was pleased to qualify and send forth a man to teach men that they must serve him with the heart; that only that life was religious which was thoroughly good; that sacrifice was smoke, and forms were shadows. This man lived and died true to this purpose; and now, with his blessed word and life before us, Christians must contend that it is a matter of vital importance—really a duty, to commemorate him by a certain form, whether that form be agreeable to their understandings or not.

Is not this to make vain the gift of God? Is not this to turn back the hand on the dial? Is not this to make men—to make ourselves—forget that not forms, but duties; not names, but righteousness and love are enjoined; and that in the eye of God there is no other measure of the value of any one form than the measure of its use?

From his affectionate letter of farewell to his congregation a few touching and beautiful sentences are here given :

And, more than this, I rejoice to believe that my ceasing to exercise the pastoral office among you does not make any real change in our spiritual relation to each other. Whatever is most desirable and excellent therein, remains to us. For, truly speaking, whoever provokes me to a good act or thought, has given me a pledge of his fidelity to virtue,—he has come under bonds to adhere to that cause to which we are jointly attached. And so I say to all you who have been my counsellors and coöperators in our Christian walk, that I am wont to see in your faces the seals and certificates of our mutual obligations. If we have conspired from week to week in the sympathy and expression of devout sentiments; if we have received together the unspeakable gift of God's truth ; if we have studied together the sense of any divine word ; or striven together in any charity ; or conferred together for the relief or instruction of any brother ; if together we have laid down the dead in a pious hope ; or held up the babe into the baptism of Christianity ; above all, if we have shared in any habitual acknowledgment of that benignant God, whose omnipresence raises and glorifies the meanest offices and the lowest ability, and opens heaven in every heart that worships him,—then indeed are we united, we are mutually debtors to each other of faith and hope, engaged to persist and confirm each other's hearts in obedience to the Gospel. We shall not feel that the nominal changes and little separations of this world can release us from the strong cordage of this spiritual bond. And I entreat you to consider how truly blessed will have been our connexion, if in this manner, the memory of it shall serve to bind each one of us more strictly to the practice of our several duties.

SPEECH IN MANCHESTER.

This speech (referred to in Memoir, p. 50) was delivered at a soirée, held under the auspices of the Manchester Athenæum, at the Free Trade Hall, in November, 1847, under the presidency of Sir A. Alison, the historian, and at which Richard Cobden and other political leaders were present. Of this meeting Mr. Emerson says in his " English Traits:" "A few days after my arrival in Manchester, in November, 1847, the Manchester Athenæum gave its annual banquet in the Free Trade Hall. With other guests, I was invited to be present, and to address the company. In looking over recently a newspaper report of my remarks, I inclined to reprint it as fully expressing the feeling with which I entered England, and which agrees well enough with the more deliberate results of better acquaintance recorded in the foregoing pages. Sir Archibald Alison, the historian, presided, and opened the meeting with a speech. He was followed by Mr. Cobden, Lord Brackley, and others, among whom was Mr. Cruikshank, one of the contributors to ' Punch.' Mr. Dickens's letter of apology for his absence was read. Mr. Jerrold, who had been announced, did not appear."

Mr. Chairman and gentlemen,—It is pleasant to me to meet this great and brilliant company, and doubly pleasant to see the faces of so many distinguished persons on this platform. But I have known all these persons already. When I was at home they were as near to me as they are to you. The arguments of the League and its leader are known to all the friends of trade. The gaieties and genius, the political, the social, the parietal wit of "Punch" go duly every fortnight to every boy and girl in Boston and New York. Sir, when I came to sea I found the "History of Europe" on the ship's cabin table, the property of the captain; a sort of programme or playbill to tell the seafaring New Englander what he shall find on his landing here. And as for Dombey, sir, there is no land where paper exists to print on where it is not found; no man who can read that does not read it; and if he cannot he finds some charitable pair of eyes that can, and hears it. But these things are not for me to say; these compliments, though true, would better come from one who felt and understand these merits more. I am not here to exchange civilities with you, but rather to speak of that which I am sure interests these gentlemen more than their own praises; of that which is good in holidays and working days, the same in one century and in another century. That which lures a solitary American in the woods with a wish to see England is the moral peculiarity of the Saxon race, its commanding sense of right and wrong, the love and devotion to that—this is the imperial trait

which arms them with the sceptre of the globe. It is this which
lies at the foundation of that aristocratic character which certainly
wanders into strange vagaries, so that its origin is often lost sight
of, but which, if it should lose this, would find itself paralysed; and
in trade, and in the mechanic's shop, gives that honesty in performance, that thoroughness and solidity of work, which is a national
characteristic. This conscience is one element, and the other is
that loyal adhesion, that habit of friendship, that homage of man to
man, running through all classes—the electing of worthy persons to
a certain fraternity, to acts of kindness and warm and staunch
support, from year to year, from youth to age, which is alike lovely
and honourable to those who render and those who receive it;
which stands in strong contrast with the superficial attachments of
other races, their excessive courtesy, and short-lived connection.
You will think me very pedantic, gentlemen, but, holiday though it
be, I have not the smallest interest in any holiday, except as it
celebrates real and not pretended joys; and I think it just, in this
time of gloom and commercial disaster, of affliction and beggary in
these districts, that, on these very accounts I speak of, you should
not fail to keep your literary anniversary. I seem to hear you say
that, for all that is come and gone yet, we will not reduce by one
chaplet or one oak leaf the braveries of our annual feast. For I
must tell you, I was given to understand in my childhood, that the
British island from which my forefathers came was no lotus garden,
no paradise of serene sky and roses, and music and merriment all
the year round; no, but a cold, foggy, mournful country, where
nothing grew well in the open air, but robust men and virtuous
women, and these of a wonderful fibre and endurance; that their
best parts were slowly revealed; their virtues did not come out
until they quarrelled—they did not strike twelve the first time;
good lovers, good haters, and you could know little about them till
you had seen them long, and little good of them till you had seen
them in action; that in prosperity they were moody and dumpish,
but in adversity they were grand. Is it not true, sir, that the
wise ancients did not praise the ship parting with flying colours
from the port, but only that brave sailer which came back with

torn sheets and battered sides, stripped of her banners, but having ridden out the storm? And so, gentlemen, I feel in regard to this aged England, with her possessions, honours, and trophies, and also with the infirmities of a thousand years gathering around her, irretrievably committed as she now is to many old customs which cannot be suddenly changed; pressed upon by the transitions of trade, and new and all incalculable modes, fabrics, arts, machines, and competing populations—I see her not dispirited, not weak, but well remembering that she has seen dark days before; indeed, with a kind of instinct that she sees a little better in a cloudy day, and that in storm of battle and calamity she has a secret vigour and a pulse like a cannon. I see her in her old age, not decrepit, but young, and still daring to believe in her power of endurance and expansion. Seeing this, I say, All hail! mother of nations, mother of heroes, with strength still equal to the time; still wise to entertain and swift to execute the policy which the mind and heart of mankind requires in the present hour, and thus only hospitable to the foreigner, and truly a home to the thoughtful and generous who are born in the soil. So be it! so let it be. If it be not so, if the courage of England goes with the chances of a commercial crisis, I will go back to the capes of Massachusetts, and my own Indian stream, and say to my own countrymen, the old race are all gone, and the elasticity and hope of mankind must henceforth remain on the Alleghany ranges, or nowhere.

ROBERT BURNS.

This speech was delivered before the Boston Burns Club, 25th January, 1859. The effect produced by it upon his audience is described by Mr. Lowell (Memoir, p. 92), and by Judge Hoar, (Tributes, p. 224).

Mr. President and Gentlemen,—I do not know by what untoward accident it has chanced—and I forbear to inquire—that, in this accomplished circle, it should fall to me, the worst Scotsman of all, to receive your commands, and at the latest hour, too, to respond to the sentiment just offered, and which indeed makes the occasion. But I am told there is no appeal, and I must trust to the inspiration of the theme to make a fitness which does not otherwise exist.

Yet, sir, I heartily feel the singular claims of the occasion. At the first announcement, from I know not whence, that the 25th of January was the hundredth anniversary of the birth of Robert Burns, a sudden consent warmed the great English race, in all its kingdoms, colonies, and states, all over the world, to keep the festival.

We are here to hold our parliament with love and poesy, as men were wont to do in the middle ages. Those famous parliaments might or might not have had more stateliness, and better singers than we—though that is yet to be known—but they could not have better reason.

I can only explain this singular unanimity in a race which rarely acts together, but rather after their watchword, each for himself—by the fact that Robert Burns, the poet of the middle class, represents in the mind of men to-day that great uprising of the middle class against the armed and privileged minorities—that uprising which worked politically in the American and French Revolutions, and which, not in governments so much as in education and in social order, has changed the face of the world.

In order for this destiny, his birth, breeding, and fortune were low. His organic sentiment was absolute independence, and resting, as it should, on a life of labour. No man existed who could look down on him. They that looked into his eyes saw that they might look down the sky as easily. His muse and teaching was common sense, joyful, aggressive, irresistible.

Not Latimer, not Luther, struck more telling blows against false theology than did this brave singer. The "Confession of Augsburg," the "Declaration of Independence," the French "Rights of Man," and the "Marseillaise" are not more weighty documents in the history of freedom than the songs of Burns. His satire has lost none of its edge. His musical arrows yet sing through the air.

He is so substantially a reformer, that I find his grand plain sense in close chain with the greatest masters—Rabelais, Shakespeare in comedy, Cervantes, Butler, and Burns. If I should add another name, I find it only in a living countryman of Burns. He is an exceptional genius. The people who care nothing for literature and poetry care for Burns. It was indifferent—they thought who saw him—whether he wrote verse or not ; he could have done anything else as well.

Yet how true a poet is he ! and the poet, too, of poor men, of grey hodden, and the guernsey coat, and the blouse. He has given voice to all the experiences of common life; he has endeared the farm-house and cottage, patches and poverty, beans and barley ; ale, the poor man's wine ; hardship, the fear of debt, the dear society of weans and wife, of brothers and sisters, proud of each other, knowing so few, and finding amends for want and obscurity in books and thought. What a love of nature, and, shall I say it ? of middle-class nature. Not great like Goethe in the stars, or like Byron on the ocean, or Moore in the luxurious East, but in the lonely landscape which the poor see around them, bleak leagues of pasture and stubble, ice, and sleet, and rain, and snow-choked brooks; birds, hares, field-mice, thistles and heather, which he daily knew. How many "Bonnie Doons," and "John Anderson, my joes," and "Auld Langsynes," all round the earth have his verses been applied to ! And his love songs still woo and melt the youths and maids ; the farm-work, the country holiday, the fishing coble, are still his debtors to-day. And as he was thus the poet of poor, anxious, cheerful, working humanity, so he had the language of low life. He grew up in a rural district, speaking a patois unintelligible to all but natives, and he has made that lowland Scotch a Doric dialect of fame. It is the only example in history of a language made classic by the genius of a single man. But more than this, he had that secret of genius, to draw from the bottom of society the strength of its speech, and astonish the ears of the polite with these artless words, better than art, and filtered of all offence through his beauty. It seemed odious to Luther that the devil should have all the best tunes ; he would bring them into the churches ; and

Burns knew how to take from fairs and gypsies, blacksmiths and drovers, the speech of the market and street, and clothe it with melody. But I am detaining you too long. The memory of Burns— I am afraid heaven and earth have taken too good care of it, to leave us anything to say. The west winds are murmuring it. Open the windows behind you, and hearken for the incoming tide what the waves say of it. The doves perching always on the eaves of the stone chapel opposite may know something of it. Every name in broad Scotland keeps his fame bright. The memory of Burns—every man's and boy's, and girl's head carries snatches of his songs, and can say them by heart, and, what is strangest of all, never learned them from a book, but from mouth to mouth. The wind whispers them, the birds whistle them, the corn, barley, and bulrushes hoarsely rustle them; nay, the music-boxes at Geneva are framed and toothed to play them; the hand organs of the Savoyards in all cities repeat them, and the chimes of bells ring them in the spires. They are the property and the solace of mankind.

SIR WALTER SCOTT.

The following address was spoken by Emerson at the commemorative recognition of Sir Walter Scott, on 15th August, 1871 :—

The memory of Sir Walter Scott is dear to this Society, of which he was for ten years an honorary member. If only as an eminent antiquary who has shed light on the history of Europe and of the English race, he had high claims to our regard. But to the rare tribute of a centennial anniversary of his birthday, which we gladly join with Scotland and indeed with Europe to keep, he is not less entitled—perhaps he alone among the literary men of this century is entitled—by the exceptional debt which all English-speaking men have gladly owed to his character and genius. I think no modern writer has inspired his readers with such affection to his own personality. I can well remember as far back as when "The Lord of

QQ

the Isles" was first republished in Boston, in 1815,—my own and my schoolfellows' joy in the book. "Marmion" and "The Lay" had gone before, but we were then learning to spell. In the face of the later novels, we still claim that his poetry is the delight of boys. But this means that when we reopen these old books, we all consent to be boys again. We tread over our youthful grounds with joy. Critics have found them to be only rhymed prose. But I believe that many of those who read them in youth, when, later, they come to dismiss finally their school-days' library, will make some fond exception for Scott as for Byron.

It is easy to see the origin of his poems. His own ear had been charmed by old ballads crooned by Scottish dames at firesides, and written down from their lips by antiquaries ; and, finding them now outgrown and dishonoured by the new culture, he attempted to dignify and adapt them to the times in which he lived. Just so much thought, so much picturesque detail in dialogue or description as the old ballad required, so much suppression of details, and leaping to the event, he would keep and use, but without any ambition to write a high poem after a classic model. He made no pretension to the lofty style of Spenser, or Milton, or Wordsworth. Compared with their purified songs,—purified of all ephemeral colour or material,—his were *vers de société*. But he had the skill proper to *vers de société*,—skill to fit his verse to his topic, and not to write solemn pentameters alike on a hero or a spaniel. His good sense probably elected the ballad, to make his audience larger. He apprehended in advance the immense enlargement of the reading public, which almost dates from the era of his books,—an event which his books and Byron's inaugurated ; and which, though until then unheard of, has become familiar to the present time.

If the success of his poems, however large, was partial, that of his novels was complete. The tone of strength in "Waverley" at once announced the master, and was more than justified by the superior genius of the following romances, up to the "Bride of Lammermoor," which almost goes back to Æschylus, for a counterpart, as a painting of Fate,—leaving on every reader the impression of the highest and purest tragedy.

His power on the public mind rests on the singular union of two influences. By nature, by his reading and taste, an aristocrat, in a time and country which easily gave him that bias, he had the virtues and graces of that class, and by his eminent humanity and his love of labour escaped its harm. He saw in the English Church the symbol and seal of all social order; in the historical aristocracy, the benefits to the state which Burke claimed for it; and in his own reading and research, such store of legend and renown as won his imagination to their cause. Not less his eminent humanity delighted in the sense and virtue and wit of the common people. In his own household and neighbours he found characters and pets of humble class, with whom he established the best relation,— small farmers and tradesmen, shepherds, fishermen, gypsies, peasant-girls, crones,—and came with these into real ties of mutual help and good-will. From these originals he drew so genially his Jeannie Deans, his Dinmonts and Edie Ochiltrees, Caleb Balderstone and Fairservice, Cuddie Headriggs, Dominies, Meg Merrilies, and Jeannie Rintherouts, full of life and reality; making these, too, the pivots on which the plots of his stories turn; and meantime without one word of brag of this discernment,—nay, this extreme sympathy reaching down to every beggar and beggar's dog, and horse and cow. In the number and variety of his characters, he approaches Shakespeare. Other painters in verse or prose have thrown into literature a few type-figures, as Cervantes, DeFoe, Richardson, Goldsmith, Sterne, and Fielding; but Scott portrayed with equal strength and success every figure in his crowded company.

His strong good sense saved him from the faults and foibles incident to poets,—from nervous egotism, sham modesty, or jealousy. He played ever a manly part. With such a fortune and such a genius, we should look to see what heavy toil the Fates took of him, as of Rousseau or Voltaire, of Swift or Byron. But no: he had no insanity, or vice, or blemish. He was a thoroughly upright, wise, and great-hearted man, equal to whatever event or fortune should try him. Disasters only drove him to immense exertion. What an ornament and safeguard is humour! Far better than wit for a poet and writer. It is a genius itself, and so defends from the insanities.

Under what rare conjunction of stars was this man born, that, wherever he lived, he found superior men, passed all his life in the best company, and still found himself the best of the best! He was apprenticed at Edinburgh to a Writer to the Signet, and became a Writer to the Signet, and found himself in his youth and manhood and age in the society of Mackintosh, Horner, Jeffrey, Playfair, Dugald Stewart, Sydney Smith, Leslie, Sir William Hamilton, Wilson, Hogg, De Quincey,—to name only some of his literary neighbours.

EMERSON AND CARLYLE.

BY JAMES RUSSELL LOWELL.

This description of the characteristics of the two philosophers (Memoir, p. 89) is from "A Fable for Critics," a sarcastic poem of great pungency, and extremely witty;—showing a wonderful facility of versification.

There comes Emerson first, whose rich words, every one,
Are like gold nails in temples to hang trophies on. . . .
A Greek head on right Yankee shoulders, whose range
Has Olympus for one pole, for t'other the Exchange;
He seems, to my thinking (although I'm afraid
The comparison must, long ere this, have been made),
A Plotinus-Montaigne, where the Egyptian's gold mist
And the Gascon's shrewd wit cheek-by-jowl co-exist;
All admire, and yet scarcely six converts he's got
To I don't (nor they either) exactly know what;
For though he builds glorious temples, 'tis odd
He leaves never a doorway to get in a god.
'Tis refreshing to old-fashioned people like me
To meet such a primitive Pagan as he,

In whose mind all creation is duly respected
As parts of himself, just a little projected;
And who's willing to worship the stars and the sun,
A convert to—nothing but Emerson.
So perfect a balance there is in his head,
That he talks of things sometimes as if they were dead;
Life, nature, love, God, and affairs of that sort,
He looks at as merely ideas; in short,
As if they were fossils stuck round in a cabinet,
Of such vast extent that our earth's a mere dab in it;
Composed just as he is inclined to conjecture her—
Namely, one part pure earth, ninety-nine parts pure lecturer;
You are filled with delight at his clear demonstration,
Each figure, word, gesture just fits the occasion,
With the quiet precision of science he'll sort 'em,
But you can't help suspecting the whole a *post mortem.*
There are persons, mole-blind to the soul's make and style,
Who insist on a likeness 'twixt him and Carlyle;
To compare him with Plato would be vastly fairer,
Carlyle's the more burly, but E. is the rarer;
He sees fewer objects, but clearlier, truelier—
If C.'s an original, E.'s more peculiar;
That he's more of a man you might say of the one,
Of the other he's more of an Emerson;
C.'s the Titan, as shaggy of mind as of limb—
E., the clear-eyed Olympian, rapid and slim;
The one's two-thirds Norseman, the other half Greek,
Where the one's most abounding, the other's to seek;
C.'s generals require to be seen in the mass,—
E.'s specialities gain if enlarged by the glass;
C. gives nature and God his own fits of the blues,
And rims common-sense things with mystical hues,—
E. sits in a mystery calm and intense,
And looks coolly around him with sharp common-sense;
C. shews you how every-day matters unite
With the dim transdiurnal recesses of night,—

While E. in a plain, præternatural way,
Makes mysteries matters of mere every day.
E. is rather like Flaxman, lines straight and severe,
And a colourless outline, but full, round, and clear;—
To the men he thinks worthy he frankly accords
The design of a white marble statue in words.
C. labours to get at the centre, and then
Take a reckoning from there of his actions and men;
E. calmly assumes the said centre as granted,
And, given himself, has whatever is wanted.

ARTICLES ON EMERSON IN ENGLISH AND AMERICAN PERIODICALS.

EMERSON, R. W. (R. Buchanan) Broadway, 2 : 223.—(J. Burroughs) Galaxy, 21 : 254, 543.—(Delia M. Colton) Continental Monthly, 1 : 49.—(G. Gilfillan) Tait's Magazine, New Series, 15 : 17.—(J. O'Connor) Catholic World, 27 : 90.—(G. Prentice) Methodist Quarterly, 24 : 357.—Dublin Review, 26 : 152.—North British Review, 47 : 319.—Westminster Review, 33 : 345.—Same art., Living Age, 16 : 97.—Blackwood, 62 : 643.—(F. H. Underwood) North American Review, 130 : 485.

—— *Address, July, 1838.* Boston Quarterly, 1 : 500.

—— *Address on Forefathers' Day.* (I. N. Tarbox) New Englander, 30 : 175.

—— *and his Writings.* (G. Barmby) Howitt's Journal, 2 : 315.—Christian Review, 26 : 640.

—— *and History.* Southern Literary Messenger, 18 : 249.

—— *and Landor.* Living Age, 52 : 371.

—— *and the Pantheists.* (H. Hemming) New Dominion Monthly, 8 : 65.

—— *and Transcendentalism.* American Whig Review, 1 : 233.

Emerson and Spencer and Martineau. (W. R. Alger) Christian Examiner, 84 : 257.

———— *Conduct of Life.* (N. Porter) New Englander, 19 : 496.— Eclectic Review, 46 : 365.

———— *Culture of.* Fraser, 78: 1. Same art., Living Age, 98: 358.

———— *Essays.* Democratic Review, 16 : 589.—Eclectic Magazine, 18 : 546.—Living Age, 4: 139; 23 : 344.—(C. C. Felton) Christian Examiner, 30: 252.—Eclectic Review, 76 : 667.— Boston Quarterly, 4 : 391.—Biblical Review, 1 : 148.—Eclectic Review, 76 : 667.—Prospective Review, 1 : 252.—Tait's Magazine, new series, 8 : 666.

———— *Facts about.* Chambers's Journal, 21 : 382.

———— *Homes and Haunts of,* with illustrations. (F. B. Sanborn) Scribner, 17 : 496.

———— *Lectures at Manchester, England.* Howitt's Journal, 2 : 370.

———— *and his Visit to Scotland.* Douglas Jerrold's Shilling Magazine, April, 1848.

———— *Lectures and Writings of.* Every Saturday, 3 : 680; 4 : 381.

———— *Letters and Social Aims.* International Review, 3 : 249.

———— *New Lectures.* New Englander, 8 : 166.—Christian Review, 15 : 249.

———— *Poems of.* (C. E. Norton) Nation, 4 : 430.—American Whig Review, 6 : 197.—(C. A. Bartol) Christian Examiner, 42 : 250.—Southern Literary Messenger, 13 : 292.—Brownson, 4 : 262.—Democratic Review, 1 : 319.—Christian Remembrancer, 15 : 300.

———— *Prose Works.* Catholic World, 11 : 202.

———— *Recent Lectures and Writings.* Fraser, 75 : 586.—Same art., Living Age, 93 : 581.

———— R. W. *Representative Men.* (C. A. Bartol) Christian Examiner, 48 : 314.—Eclectic Review, 95 : 568.—British Quarterly, 11 : 281.

———— *Society and Solitude.* Fraser, 82 : 1.

———— *Writings.* (F. H. Hedge) Christian Examiner, 38 : 87.— (J. W. Alexander) Princeton Review, 13 : 539.

Books, Pamphlets, &c.

Emerson : His Life and Writings. By January Searle : London, pp. 48, 1855.

Ralph Waldo Emerson : His Life, Writings, and Philosophy. By George Willis Cooke. Boston: Osgood. London: Sampson Low, Marston, & Co. 1881.

Ralph Waldo Emerson : Philosopher and Poet. By Alfred H. Guernsey. New York : Appleton, 1881 (Appleton's New Handy-Volume Series).

Transcendentalism in New England : A History ; by Octavius Brooke Frothingham. New York : 1880.

In Memoriam ; Ralph Waldo Emerson : Recollections of his Visits to England in 1833, 1847-8, and 1872-3.—Extracts from unpublished Letters, &c. By Alexander Ireland. 1st Edition, pp. 120 ; 2nd Edition, pp. 346, with Three Portraits. 1882. London : Simpkin, Marshall, & Co.

Emerson at Home and Abroad: By M. D. Conway (announced for publication in Nov., 1882). London : Trübner & Co.

Correspondence between Emerson and Carlyle, from 1833, edited by Mr. C. E. Norton, is announced as in preparation.

"The Literary World" (Boston) of May 22nd, 1880, devotes twelve pages to Emerson, consisting of articles upon him in his various aspects.—The Man, by C. A. Bartol ; The Founder of a Literature, by T. W. Higginson ; The Philosopher and Poet, by F. H. Hedge ; His Books, by Walt Whitman ; "The Dial," by G. W. Curtis ; His Friends, by F. B. Sanborn ; College Days, by W. Bancroft Hill ; Literary Methods, by G. W. Cooke ; His Home, Tributes, Table-Talk, Bibliography, &c.

Magazine Articles, &c., since his Death.

Emerson's Gospel : The Religion of Nature. By the Rev. R. Heber Newton, a discourse delivered in All Souls' Church, New York, May 28th, 1882.

Illustrated London News. Memoir (with full-page portrait), May 6th, 1882.

The Graphic. Brief Memoir (with full-page portrait), May 6th, 1882.

Ralph Waldo Emerson: by M. D. Conway. [In this article, Mr. Conway proves that Emerson advocated and set forth the doctrine of Evolution five years before the appearance of Darwin's and Wallace's papers on the subject in the Journal of the Linnæan Society, 1858.]—"Fortnightly Review," June, 1882.

Emerson in England, by M. D. Conway.—"Harper's Weekly," June 10th, 1882.

Emerson as a Poet, by Edwin P. Whipple.—"North American Review," July, 1882.

Emerson's Personality, by Emma Lazarus.—"The Century," July, 1882 (with engraving of bust).

Ralph Waldo Emerson, by Julian Hawthorne.—"Harper's Monthly Magazine," July, 1882 (with portrait).

Some Recollections of Ralph Waldo Emerson, by Edwin P. Whipple. —Ditto, September, 1882.

Ralph Waldo Emerson, by W. T. Harris.—"Atlantic Monthly," August, 1882 (with portrait).

Ralph Waldo Emerson: A Letter to the Editor.—"The Modern Review," October, 1882.

FOREIGN TRANSLATIONS OF, AND ARTICLES ON, EMERSON.

Edgar Quinet, in a volume of Lectures on "Christianity and the French Revolution," 1845, devotes one to "America and the Reformation," in which he thus expresses his opinion of Emerson:—"In this North America, which is pictured to us as so materialistic, I find the most ideal writer of our times. Contrast the formulas of German Philosophy with the inspiration, the initiative, the moral *élan* of Emerson. The author I have just named is proof enough that bold pioneers are at work in America pursuing the quest of truth in the moral world. What we announce in Europe from the summit of a revived past, he also announces from the germinating solitude of a world absolutely new. On the virgin soil of the new world behold the footsteps of a man, and a man who is moving toward the future by the same road that we are going."

In the "Revue Independante," 1846, the Countess D'Agoult, under her pseudonym of "Daniel Stern," has an article on "The Literary Tendencies of America," in which Emerson is highly appreciated. Philarète Chasles also wrote about him.

Emile Montégut, in the "Revue des Deux Mondes," has written on Emerson in an article entitled "An American Thinker and Poet," 1847. "Hero Worship: Emerson and Carlyle," 1850. "English Character judged by an American," 1856.

Herman Grimm, in 1857, published a translation of Emerson's "Goethe" and "Shakespeare" in "Representative Men," with a criticism on his writings. Some sentences from this criticism, as well as from another work by the same author, "New Essays," will be found at page 117, "Memoir."

H. Wolff gives a life of Emerson in a Dutch work, published at Bois le Duc, 1871, entitled "Prophets of Modern Date."

ADDENDUM.—The portrait of Emerson taken by David Scott in Edinburgh in 1848 (Recollections, p. 161), is in the possession of the widow of the late Dr. Samuel Brown. This lady is resident in Edinburgh.